HEART *of a* TIGER

HEART *of a* TIGER

GROWING UP WITH MY GRANDFATHER, TY COBB

HERSCHEL COBB

ECW PRESS

Published by ECW Press
2120 Queen Street East, Suite 200, Toronto, Ontario, Canada M4E 1E2
416-694-3348 / info@ecwpress.com

LIBRARY AND ARCHIVES CANADA CATALOGUING IN PUBLICATION

Cobb, Herschel
Heart of a tiger : growing up with my grandfather, Ty Cobb
/ Herschel Cobb.

ISBN 978-1-77041-130-2
ALSO ISSUED AS: 978-1-77090-381-4 (PDF); 978-1-77090-382-1 (EPUB)

1. Cobb, Ty, 1886-1961—Family. 2. Cobb, Herschel—Family.
3. Baseball players—United States—Biography. 4. Grandparent
and child. I. Title.

GV865.C6C63 2013   796.357092   C2012-907507-8

Editor for the press: John Paine
Cover and text design: Tania Craan
Cover images: Ty in the dugout © Associated Press; Herschel
Cobb, 1946 and Hershel Cobb, age 6 courtesy Herschel
Cobb; Herschel in 2012, at Ty Cobb's Lake Tahoe cabin ©
Tyrus Charles Brogan Cobb
Printing: Friesens   5   4   3   2   1

FSC
www.fsc.org
MIX
Paper from
responsible sources
FSC® C016245

PRINTED AND BOUND IN CANADA

To my children, Madelyn and Ty,
who inspired and made this book possible.

When Madelyn, our daughter, was of an age to be curious about
me, we were looking at a photo of her as a young child chasing a
duck along the edge of a large pond. I smiled to myself, recalling
her childhood joy. She suddenly said, "Daddy, tell me about
when you were a little boy." I started to say something, caught
my breath, rocked back on my heels, and stood speechless for
a moment. I could not think of one single time with my father
that was not filled with dread and terror. Each flashing memory
of him made my stomach sick, my throat clamp shut, and my
heart pound. Quickly, I grasped onto a story of catching crawfish with my grandfather at Lake Tahoe. I had been teasing my
sister with the crawfish until she appealed to Granddaddy to stop
me and he suggested one of his favorite pastimes, going out for
ice cream. Madelyn and Ty, our son, wanted to hear more stories about Granddaddy, Lake Tahoe, his home in Atherton, and
my adventures with him. Lyn, my wife, suggested I write them

down before they were lost. I did and soon realized how much these times meant to me, and how I privately held onto them as a lynchpin between me and my grandfather, who had helped me so very much.

I decided there was a useful story in my childhood with Granddaddy. Growing up, my time with my grandfather was my bedrock. Those experiences were etched in my emotional memory, providing strength and guidance, in stark contrast to my life with my father and mother. I had steadfastly kept my recollections of Granddaddy private, not wanting share them for fear of seeing them and my grandfather float away from me. My children opened a part of my heart that I feared I would lose if I talked about it. Not so. Just the opposite. Madelyn and Ty laughed and giggled at stories of me and Ty Cobb, quizzed me for details and more stories, then retold the stories to their friends, who were fascinated. I realized the power of a grandparent to provide laughter, love, protection, and comfort to pass on to the next generation.

I knew that my story had to include my father and mother. The first chapters of this book were not easy to relive and write down, perhaps not easy to read, but nevertheless true. I am very lucky to have had my grandfather. The later chapters are about him. And me.

After a few years of writing in the evenings, there was a story, perhaps a book that others would read and see something they could relate to. I asked Madelyn to read some chapters. She told me, "Dad, you've written a story from your heart, now write a book other people can read." I sought out an agent and was fortunate to be introduced to Jake Elwell, a sensitive and professional literary agent of the highest caliber and an endless resource. He introduced me to John Paine, a professional editor who helped me transform pages written from my heart into a book others might enjoy reading. Lyn, my wife, has been supportive and insightful throughout. Her encouragement to open up and tell full stories always produced a better chapter. The folks at ECW Press have been kind, incisive, and professional at every juncture. I thank all of these wonderful people. I especially thank our children, Madelyn and Ty, in whom I see the fruits of my grandfather's true heart.

Herschel Cobb
Menlo Park, California, 2013

CHAPTER ONE

The Snake River, Idaho, 1949

I sat between my father and my grandfather in the front seat of my father's Packard, being bounced around as we inched down a rutted dirt road. High above in the darkness loomed the rim of the Snake River Canyon. We were headed to my father's small boathouse, set on the river's edge. The headlights jumped up and down, left and right as we lurched from pothole to pothole. My father also shined a spotlight along our path with his outstretched left hand as he steered the car with his right, wanting to avoid a fallen branch or startled deer. From our house to the dirt road had taken only twenty minutes, but we would need another twenty-five minutes to wind down the face of the canyon. My dad told me we'd sleep at the boathouse, then get up before dawn to go duck hunting. I was dreading the opportunity. I was frightened whenever Dad had a gun in his hands, and this afternoon he had said it was time I grew up and learned how to shoot.

Granddaddy had arrived earlier that evening to visit us in Twin Falls, partly to hunt ducks with my dad, but really to see how my father was spending the huge sum of money he had given him a few years before. My father's latest purchase was a new Chris-Craft speedboat, which was moored at the boathouse. My father was grim-faced as he drove. Both he and my mother despised being held accountable, resented any intrusion on how they spent the money that was given to them.

Granddaddy had visited us last year, and I had a vivid recollection of him. The hair on his head was thin, and he was roly-poly in the middle. Yet his voice was warm and direct, and when he picked me up, his grip was strong yet gentle. He took in everything around him, seemingly looking right into me and at the same time noticing every look and motion I made, and when he smiled, his eyes twinkled. When he greeted my sister, Susan, and me, I felt like he had come all the way to Idaho just to see us. He adored Susan, two years older than me, with her light red hair that hung in large curls and her lovely smile. She paid special attention to him, prompting him to laugh and tell her stories. He loved to sit her on his knee to talk about almost anything.

By the time of his visit this year, the leaves on the trees had already turned golden, then rust, and drifted listlessly to the ground. I liked autumn because snow would soon fall and I would have my seventh birthday at the end of the year, in December. So, I was excited my grandfather was coming—until Dad told me I was coming along with them to learn how to shoot a shotgun.

Granddaddy had come for dinner before the three of us were to leave for the river. Dad wanted to fix a fancy meal, but my mother objected. During the afternoon they started drinking whisky, arguing and yelling at each other. I watched from behind a doorway. My mother felt a special tension on these occasions.

2

She knew how much Granddaddy disliked her. He regarded her as a grasping freeloader. He had heard an earful of her complaints that she expected to live the life of a socialite in L.A. and "your son isn't moving fast enough." He never forgot her selfish whining or forgave her liquor-fueled gripes. In revenge, she relentlessly belittled and henpecked my father.

When Granddaddy came to visit, she chafed at his disgust, but she didn't dare say anything. She yelled at Dad instead, saying it was her house and she didn't like his father telling her anything.

Dad became more agitated as the afternoon passed. He knew he would have to account for his new speedboat. As his anger built, I crept upstairs to hide. I knew his temper would rise like the pressure inside a geyser. Anything around him was in danger of being hit, smashed, and destroyed, and if he saw me, he would surely grab me and give me a beating. Susan was already hiding in her room, and when I appeared at her door, she told me, "I knew this would happen."

Granddaddy arrived wearing hunting clothes, and he put his guns and gear straightaway in Dad's car. His boots were laced up just below his knees, his pants were thick and stiff, and he wore three shirts bunched up by suspenders clasped onto his belt. He carried his tin cloth–hunting jacket on one arm. I knew he hunted every year with his friends in the mountains of Wyoming, and I wondered if he wore the same clothes there.

When we heard the doorbell, Susan and I rushed downstairs. Mother quickly emptied her glass of whisky into the sink. When she opened the door, Granddaddy brushed right past her and picked up Susan, hugging her and then me. He sat down in a big easy chair, put Susan on his knee, and began talking and laughing with her. I rested my chin on the armrest, hoping to be noticed. His big right hand came over and squeezed my nose, as if to tell

3

me I was next. My brother, Kit, who was just two years old, sat nearby playing with his toys.

Yet beneath the surface, trouble was brewing. We knew the danger signals in our house. Mother was already mad. Dad appeared, ready to yell at her, saw his father, and abruptly left the room. When he returned, he suggested we have dinner right away because we had to get to the Snake.

Susan and I were used to eating dinners on tenterhooks, awaiting an explosion of anger, but we were spared that night. Granddaddy's presence kept my parents at bay. They didn't have their usual glasses of whisky at the table, and the meal passed without any of the yelling I had feared.

Mother even tried to be interested in Granddaddy's chatter about duck hunting. Yet when she dared make a remark, he glared at her and bluntly asked, "Say, what happened to that fellow whose house your husband filled up with water?"

Mother started to fire right back, but stopped with her mouth open, unable to yell at my grandfather the way she would with my father. Instead, she sprang to her feet and retreated into the kitchen. Susan and I exchanged glances, hiding secret smiles. We knew what had happened.

The previous summer, we had returned from a June vacation to discover that the entire outside of our house had been painted bright pink. The scale of destructive pranks Dad and Mom played on their circle of friends had escalated over the past few years. Even though they paid for repairs, their antics had passed the point of being funny or clever, becoming more ruinous and grotesque. Dad was furious and stormed around the neighborhood, knocking on doors trying to find out who had painted his house. Eventually, Dad found out the culprit.

In August, the man and his family left town on their own

4

summer vacation. The next afternoon, Dad called, "Hersch, come with me. We're going to have some fun."

I followed him to the man's house. He found a window he could open, ran a garden hose inside, turned the faucet on full blast, made sure the room was filling with water, and left. Two weeks later, the family returned home to find the whole first floor and everything in it floating in three feet of water—all of their things had been ruined. The man stormed to our house, waving a shotgun, looking for my dad. My mom called the police, and they forced the man to give up his shotgun and took him away.

Dad complained that he was "just getting even." Although he paid for all the damage, he never apologized, and the episode became a story he bragged about to everyone. It was easy for him to lash out, destroy things, because he never had to suffer the consequences. He did have to suffer, however, the humiliation of his own father calling him out on his vicious prank. That was another reason I was dreading going to the Snake River to hunt. The pressure inside my father was building, and just about anything now was liable to make him blow up.

We slowly wound down the narrow dirt road toward the Snake River, bounced around by ruts and hairpin turns. Babe, our small chocolate Labrador retriever, rode in the back seat. Each time I bumped into Dad, he gave me a shove with his elbow and told me to watch out. After an extra hard shove, Granddaddy cradled his arm around me and pulled me over toward him, and we bounced together.

"How far to your place?" Granddaddy asked.

My father glanced over at us. "Not that far, but with these switchbacks, twenty minutes or so, maybe a little longer."

Granddaddy responded, "Well, then, take it easy. It's bumpy as hell. Oh, sorry, Hersch." He looked down at me, apologizing

5

for the swear word he'd used. He had to be aware that I heard far worse in my household. He lifted his left arm off my shoulder and unzipped the gun cover he was holding next to his legs. Twin barrels of a shotgun appeared, and Granddaddy flicked on the dash light and the overhead. The barrels were nearly black, with a dull sheen finish. He pulled the gun cover down the barrels, revealing the steel near the trigger guards and part of the stock.

"You sure that's empty?" Dad asked.

"Sure. I'll show you." Granddaddy broke open the barrels and stuck his fingers up inside. "Safe as can be."

My father had plenty of guns, but he had never shown me how they worked and I was not allowed anywhere near them. I was fascinated to be sitting so close to a real shotgun.

Granddaddy nudged the gun cover toward the floor and the rest of the shotgun emerged. It was still broken open where the ends of the barrels met the stock. He smiled at me and said proudly, "There you go, Hersch. Twelve-gauge, side-by-side, double triggers, forward and back. Beautiful."

I didn't know what he was talking about, but I did notice that the whole steel plate above the trigger guard and half of the barrel was carved with a hunting scene of a small lake, reeds, a hunter holding a gun, birds flying overhead, and engraved words.

In the dim light of the dash, I could read, "Presented to Ty Cobb" and "City of Detroit." There was more writing and a date. I knew the words "Ty Cobb"—that was my granddaddy. But I'd never heard of "City of Detroit" and didn't know what that meant. That didn't bother me, though, because I was awed that someone was able to carve into steel so beautifully. I touched the barrel and the side plate, tracing "Ty Cobb" and the hunting scene with my fingertips.

Granddaddy put his left arm back around my shoulder and

6

held his shotgun in his right hand, braced against his leg. "I haven't used this much, Hersch. It's mostly for show. But I thought I'd bring it along to show you, and maybe test it out." He turned out the overhead light but left the dashboard light on. I sat in silence, eyeing his shotgun and looking out the window, hoping to see a deer or some other animal.

Nobody talked for a while, until Granddaddy asked my father what I liked to do best. "Does little Hersch like to hunt or fish more?"

"Neither, really. Hasn't fired a gun yet. Still a sissy, I think. Plays with his stuffed toys."

Daddy's voice was muffled, but the gruff answer cut into my thoughts. I was always on alert if he sounded like he was angry. I didn't know what "sissy" meant, but it was true that I liked my stuffed animals. Granddaddy's hand squeezed my shoulder and then patted it. He didn't say anything but winked at me. I liked that he thought stuffed animals were just fine.

The deeper we descended into the canyon of the Snake, the darker it became. I was afraid of the dark because nighttime was full of bogeymen, or so Dad told me. He had told me about the bogeyman from the earliest time I could remember. Every time I didn't behave or he wanted me to do something, he told me the bogeyman would get me.

A wave of anxiety overcame me, and I suddenly pleaded, "Hurry up, Daddy. The bogeyman's out there." I pointed out the windows of the car.

"The what?" my grandfather boomed in my ear. "What did you say? What's out there?" he was asking my father.

"It's nothing, Dad. I'll tell you later," my father responded quickly. "Hersch," he said, "stop your fretting. We'll be there soon enough." He gripped the top of the steering wheel with his right hand, curling his shoulder upward, partially shielding his face from view.

With the dash light still on, I could see Granddaddy was examining his son severely. He'd heard what I'd said. I moved closer to Granddaddy. His arm wrapped around me, and I relished the comfort it provided. My father never held me this way.

Granddaddy didn't say anything the rest of the way to the boathouse, and I didn't dare open my mouth. I knew Daddy was seething because he drove faster, hit the bumps harder, and wrestled the car sharply around the tight turns. I didn't know what scared me more, the bogeymen outside the car or my father inside.

"We'll be there any moment now," my father finally announced. He rolled down his window, letting cold air and the rushing sound of the Snake River fill the car. I breathed in deeply. The air tasted clean and exciting. Even though I knew what was lurking out there in the dark, I loved the excitement of just barely being able to see through the trees, and at the same time, being able to look straight up, overhead, and see millions of stars.

Daddy parked in front of the boathouse, rushed to open the front door, and yelled back to us, "Wait a minute, I'll get the lanterns lit." The boathouse didn't have electricity, so we used kerosene lamps for light and a propane stove for cooking. It had an icebox, but we didn't bother to bring in any blocks of ice because we weren't staying long enough.

Granddaddy opened his door and said, "Come on, Hersch, we'll unload the trunk."

I scooted out and stood upright, holding onto the car door. My eyes hadn't adjusted to the dark, and I couldn't see anything beyond the car. I felt Granddaddy's hand take mine and shove something heavy into it.

"Here, take this. You hold the light, and I'll open the trunk."

He led me around to the rear of the car and opened the hatch. Inside lay the shotguns in their cloth cases, resting on top of sleeping bags, a box of food, and a dozen boxes of shotgun shells.

"Your dad packed enough guns, that's for sure," he said almost to himself. "I've got my side-by-side up front, my twelve-gauge over-under here. Really nice gun, Hersch. Bit much for you until you're bigger, though. And I see your dad's twelve-gauge, a twenty-gauge over-under, and two others." The sight of them made him pause. "Wonder what he wants those for? Well, I suppose he wants all of them inside."

Giving me a job, he moved the guns to one side and handed me the box of food. "Sure hope there's some ice cream in there, Hersch." He smiled as he handed the box to me. "Go ahead. The light is on inside, so leave the flashlight here."

Where one of the lanterns in front of the cabin provided a funnel of light, I peeked in the box of food, and sure enough, I saw a carton of ice cream, marked "chocolate." It still had that frozen hard look. I knew Granddaddy loved ice cream, so I put the box on the small countertop, took out the ice cream, and put it into the icebox even though we didn't bring ice.

With my father's large bulk filling the space, I remembered how small the cabin was. The cabin and boathouse were really one building, with the cabin erected on the bank of the river and the boathouse built out over it. The light from the lanterns reflected off the yellow linoleum countertops and the yellow linoleum floor. Except for a small throw rug, the floors were bare. The small kitchen adjoined a small eating area, which was right next to the built-in bunk beds. The bottom bed was larger, and sometimes we used it to sit on while we ate at the table. The toilet was outside and around the corner, outhouse style. The living and eating areas were close and crowded and not very comfortable, but that wasn't the purpose of the boathouse. It was supposed to protect Daddy's new speedboat, moored in the water, always ready to go. The doorway down to the boat was right behind me, guarded with a padlock.

Granddaddy walked in, carrying three guns over each shoulder, and nearly shouted, "Well, where is this beauty?" He was talking about Daddy's new Chris-Craft inboard. The speedboat had arrived in June, and Daddy had showed it off to all his friends during the summer. "I want to see where all that money you're making is going."

I wasn't sure exactly what he meant by this, but the tone of his voice was more of a demand than a question. Daddy had bought an airplane a couple of years before, and I overheard him when he called Granddaddy to tell him about it. The phone call turned into a shouting match. I could tell Granddaddy wanted to know why he had bought an expensive airplane because Daddy kept yelling louder and louder that he needed it for something or other.

"Be right there," my father said. He was looking over his shoulder, fiddling with one of the kerosene lamps as he answered. "Got to get this lamp set so it doesn't fall over. The key to the padlock is in the drawer, right behind Hersch. Taped to the left side in the rear."

I knew what he meant and immediately opened the drawer to look for the key.

"Hersch, leave that alone," he ordered me, his voice loud and sharp. I could tell that he was close to yelling at me: his eyes and face were rigid, holding back a torrent of anger. I quickly backed away from the drawer and let my arms hang stiffly at my sides.

Granddaddy set the guns and cases in the corner and walked

over to the drawer. He felt along the left side with his hand. "Hersch, I think I feel it, but my hand's too big. See what you can do."

Glad for the chance to help, I stepped forward, quickly found the key taped to the side, and pulled it off. As I handed the key to Granddaddy, Dad advanced on us, breathing hard. He didn't like anyone countermanding his orders. His face was flushed, but he didn't say a word. He grabbed the key to open the back door himself.

Yet he fumbled with the padlock, unable to fit the key into the slot. One of the kerosene lanterns was shining a flood of light onto Daddy, and I could see his left hand gripping the lock so tight, his knuckles were white. Frustrated, he kept trying to jam the key into the lock. He started cursing under his breath; I knew that something like this was sure to set him off. I slipped around behind my grandfather and quickly edged toward the bottom bunk, wanting to be as far away as possible.

He muttered under his breath, yanked the padlock futilely, cursing in a low voice, "Goddamn lock. I should have gotten the key myself."

I had seen him like this hundreds of times before, when his temper built to a peak and he lashed out in violence. The eruption could happen in an instant. Yet as mad as he was getting, he kept himself in check. Granddaddy was slightly behind him, leaning against the counter, watching. I realized that Granddaddy was the reason he hadn't exploded. My father didn't dare fly into a violent rage with Granddaddy around.

I watched with intense interest. I had rarely seen my father hold back about anything. My eyes darted back and forth between them, waiting to see what would happen. The yellow light of the kerosene lamp glowed eerily over my father and grandfather, and they seemed to stand still like a tableau. Deep inside, I felt an invisible wish to be as powerful and confident as my grandfather. He watched for another few seconds and said, like he didn't care one way or the other, "Herschel, want me to take a try?"

"Shit, Dad. Something's wrong. Goddamn lock," Daddy replied, while moving aside. He handed the key to Granddaddy, then leaned on the counter, gripping the edge tightly. He glared at his father but didn't look at me. I barely breathed, not wanting to draw his attention.

Granddaddy turned the bottom of the padlock upward, peered at it, then retrieved a small pocketknife from his pants pocket. He stuck a blade into the cylinder and jiggled it a few times. When he tried the key again, it slid smoothly into the cylinder chamber and turned. He let the open padlock hang on the hasp and tossed the key onto the countertop. When it landed, it made a dull clink, but the room was so quiet, it sounded as if someone had hit a doorbell.

They stood side by side, and though they were about the same height, Daddy was much bigger. He often said that he had to "stay away from three hundred." And I knew he meant how much he weighed.

Granddaddy stepped aside and said in the same even voice, "Lead the way, son."

My father's knuckles were white from gripping the countertop, and I half expected him to rip it off. Instead, he took a deep breath and grabbed the lantern hanging on a nail, pulling it so hard the nail sprang out of the wall. Even more embarrassed by that, he barged through the doorway and down the stairs to where his new Chris-Craft was moored.

Granddaddy turned to me and held his palms out, telling me to stay put. He must have sensed the building rage as much as I had.

As I sat on the edge of the bunk bed, Babe came over to me, nuzzled my leg, and wagged her tail happily.

"Well, come on. Here she is," my father said in the distance. His voice was full of disgust and finality, wanting to get the examination of his boat over with as soon as possible.

Granddaddy went down the steps to where the Chris-Craft inboard was tied up. I could hear the sound of the river splashing against the poles holding up the boathouse and the voices of the two men. The sounds bounced off the water and the sides of the boathouse and echoed up through the door to the kitchen.

"That's her," I heard my father say. I imagined he was pointing to his new inboard.

"So, this is what I gave you all that money for. And the airplane. Toys. I hope you sell plenty of Cokes," replied Granddaddy. He sounded like he didn't care what the Chris-Craft looked like.

I heard someone climbing the steps, and my grandfather appeared. That night I didn't understand what he meant about the money, but some years later I learned how Daddy was able to buy a Coca-Cola franchise in Twin Falls, a house, airplane, speedboat, racing boat, plus two new cars. He seemed to prosper selling cold soft drinks in a place that ironically was cold eight months out of the year. My grandfather knew where the money came from; it was provided by him, and he didn't like what he saw.

I now knew my father would not explode that night, not while Granddaddy was around. I was very sleepy, and I wanted to crawl into a warm bed and pull the covers over my head. Luckily, Granddaddy unhooked the rollaway bed set against the wall, opened it up, and motioned for me to help him arrange one of the sleeping bags on it. I climbed into the bag with my clothes on.

Granddaddy whispered to me, "What, no pajamas?"

"No, Granddaddy," I replied, "too sleepy, too cold." I peeked over the end of my sleeping bag, watching him. He unrolled his sleeping bag on the lower bunk, spread it over the mattress, and arranged the pillow he brought. He tossed another bag onto the upper bunk. My father was still down below with his new boat.

I was in my sleeping bag, with my head covered, squirming around to make it warm inside, when I heard my father's footsteps come up the stairs. A loud slam on the kitchen counter followed. I sensed he had been on the verge of exploding all day. His temper was short, his voice strained and so tense that conversation of any sort didn't last more than a sentence or two. Frightened, I pushed deeper inside the sleeping bag, kept my heard buried, and froze every possible part of me.

"What the hell's that for?" It was my grandfather's voice. "Keep it down. Little Hersch is sleepy, and we got an early morning. Let's just turn in."

I put the pillow over my head but could hear more mumbling between them. My grandfather put an end to it by saying, "Not tonight. I'm too tired to talk about money. I'm going to sleep. You get the upper."

I eased the pillow off my ear and heard the squeaking of the wood planks of the bunk bed, along with footsteps on the other side of the room. I guessed that my grandfather was climbing into the lower bunk and my father was still fuming. I lay as still as I could, pretending to be asleep, hoping the light would go out and put an end to the evening. My body was tense, and my ears picked up every little sound.

In a few minutes the shuffling ended, and the lights went out. I heard my father climb into the upper bunk. He bumped his head on the ceiling and cursed, but only the swishes of his working himself into his sleeping bag followed. I relaxed and the tension of impending catastrophe slid away. The warmth of my sleeping bag and quiet in the room were soothing, but even more comforting

14

was the knowledge that while my grandfather was around, I was safe from harm.

I slipped my arm out of my sleeping bag and searched around the floor until I found Babe. I patted her, then covered myself up again, got really warm, and drifted off to sleep.

I woke up a couple of times during the night to a loud growling noise. It was Granddaddy snoring. I went back to sleep, but the final time I was awakened, the sound was a frantic one—a combination fire truck and circus parade ringing right next to my head. The alarm clock. I pulled my sleeping bag away from my face until the cold air hit me. It was totally dark and I couldn't see anything.

My father's yelling jarred me. "Turn that damn thing off, will you?"

The alarm kept ringing and my father kept yelling. Granddaddy didn't stir at all. I lay still and waited, but nothing changed. My dad yelled louder and louder, and the alarm kept ringing. I heard shuffling and creaking, and finally my grandfather's voice: "What? Oh, yeah. Sorry. Sorry. Hold on. Can't find it." He was moving around at the same time, and the words came between his breath heaving. Just as suddenly as the ringing started, it ended.

"Christ almighty, Dad. Wake the dead. You all right? Hold on while I light this damn thing." The sound of a match being struck was followed by a flash of yellow light. The kerosene lamp began to glow, slowly lighting the room. The clock said 4:00. I was cold, and it seemed like the middle of the night; my body was moving, but I was not awake.

My grandfather rubbed me on the outside of my sleeping bag. "Time to hit the deck, Hersch. Sunrise is in an hour or so, and we want to be ready. Come on. You can have Granddaddy's jacket. I slept with it, so it's warmed up for you. Come on, boy; let's move." 15

He smiled down at me and his voice sounded ready for an adventure, sharing his excitement. He tugged my arm, pulled it out of the bag, and, at the same time, slipped it into his jacket sleeve. It was warm, just as he had promised. I began to wriggle out of the bag on my own and put on his hunting jacket, although I was nearly lost inside because it was so big. Granddaddy turned to my father, who was still on the top bunk, and said, "Herschel, it's cold as ice in here. Can we turn on that stove and get some heat going?"

My father replied harshly, "Yeah, yeah, yeah. Hold your horses. I've got to get out of this damn thing. The zipper's stuck."

The lantern hissed, casting a spotlight over my father as he tried to free himself. He was facing us with the lower half of his body still inside the bag. He yanked the zipper, then grabbed and pulled the material of his sleeping bag on each side of the zipper, trying to make the zipper open. His arms tugged and pulled furiously. His breathing was getting heavy, his face was red, and he was cursing under his breath. He couldn't get the zipper to budge. An explosion was coming, I could feel it. Granddaddy was sitting on the edge of the lower bunk, watching but not saying anything. Finally, my father grabbed material from each side of the bag, wrapped it around his hands, and gave a mighty yank. The material ripped apart, the zipper popped, and my father kept pulling savagely until the rip went all the way to the end of the bag, where his feet were. White feathers flew everywhere.

Granddaddy stuck out his hand, as if he could catch them all, saying, "Jesus, Herschel, that's a brand-new down bag."

"Forget it, Dad, just forget it. I'll get another one. Damn. What a mess," he said hotly.

Dad eyed the feathers floating downward, then looked over at me and ordered, "Hersch, get over here. Help me clean this up!"

I shivered, not so much from the cold, but because I knew Daddy wanted a target for his anger. I'd seen things go downhill before, when he exploded into a fit of rage, targeting anything he could see to hurt or destroy. I was still half asleep and cold, trying to force my body to climb out of the warm sleeping bag. I pushed and pulled, panicked by the prospect of my father erupting in a fit of rage.

In the stillness I heard Granddaddy's voice, "Cut it out, Herschel. You're the one that made the mess. Just leave it. We'll get it later. Move the damn light so you don't start a fire." His voice stopped both of us short. He didn't yell, but the intensity of his voice said he expected to be obeyed.

By this time, I was standing upright on the cold yellow linoleum floor. I didn't move a muscle. I watched my father's head slowly rise up from watching the feathers settle on the floor. He stared at Granddaddy for a full second or two. His eyes were glazed, and he was moving like he was in slow motion. He slowly shifted out of the bag, causing more feathers to cascade downward, and turned to reach for the lantern. Dad's hand closed around the handle of the lantern, but he did not move to get out of the bunk.

I heard the low rumble of cursing, half-swallowed back into his throat. I edged backward, getting as far out of the way as possible. But then, as if nothing had happened, Granddaddy walked across the room and stopped in front of the propane stove. "So, how do we start this thing?" he nearly shouted. "Let's get some heat going and make some coffee. I want to get going."

He looked funny, a grizzled old man. His thin hair jutted in all directions, and his whiskers darkened the lower part of his face. He'd slept in his pants, and they were baggy and wrinkled. His belt was unbuckled, and his boots were untied and flopped open. I could see he didn't have any socks on. His undershirt was gray,

17

the two top shirts unbuttoned and open. His belly was round and soft, and his face showed that he had just slept on it.

My father did not respond. I could sense all his energy welling up. Then he lashed out. My father pulled his right arm across his body, twisting himself up, and unleashed a huge swing. His fist hit the wooden side panel at the end of the upper bunk, causing a thunderous clap. The blast shook the wall and rattled the whole boathouse. The lantern swung back and forth on its hook but didn't fall. It was as if someone hit a huge, thick gong, sending dull, ugly echoes resounding off the walls and filling all the space in between. My mouth suddenly tasted bitter with acrid fear.

Granddaddy's shoulders flinched upward at the sound, and he turned slightly, looking out of the corner of his eye at my father. Daddy didn't move. He was still twisted around, facing the back of the bunk, suspended on its edge.

"Hersch, let Babe outside so she can do her business." Granddaddy's calm voice startled me. It lanced the dread I was feeling, allowing me to move. I had backed up against the wall farthest from the bunk beds, my hands held up in front of me for protection. I was entirely focused on my father, expecting him to leap down and bash anything in sight, but he kept himself in check.

Seizing my chance to escape, I opened the door and Babe hustled outside. Cold air rushed over my face as I stood in the open doorway, breathing in as deeply as I could. When I turned around, I saw Daddy had gotten down from the upper bunk and was walking, with fists clenched tight, slowly toward the counter where Granddaddy was standing.

Daddy had been a Golden Gloves amateur boxing champion in the heavyweight class. I had seen his gloves and equipment and watched him pound his punching bag, hung like a sack from a hook on a round flatboard. I had watched him sweat,

18

beads pouring down his face, neck, back, and shoulders when he worked out on his heavy bag. That bag was as big as I was, only much heavier, and when he hit it hard, stuffing flew from its seams and a loud "ouaf" jumped off the leather. He once told me, "Men box." I didn't really understand what he meant, but I knew he hit people and liked it. He'd hit my mother and knocked her down, causing blood to dribble from the corner of her mouth before she ran screaming out of their bedroom. I'd heard him brag about beating men into a bloody mess.

I was ready to run, but my grandfather held his ground. His head was slightly tilted toward the propane stove, but cocked at a slight angle, watching my father out of the corner of his eye. He shifted his feet so they were slightly apart, bent his knees just a little, and moved his weight forward. His posture transformed him from an old man into a huge cat, poised and ready to pounce.

As Daddy stomped up next to him, Granddaddy calmly asked, "Herschel, where's the turn-on for the propane? I can't find it anywhere." He didn't even glance up at my father but kept surveying the top of the stove and around the front and sides, moving the lantern back and forth so the light illuminated one spot and then another.

Daddy rolled his fingers tighter into his clenched fists. The back of his neck was bright red, wet with sweat. His shoulders were hunched and he was heaving, not breathing. He was kneading his palms with his fingers, the fists getting tighter and tighter, and his forearm muscles working harder and harder.

I moved away from the door and crouched behind the eating table, wanting to stay out of sight. My fingers gripped the top, and I peered over its edge, expecting a fistfight to erupt in front of me. Nobody moved for what seemed like minutes. Daddy was standing almost right next to Granddaddy, staring at him. Granddaddy kept

19

his alert stance. Throughout his search for the pilot light, I knew he was watching my father too. He was ready for anything.

Daddy began rocking back and forth ominously. He lifted his arms and fists slightly away from his sides, then thumped them hard down against his sides. Yet he managed to keep a semblance of control. His head rolled back, and he hissed, "Shit, right here." He reached behind the stove and turned something. He swung around on his heels and stormed out of the cabin, slamming the door. The cabin shook a second time.

I stood up and at the same time Granddaddy looked over at me. The corners of his mouth were turned up in a smile, and his eyes twinkled. "Hersch, about ready for some breakfast?"

I was too shocked to answer. The room had been crackling with Daddy's rage and I expected to see something awful, like him take a swing at his own father and thrash him. I'd seen him put his fist through doors, rip cords out of plugs, smash furniture in our house. I was relieved that he had gone outside, but my stomach was curdling with memories of all the times he had whipped my bare butt with a belt or crowded me into a corner, trapping me with his legs, pressing me hard against the walls until I cried "uncle" or just cried. I could hear him down by the water, cursing and knocking things around. Meanwhile, Granddaddy was lighting one of the burners with a match, adjusting the flame.

"I have to go to the bathroom," I muttered, suddenly aware of my own urgency.

"Oh, sure," he replied, looking around the cabin. Then he motioned with his head toward the steps down to the boathouse, where the Chris-Craft lay in the water. "Why don't you go down there, might be warmer. Into the water, I mean."

I realized in a flash that the suggestion meant I didn't have to go outside and possibly meet up with my father. I hurried toward the steps leading down to the small gangway next to the Chris-Craft. He handed me a flashlight as I passed and asked me if I wanted some hot cocoa. I nodded yes, and closed the door after me and disappeared into the dark.

When I returned, he was stirring a pan of milk on the stove, putting cocoa into it a little at a time. He'd set a box of Wheaties on the table, along with a bottle of milk, two bowls, and two huge spoons. "Go ahead and eat. We have to hurry up. Otherwise, we'll miss the shoot."

I poured Wheaties into the bowl and had the milk bottle poised over them when Granddaddy grabbed a box of sugar. He spread so much sugar over his cereal, the flakes were completely covered. Milk followed and he munched away while I watched in delighted amazement.

"Here," he said, offering the box to me, "those are like eating paste without something on them." I gladly added sugar, poured some milk, and started eating.

I finally realized what my half-dressed, unbuttoned grandfather looked like: a disheveled old elf. I half swallowed my cereal and laughed, almost losing my mouthful. He looked at me with the oddest expression and asked, "Well, what's so funny?"

I was embarrassed to tell him, so I muttered, "Oh, nothing." But I could tell by the way he glanced down at his open shirt and undone belt, the cuff of his sleeve soaked with milk, the sugar and flakes all around his bowl, and how he immediately wiped off the milk dripping from his chin, that he knew how funny he looked. He didn't care. He just kept on eating.

The tension of a few minutes ago had faded. I was relieved that my father wasn't looming over me, but I felt something more than that. I'd never sat alone with Granddaddy. I really didn't know him. The only man I knew was my father, and being with him was scary. Granddaddy seemed easy and comfortable, acted as if he liked having me around. He didn't talk much, just a few words between bites. He asked me about having enough warm clothes and cookies, and did I like school, and what books I liked. By the way he kept asking questions, I could tell he was actually interested in me.

"I think your father is busy outside. I don't think he's coming back in," he calmly remarked after a few more big bites. He spoke as if he knew this for a certainty, even though neither of us had looked. "So, let's finish up and get going. Hersch, why don't you put the food and drinks in that box? I think your cocoa is ready. You can bring it with us in the thermos. I'll take care of the hardware."

I knew he meant the shotguns. I kept eating, wondering if he would say anything about nearly being attacked by my father. He didn't, and I was glad for that. My father and his rage had left the cabin, and I could relax. I could feel the stove warming up my body. I finished my breakfast, put on more clothes, my shoes and galoshes, and started storing our food and drinks in the cardboard box. By the time I finished, Granddaddy had washed his face, combed his hair, straightened his shirts and pants and put on his boots and heavy jacket, and was gathering up his two shotguns and the four that Daddy had brought. I set the box of food on the table and stood behind it, watching him, ready to go.

He smiled at me. "You're all ready. Good. Good job."

I was struck dumb. I never had anybody tell me that I'd done a good job. I felt so good, I didn't know what to do. The expression on my face must have surprised him. He looked at me intently, then winked and said, "Well, let's go. We'll have some fun with Babe."

Outside, the sky was dark except for the sparkling stars. The gorge was dark too. I'd turned off the lantern inside the cabin, but we both had flashlights. Down by the river, I saw a light moving around and heard the thuds and clangs of stuff being thrown into the metal runabout and knew it was my father. We'd use this runabout, mounted with an outboard engine, to motor out to one of the small islands in the middle of the wide river. I followed behind Granddaddy, not knowing what to expect.

The bow of the runabout rested on the sandy beach. Granddaddy stepped in and handed the shotguns, still in their cases, over to Daddy, who was standing in the stern. Granddaddy then climbed into the center, took the box from me, and extended his hand. I'd never grabbed Granddaddy's hand before, so I didn't realize how huge it was or the tremendous strength of his grip. His hand took hold of me gently, but I felt it wrap fully around my own and part of my arm, practically lifting me into the boat. He set me down exactly in the middle of the forward bench.

"Let's get going." Dad's voice was gruff and insistent. He pulled hard on the cord to start the outboard, used an oar to push off from the bank, and we headed up the river. Babe was seated next to me, wagging her tail and licking the sugar and milk off my face. I faced forward, feeling the cold air rush across my face, and squinting into the darkness. Overhead, the starlight had faded and the slightest steel-gray tinted the pitch-black sky. I didn't hear any conversation behind me, just the change in the engine noise as we humped over small waves, fighting the river's current. We motored for about twenty minutes and passed a number of small islands. Finally, with my eyes more accustomed to the dark, I could see a good-sized island up ahead, covered with short, broad leafy trees that would provide the cover my father called a blind. Early in the morning, around dawn, the ducks fly upriver, over the islands, or out over the water. Wearing brown clothes, Daddy would hide under the branches, take aim from his blind, and shoot. Ducks fly fast in small flocks. Without warning, they pull up and head down

23

to the water, hunting for food or returning to a favorite feeding spot. The decoys and duck calls are supposed to trick them into slowing down near us or alighting in the river. If Dad shot a duck, it went down in the river and Babe would retrieve it. By the time sunlight touched the top of the canyon rim in two hours, no ducks would be flying, the hunt would be over, and we'd go home. We ate all the ducks Dad shot, or gave them to families who ate them. They were bigger than chickens, and one easily fed an entire family.

The year before, I had come with Dad and Babe to a similar island on the Snake and watched Babe work. Retrieving ducks was a game to her. After dawn had broken, Dad fired four times very quickly and called to me to hurry over to the edge of the island, pointing to Babe splashing into the river. He'd hit three ducks in total. Two dropped into the water far out and one close in, all being carried away by the current. Babe watched them fall and swam to the first duck that hit the water. She snatched it in her mouth and swam to the second duck. There, she let go of the first duck and took a hold of the second one and swam with it to the third duck. She let go of that duck, grabbed the third duck, and swam with it to the island. She dropped it at Daddy's side and went back into the river, found the first and second ducks, and retrieved both of them. They had been carried a long, long way downriver by the current, but she never lost track of them. Babe had what was called a "soft mouth," so the bird's feathers were wet and ruffled, but the flesh was not chewed or broken.

My father powered down as we approached the shore. Taking this as my cue, I retreated to the middle of the boat, causing the nose to rise and allowing it to run onto the sand so we didn't have to step into the water. Babe jumped out right away, and then Granddaddy climbed past me, onto the island, and pulled the boat as far up as he could. I climbed out with the box of food, and Dad handed the shotguns and ammo bag to Granddaddy. Dad had already told me to be quiet and stay under the branches, out of his way. He hustled his gear to the other side of the island, set things down under a tree, and quickly put on his hunting jacket and green hat. The tree branches and bushes on the island provided perfect cover from overhead, and I could barely see the sky and high sides of the gorge from under the tree where I was standing. The Snake flowed fast, changing color from the black of the night sky to the steel gray of predawn. Granddaddy waded out and planted four decoys in the water; they had anchor weights and were attached along a strong line we would use later to pull them back to shore. Both Daddy and Granddaddy had a string of duck calls around their necks. Daddy ignored me, which was fine, so I just watched Babe. Excited, she ran from the edge of the river over to my father and then to me. Back and forth and back and forth. She knew what was coming.

I heard the sound of shotgun fire echo off the walls of the gorge at the same time I heard my father say, "Shit, sonofabitch. Who in the hell is that?" He didn't direct the question at Granddaddy or me. He was feeding shotgun shells into his pump-action twelve-gauge as fast as he could, pacing back and forth under the outer branches of the small tree he chose for his blind. He was watching the sky and loading at the same time.

"It's still dark, dammit. That sonofabitch can't even see." He faced the river, creeping close to the edge of the overhanging branches. He muttered and cursed to himself, peering into the sky. Whoever had fired his shotgun had stirred his wrath. He wanted the whole Snake River to himself and was livid that somebody had spotted and fired at a duck before he did.

Granddaddy stood quietly among three small trees, looking

up at the dark sky and then at me peeking out from under my tree. He came over, reached in the food box, and opened a bottle of Coca-Cola. Perched with one knee on the ground while he drank a huge gulp of Coke, he tousled my hair. His hand shifted to my shoulder and he held it firmly, saying, "Hersch, you stay here. Don't follow your father. If you want, come over to where I am. I'll be up there, behind that group of trees. Now, be careful and stay low if you come. Here, here are some cookies." He pushed the bag of cookies into my lap, tousled my hair again, and walked away. I watched exactly where he went, planning a pathway to him if needed.

I sat, waiting in anticipation for the gunfire to begin. The sky changed color in just the few minutes I sat still. I heard Granddaddy's voice call in a muffled voice, "Herschel, 11:00. Three mallards." His duck call squawked as loudly as he could blow. He wanted his son to take the first shots.

The explosion from my father's twelve-gauge startled me, even though I expected it. I instinctively ducked, curling my shoulders and head into my lap, covering my ears with my hands. Yet my fear lasted only a moment. I got to my knees, stuffed a cookie into my mouth, and scuffled around to find a position to see the sky through the tree branches. I squinted hard, just barely making out dark forms flying over the Snake. Ducks, lots of ducks. They were barely visible against the side of the canyon, but as I changed position, I saw that the steel-gray sky behind them cast them in silhouette. Part of me rooted for them to fly fast so they'd escape, and another part remembered how delicious they tasted.

I gradually maneuvered myself away from my father and toward Granddaddy. Both of them were taking shots, ducks were hitting the water, and Babe was jumping in and out of the river as fast as she could swim and retrieve. Dad called out after each duck he shot hit the water, while Granddaddy kept spotting the ducks up river before Dad did. At times the sky was filled with ducks and for long periods there were none. The light changed from pitch dark to light gray to silver-blue to very pale rose. The morning was icy cold, and I kept eating as I watched. When Babe was not retrieving, she came to me and I held her wet, cold head, feeding her cookies.

The faint blush of early dawn gathered more orange and then the sky settled into a pale, pale blue. Fewer and fewer ducks flew up river. Granddaddy and Dad had plenty of shooting over the past couple of hours. I was sitting near a string of two dozen ducks. On my haunches, with my feet under me, I pretended I was a duck waddling along. Since I hadn't heard any shots for a while, I was hoping it was time to go home.

"Hersch, come over here," my father ordered. He stood near a tree branch that extended out horizontally a few feet above the ground. He was holding his double barrel under his arm, the tip swinging back and forth. "Bring some of that stuff in the box. Find an empty bottle and some cans. Come on, hurry up," he growled. I didn't know what he was going to do, but I obediently scrounged around, grabbed a milk bottle, an empty shotgun shell box, plus a tin can, and hustled over to him.

The smell of burnt gunpowder lingered around him.

"Put those on this branch, Hersch. Set them up nice and tall." He stood over me, watching, and then headed over to where he had put the other shotguns. I balanced everything along the branch and turned to face him. He unzipped the case of one of the shotguns he'd brought. "Comehere." The words ran together, and my mouth tasted bitter with fear as I walked toward him. He had a shotgun in his right hand, holding it under the stalk, extending it slightly to me.

27

"Daddy, I don't want to shoot anything," I said. The shotgun was nearly as tall as I was. I measured barely three and a half feet and weighed fifty-seven pounds. He took hold of my arm as I approached and yanked me over to him.

"You gotta grow up, Hersch. You gotta quit being a baby. Now, come on." He was bent over me, his face just inches away. His mouth and lips tensed as he spat out, "You're going to do this! Do you want a spanking, right here? Now, come on. This is a twenty-gauge pump-action, holds more than ten rounds. I'll put in just a few. Now watch me, understand?"

He grabbed hold of my hands, shoved two shells into my palm, then pushed my fingers and the shells toward the slot on the side of the barrel, trying to load them. My fingers felt wooden, but he kept shoving until he jammed them into the loading slot, slicing open a cut that gushed blood onto the gun barrel and my hand. "Dammit. Now look what you did!" He wiped the gun off and stuffed the cloth into my hand, saying, "Christ, Hersch, push on that bleeding and stop it. We're going to do this."

He shoved more shells into the loading chamber. I held tight on my finger where it was sliced and watched him fill the chamber. When he stood up, he held the shotgun in his right hand and put his left hand on the middle of my back. He pulled me forward, placing the butt of the shotgun against my right shoulder. I was so afraid, all of my senses were on full alert. The wood on the stock and handle was pale dirty-yellow, and the barrel and trigger guard were black steel. The butt had a steel guard on the end, and this was what I felt against my shoulder. "Here, get your left hand under here, and hold on." He wrapped my left hand around the wood under the barrel.

"Daddy, I can't hold it up. It's too heavy." Struggling to keep my balance, I had to stretch awkwardly to reach the wood with my left hand. At the same time, my right arm was just long enough to reach around to the trigger guard. That forced the butt tightly against my shoulder.

"Don't argue, Hersch. Just do as I tell you." His voice had the force of a wild scream, but tightened down so it came out with hot, smelly breath all over my face.

From a distance I heard Granddaddy calling to my father, "Herschel, what are you doing? What are you doing over there?"

"Quiet, Dad. He's going to learn. Got to grow up." My father didn't turn his head. He was busy pushing my scared hands and fingers around the wood support and onto the trigger.

"Wait, Herschel. Stop that. That's way too much gun for him." Granddaddy sounded insistent, though I couldn't see him.

"It's okay, Dad. Just leave me alone. Stay out of this." He stood up next to me, holding my left hand under the barrel and my fingers on the trigger.

I wanted to beg him to let go, but the words wouldn't come out. I saw the tension in his lips and the brutal determination in his eyes. I didn't have a chance, anyway, because he held me tighter and told me fiercely, "Now. Look down the barrel and pull the trigger. Now, Hersch, now."

He let go of my hands. I pulled the trigger.

The explosion next to my face and the searing pain in my shoulder happened simultaneously. I was knocked backward by the recoil and landed on my backside flat on the ground. My chest and shoulder felt like someone had hit me hard with a bat. My ears were ringing, and I couldn't hear a thing. The acrid smell in my nostrils and throat was choking me. If that wasn't enough, when I fell, I had put my hands out behind me and now they were scraped with small rocks stuck in my skin. Tears welled up inside me. I had let go of the twenty-gauge, but Daddy had caught it and was standing above me, looking down, sneering mockingly. He grabbed me under my right arm and yanked me up. "You missed. Let's do this again, and this time, get it right."

I tried to wriggle away, but his grip was like iron. He was not going to let me go. I was half crying, mumbling a protest, but no real words came out. Daddy again put the shotgun in my arms. My shoulder was throbbing with pain, and my body was trembling. I was so scared, my eyes saw the cracked veins in the whites of his eyes, every line in his face, every mark on his teeth, every movement of his tongue, and every bead of sweat on his forehead. The awful pain was going to happen to me again. He forced my left hand tightly under the barrel and pulled my right hand onto the trigger, saying, "Now, you're going to do this, or else. Look down the barrel and pull the trigger."

I was terrified, certain he would hit me if I didn't do as he said. I looked down the barrel, trembling. My shoulder ached with the pressure of the shotgun. I felt utterly doomed.

Out of nowhere, a hand grabbed hold of Daddy's wrist. The fingers wrapped around and squeezed. The hand that was holding my finger on the trigger grew still.

"Enough, Herschel. That's enough. Leave the boy alone! Do you hear me, leave him alone!"

Granddaddy's voice was strong and determined. His face was wedged between Daddy's and mine. I watched his grip tighten around my father's wrist and fingers. Granddaddy's knuckles turned white and the muscles of his forearm stood out, quivering. His wrist looked huge, and his fist looked like iron. He was not going to let go.

"Herschel, enough. Do you understand me, I said enough.

You're not going to hurt him. We're going home. Now!" The intensity in his voice was palpable. This was a man who would never back down.

I was only inches away from both their faces. Granddaddy's whiskers were dark, and his jaw was fixed. They looked directly into each other's eyes for what seemed like forever. I could feel the heat of their breath and smelled their sweat. I was still trembling when I felt my father's hands let go of mine. As he stepped away, Granddaddy caught the shotgun.

My father uttered a piercing, loud, "Shit!" as he stormed away.

Granddaddy didn't pay him the slightest attention. He rubbed my shoulder, knowing how much it hurt. "Hersch," he said evenly, "I want you to get your stuff together and stay here."

He let go and I stood in a daze. My head was still ringing, and my shoulder and chest hurt. I didn't have words to thank him, just feelings. They flowed throughout my entire body. My father would have never stopped. I was certain my grandfather saved me.

The hunt was over. My father deposited his guns in the boat. Granddaddy gathered up the dead birds and put them into the boat, then returned for the rest of our stuff. I followed him to the outboard and scrambled to the bow, where I slid down and crouched between the forward bench and railings. Dad grabbed the tiller, and Granddaddy sat on the middle bench.

Riding with the current, we motored swiftly toward the cabin. My fingers clung fast to the railings; I pulled up my jacket collar to cover my cheeks and hoped nobody said anything. I tried to keep looking ahead, but sat sideways so I could steal an occasional look at the two large men behind me. Daddy's eyes were frozen on the hazy distance in front of us, refusing to acknowledge me. Granddaddy sat hunched over, glancing back and forth at his son and at me. When his gaze landed on me, he seemed apologetic,

31

almost mournful. When he looked at his son, his jaw muscles tightened, as if haunted by what he had witnessed. He knew his son was a bully, but he had never seen the brutality taken out on a little boy. He looked like he might throw up.

Later, when I was a teenager, I once asked Granddaddy about this trip. His answer was a clipped, unintelligible whisper, and that terseness stopped me from asking again.

Shame and disgrace had soured the hunting excursion. Nobody spoke while we motored back to the cabin, or while Daddy tied up the boat, put his engine away, and Granddaddy loaded the shotguns and gear bag into the Packard. I stood near the car, rubbing my sore shoulder. Nobody went inside the cabin, and we left the sleeping bags and all the feathers. Daddy shuffled with his head down to the driver's side and climbed in. Granddaddy got in the other side, and I hurried into the back seat, not looking up. I wanted to disappear, become invisible. Daddy started the car, gunned the engine, and spun the wheels as he accelerated in a roar. Soon the bumpy road slowed him down.

I was overwhelmed with tiredness and couldn't keep my eyes open. Battling my fleeting relief at not being hurt, I felt an overwhelming sadness, like a wound, open and sucking my energy. I pushed on Babe to make room for me to lie down on the seat. I wanted only to sleep.

When I woke up, I was lying on top of my own bed, at home, with a quilt over me. It was the middle of the afternoon. I lay motionless and listened. I didn't hear a sound. As I pushed myself up on one arm, I felt something in my hand. It was a crumpled-up part of an envelope. I tiptoed over to the window and looked out at the front yard, dreading the sight of my father. Yet I saw no cars in the driveway. Granddaddy had left. Mom and Dad weren't home either.

I smoothed out the paper in my hand. Written in dark green ink was a message, which I read and re-read and savored with hope:

Hersch,
Remember I love you,
Your Grandfather

CHAPTER TWO

223 Pierce St., Twin Falls, Idaho

I crawled back into bed, lay as still as I could, with just my eyes peeking out from under the covers. I held the message from my grandfather in my left hand. Drawing encouragement from it, I pulled the top of my head slightly under my pillow, so as not to be seen. My grandfather had left, and that meant I was vulnerable once again.

All of my memories of guns and hunting were terrifying. In the hands of someone who couldn't control himself, a gun stopped being the weapon of a sportsman. My father paid little attention to the usual boundaries that are kept and respected by most men and women. This was hardly my first encounter with the raw power of guns. When I was four years old, my father took me pheasant hunting with him. We had found a spot he liked, and he reacted as if having a tantrum when several men drove up in their pickup truck. He wanted the place to himself. So he pointed his shotgun at them and fired, over and over again, until they backed up and drove away in fear. He did this so easily, as if shooting somebody meant nothing to him. All he cared was that they didn't poach the spot he had claimed.

In later years I realized that my father lacked the ability to feel shame for the pain he inflicted on others. He acted on his impulses, and many of them were violent. He allowed himself to be ruled by them. He derived intense pleasure from the power he wielded while acting upon them. It was terrifying and paralyzing. So while I feared his violent rages, I never could be certain that he wouldn't inflict his sadism just out of sheer sport. That's what happened the previous summer after he purchased a new BB pistol.

I was playing outside, wearing shorts, when he called, "Hersch, do you want to play?"

As soon as I heard his voice, my entire body went on alert, tensed and on guard. I looked around but could not see him. He did not sound angry, so maybe he really meant what he said. His voice had come from the side of the house by the garage, and I ran across the lawn, around the corner, and saw him standing near the side door. He was unwrapping brown paper that bound a package. He told me he had ordered a new BB pistol, better than the one he had. He ripped apart the paper on the package, opened the box, and took out a pistol and a sack of BBs.

"I want to try this baby out," he announced. He filled the handle with BBs. Under the barrel was a small tube that fed the BBs into the firing chamber and a pump on the handle to create the air pressure to fire the BBs. He pumped until he could hardly move the lever on the handle, then took aim at a tree growing on the divider between the sidewalk and the curb and shot. I heard a little poof-pop from the pistol and a thud on the tree.

Excited, he shook the pistol, rattling the BBs in the handle, and fired again. Poof-pop, then thud. "Now let's see if it really works." He took a couple of steps back, aimed at my bare legs, and shot. The sting made me flinch and jump away. He shot again and again before I even knew what was happening. The stings felt like sharp needles pricking all over my skin. As I flinched to one side, he shot again, hitting my calf. Although I didn't see blood, the stings left small red blotches all over my legs. He shot ten or fifteen times and then had to stop to pump the lever.

I started backing away, but he yelled at me to stop. "Stay right there, Hersch. Don't be such a sissy." When he shot again, I tried to cover my legs with my hands, but the stinging on the back of my hands, with hardly any flesh, hurt far worse. He yelled to get my hands away, kept shooting, then pumped a few times and shot some more.

I looked around, desperate. I wanted to run or have someone help me, anything. He yelled for me to stay put and shot the ground around me so if I moved I would be hit. I was stunned. More than anything, I was afraid of getting shot in the face and waved my arms spastically back and forth between my eyes and my knees. The thrill of his new toy had totally overtaken him. He pumped the pistol handle and kept shooting at the same time. He had poured hundreds of BBs into the handle. BBs hit all around me on the ground and all over my bare legs, as fast as he could pump and fire.

I heard the side door of our house open and my mother appeared. She had on an off-white summer dress with puffed sleeves and a cloth waistband. I was too dazed with pain to yell out loud, but I so badly wanted her to help me. I looked down at my legs, covered with red welts.

She came up beside him and slipped her hand under his arm, the one firing the pistol. She lightly held him while he shot me some more. She watched as I hopped madly back and forth, hopelessly trying to dodge the BBs. She did nothing. He kept shooting, and pumping, and shooting. She stood there, watching me. I was standing, dodging, looking up at my dad, over six feet tall, nearly three hundred pounds, towering over me, and my mom, standing next to him, watching him shoot me. I didn't have any words. My head was numb, blank, and dark. I was stunned. Only my heart screamed, not in words but in feeling, screamed so loudly that it felt like a white lightning bolt piercing through my bones, my muscles, my veins, every bit of my being: *I will never, ever need or trust anybody ever, ever again!* I was not crying. I was spent. Dad kept pumping and shooting, but luckily, fewer BBs came out. At last he was out of ammo.

As he reached for the sack of BBs on the ground, I ran for my life. Their voices faded as I ran across the neighbor's front yard. There was no fence or hedge to shield me, and I kept running as fast as I could. I didn't slow down until I had run past several houses and reached the end of the block. Everywhere else the world was normal. The sun was warm, the sky was clear and blue, and I heard the voices of other families, grown-ups and kids, talking and playing. A car came around the corner, and the driver waved, even though I did not know her. Yet all I could feel, throughout my stomach and chest and legs and arms, was the danger lurking nearby. My father wanted to kill me, and my mother didn't care. This feeling settled in me, not as thoughts or something I figured out, but penetrating into my emotional core.

I reached the end of the block and sat on the curb, looking across the street at the edge of town. Across the way was a field filled with the straw-colored husks of stiff reeds, standing taller than I was and thick enough to hide all kinds of birds and animals. I wondered if I could live there, hidden and safe. Encouraged by

37

that thought, I took a running jump, leaped over the irrigation ditch, and scurried into the stalks. I felt a sharp pain in my little finger on my right hand. I'd landed hard on the stubble and tore a ragged hole at the first joint; blood spilled out. I might try to hide, but the pain reminded me that inevitably I would have to go back home.

My father enjoyed these games with a little person at his mercy. I knew that full well by now, because they had started when I was much younger. An earlier version of the BB gun was his bullwhip. During the summer I was four, he taunted me to run across the lawn and jump over the front walkway, running from the street to the front porch. When I ran and jumped, he whirled his bullwhip and snapped at my legs. The sting was like a swarm of bees had attacked my thigh all at once. He ordered me to keep running and jumping or else he'd catch me and tie me up. Sometimes I made it across without getting snapped, sometimes not. He laughed and laughed at his increasing success as I grew more and more tired. Finally, I gave up. I was so tired and my legs hurt so much that I didn't care anymore. I stood in front of him, and he wrapped his whip around my neck, gave a little tug, but then oddly uncoiled it. Set free, I wondered why he hadn't yanked on it. That was the obvious end of the game. Yet when I turned around, I saw the mailman walking up the street toward us.

The bullwhip was a modification of a more primitive game that he had initiated earlier, when Susan and I were still small enough to share a bath. We immensely enjoyed the nights when Ayako, our maid, made us a bubble bath. It was like magic to be able to disappear under the bubbles or make funny shapes. In the wintertime, I liked to take a bath, get really warm, put on my PJs with feet, and climb into bed right away. The warmth was like being held and hugged in just the right way.

These times of innocent pleasure were destined to be interrupted by his sadism. One night Susan and I had finished our bath and were drying ourselves when Daddy burst into the bathroom. He stood in the doorway, towering over us. He took Susan's towel from her and sank about half of it in the bath water while Susan stood naked next to the sink. She must have known what was going to happen because she started pleading, "No, Daddy, please no, please no." He wrung the water out of the towel, took a corner of it in each hand, spun it around until it was like a thick rope that bellied in the middle, and snapped it at her butt, using the tip of the towel like a whip. She had already started to cry. The towel made a cracking sound when it snapped, and a red splotch immediately showed on her behind. I gaped, my eyes wide open, instinctively pulling my towel as close to my body as possible. Susan was crying and pleading at the same time, crouching down, trying to cover her butt and legs with her hands. King of the game, Daddy flipped the wet towel around and around again, sizing up both of us. He hit Susan again, and then yanked my towel from me and threw it on the floor out of reach. He coiled the wet towel in his hands, telling me, "You're next. Get ready, Hersch."

I turned, trying to protect myself, but got whipped in the back of my right leg. The snap felt like I'd been smacked with a belt. I grabbed the spot with my hand, bending over at the same time. Tears welled up in my eyes. I thought we were done for. Susan pushed herself up against the wall as hard as she could, still naked.

In through the open bathroom door waltzed my mother. She had her glass of whisky in her hand and said, "What are you doing? You know it's the kids' bedtime. Now let them go."

"I'm only playing with them."

Disregarding our terror, she walked away, calling to Ayako to come and put us to bed.

Susan began sobbing. Caught in his game, Daddy looked at the red splotch on her leg and told her, "Put some cold water on it. It will be all right." He then dropped the wet towel in an ugly curl on the floor and left the bathroom.

Realizing that she couldn't use it, I handed my towel to Susan. She dried herself, telling me at the same time, "You better be careful. He did this to me last year too, when it snowed."

I couldn't take my eyes off her leg, not understanding what had just happened. I asked her if it was a game. What did the snow do? She told me it was not a game at all, it just hurts. She told me that Daddy had chased her all around the upstairs, snapping at her as they went, and when she was cornered in her room, he snapped at her feet to make her jump.

Daddy called his game "Rat's Tail." It did not matter if we were taking a bath or not. Sometimes he caught us in the hallway or when we were in our rooms playing. He would snap a few times in the air, coil his towel again, and snap, snap, snap. That demonstration was enough to send me scrambling. As I ran, he chased me and snapped. Most of the time I had my PJs on and it didn't hurt so badly, unless he lashed my hands or arms.

I wanted to learn how to make a Rat's Tail, so one night he gave me a small towel. He said he would teach me. The towel was larger than my washcloth, but smaller than the one I used to dry myself. He told me to watch and began to show me. He immediately whirled his wet towel around and around into a belly-laden whip and snapped me in the hands. It stung like blazes. Smarting from the pain, I dropped my towel, only to have him snap at me again. Then he picked up my little towel and handed it to me and said to watch him. He flipped his towel around and around again into a whip and snapped me in the hands again. This time it hurt even more.

I was backing away from him, wanting the "lesson" to end, but he picked up my towel, rolled it the right way, and handed it to me. It was soft and dry and I tried to snap him, but all that happened was the towel unraveled. He laughed and laughed. "Come on, Hersch, hit me!" He held out his hand for me to snap with my towel. I fumbled to roll it up again, but I was really just waving my dry towel at him.

While I was fumbling, he rolled his wet towel into a whip and snapped me expertly on my bottom. I jumped with pain, and he laughed some more. "Hersch, you better practice," he commented, and left my room. I rolled up my towel a few times, trying to make a whip, but it never worked, so I put it over my head instead and pretended I was invisible. He said he was going to show me how, but really it was a trick and a lie.

The fear of pain and certain doom started before I actually could conceptualize the world any other way. It was as much a part of my day as getting up, brushing my teeth, and eating. When I was still too young to participate in his sadistic games, when I was three years old, my father first started in with his tales of the bogeyman. He told me that if I didn't behave, the bogeyman was going to get me. If I made a noise or any type of commotion, he told me to "watch out." He was dead serious, and I believed him. He went on to describe the creature in lurid detail. He told me about its huge claws and long fangs and gooey, stinky mouth. He told me it could fly and would take me away and I'd never come back. I'd have to live in a cave and eat dirt and never see my family or friends again. I became so scared that at night I hid in the center of the house, near the stairs, where there was a light, away from any windows.

One night he made me get my plastic tomahawk and a flashlight and took me out to the backyard. He had me stand next

41

to a large tree and told me to stay there until I was sure that nothing out in the dark would get me. He then left me alone, shaking and scared. After a few minutes, something grabbed me from behind. I was scared out of my mind. It was the bogeyman. I felt its huge, strong claws grip my arms and side and hold me so I couldn't move. I yelled and kicked, but it picked me up. I could not turn around, but I could hear it growl and breathe on me. I was doomed. I knew it was going to take me away to its awful cave. I twisted and kicked for dear life, but it held me so tight I couldn't breathe. It started to carry me away, and I felt sick and everything went dark.

The next thing I saw was my father next to me, telling me to go inside the house. I looked around in surprise and relief; the bogeyman was gone. My father headed toward the back door, breathing hard. I backed a step away before he yelled at me to hurry up or else. I rushed into the house and ran upstairs to my room, the only place I felt safe.

The most crushing, both physically and mentally, of the "games" my father played with me took place during several winters. In the evenings he would pluck me up to wrestle with him on the big bed in his bedroom. At first I didn't know what wrestling meant and was just excited to play with my dad. He put me on the bed, sat next to me, and we pushed back and forth. I pushed as hard as I could and Daddy fell backward, lying on the bed. I felt very strong and kept pushing on his hands. Suddenly, he picked me up under the shoulders and held me in the air. I swung my arms, trying to reach him, but it was no use. My arms would not reach him. He then tossed me up in the air and caught me when I came down. It was fun. I laughed and laughed and wanted more. So he tossed me up and down a few more times.

Then the game changed. He caught me, brought me down

and put me between his legs. He locked his ankles together and started to squeeze. His legs were locked around my middle, and I struggled to get loose. The harder I struggled, the tighter he squeezed. His legs were big, and I could sense their immense power. At the same time he squeezed, he wiggled both legs really fast, tossing me like I was in a mixer, being wiggled faster and faster back and forth. My head flopped around at one end and my legs flopped below me. The squeezing became tighter and the shaking faster. He called this his "scissors lock."

I was pushing as hard as I could on his knee to make him stop when Mom came into the room. I called out to her for help. She said, "Will you two please stop it? I want to use the bathroom." She walked past us and Dad let go of me. I scrambled off the bed as fast as I could and shot out the door. Dad closed the door behind me, and I heard them yelling at each other as I searched for Susan.

Daddy wrestled with me many times that winter. I couldn't say no because he had already picked me up and had me on his bed, holding my arms so I couldn't move them, or my head so I couldn't reach him, or my legs so I couldn't get away. Most times he put me in that scissors lock, squeezed hard, and only let go when I cried "uncle." I fought as hard as I could and got hot and sweaty. I tried to hide at night before I had to go to bed. I would find a place I thought was safe and remain still, afraid to move. Sometimes he ignored me. Yet if he wanted, sooner or later he found me. There was no place that was safe. I tried to become invisible, but even stopping breathing didn't make me invisible. One night he found me buried under all my stuffed animals on my bed. I thought I looked like part of my pile of animals.

He slung me over his shoulder and carried me into his room. "So, are you going to cry and say 'uncle'?" I said no. I meant it. I

43

promised myself I would never say "uncle" again. He laughed and poked at me and, putting his huge hand on my head, held me at a distance while he pinched my legs and stomach with his other hand. I swung and pushed at him, but it was no use. My arms were too short to reach him. He shifted higher up on his bed and swung his legs up next to me.

I knew what was coming and fought with all my might to get loose. His grip on my head tightened and he grabbed both of my wrists in his left hand. I couldn't pull loose. Laughing, he said, "I got you, don't I?" My head was pushed downward until I could only see his shirt and belt. I started to kick at his stomach as hard as I could. He told me not to do that and grabbed my leg and twisted me until I was between his legs. They locked together and I was caught.

He squeezed tight and told me to cry "uncle." I said, "No." He squeezed tighter and tighter, and each time told me to say "uncle." I refused to give in. He started to shimmy his legs, making me bob more and more rapidly, telling me to say "uncle." I cried no. He squeezed and shimmied tighter and faster. My body vibrated from my head to my feet. I began to beat on his legs with my fists. I knew that made him mad because the pressure from his legs increased until it was hard to breathe. He demanded that I say "uncle." By this time I was gasping. "No." His face was turning red and he was panting. Almost with each breath, he said, "Now say 'uncle.'" I didn't say anything. I fought to get air and pushed as hard as I could. I felt his legs come together like giant pincers around my middle. They were crushing me. I saw two of him, then three or four of him, all blurring together and rolling around. I gasped for air, but couldn't breathe. The room swirled, and then everything went black.

I woke up lying on my own bed, with a damp washcloth over

44

my forehead. I was alone in my room. My middle hurt, and my hands hurt, and I felt awful, like I was going to throw up, only I knew I wasn't. I pressed the washcloth against my forehead and looked around the room without moving my head. I took short breaths because my stomach hurt so badly. After a while, my dad walked into my room and sat next to me. He said, "I guess we got carried away, didn't we, Hersch? Well, that's okay, you'll be just fine." He turned the washcloth over so the cool side was against my forehead, got up, and left.

I lay there, feeling perfectly empty. It was like all my feelings had gone somewhere to hide. My world, the one where I lived, was too full of danger to let them loose. I was warm and comfortable, but in bed I noticed how tense my body was. My muscles in my legs had tightened up, my hands were clenched into fists, and my neck and shoulders were rigid. I had a slight headache but didn't connect it to how rigidly I was holding my body. I tensed my muscles so I couldn't feel waves of terror and fear flow through my body. This became my habit. I wanted to be numb to all these feelings. My responses to other people did not come from how I felt; they came from carefully watching what others said and did, and quickly acting in an acceptable manner. I had to figure out what was going on and how to talk or act.

After that time my dad would say, "Let's play, Hersch. You can trust me. I won't do anything this time. Come on." Then he would start. First, holding my head away from him and poking me in the ribs, then eventually getting me into the scissors lock. Sometimes, he would merely toss me on his big bed and let me alone. He wouldn't grab me or squeeze me. Yet I remained on guard. I lost all trust in him. I didn't know when he was going to hurt me.

These mean-spirited games were only part of a larger pattern, the full extent of which I didn't comprehend until much later. My father was bitter, seething with resentment against the world, perhaps because his own father was so famous and successful. His relationship with my mother was caustic. Rancor and animosity ruled. I learned why many years later, at age thirteen, when Susan told me, "Mom turned frigid on Dad. She wouldn't let him touch her. I think she liked someone else." I immediately remembered the summer I was six years old, clearing a vacant lot two doors down from our house for a playing field. A car parked in front of our house, and a man got out and went inside. Shortly after that, Ayako left. A while later, I was thirsty and went to the side door to get a glass of water. It was locked; so was the front. I got water from the garden hose and didn't think about it. But the same thing happened a week later, and then a week after that. Ayako left both times the man went inside. Susan's revelation to me struck a chord.

In Twin Falls, all I knew was that at home my father was always erupting. His anger would explode for almost any reason. Many times spankings occurred when the reasons were impossible to fathom. When his anger raged, he grabbed whoever was near, my sister or me. He yanked his belt from around his waist, pulled our pants and underwear down, and beat our bare bottom until it was red. I watched my sister get beaten. She watched me. Watching was terrifying because whoever watched was next.

One time, when I had just turned five years old, I opened the box where he kept his cigars, took one out, and asked him what it was. He told me he'd show me. He clipped the end off one, walked over to a closet, and pulled out all the clothes from the rack. At this point I was still curious about what he was going to show me. Then he lit and put the cigar in my mouth, pushed me into the empty closet, and told me he'd let me out when I sucked on the thing until it was gone. After a few minutes, I became sick and threw up.

When he smelled my vomit, he opened the closet and whipped me with his belt for the mess I'd made. I was sickened by the awful taste of vomit, but he liked the fact that I was so helpless. That added to the control he felt. When he had whipped me to his satisfaction, he stopped yelling at me. In a calm voice he commanded me to get ready for dinner. It was as if, to him, nothing had happened. He left me still sick to my stomach, my bladder about to burst, and quivering in fear. I managed to splash water in my mouth, removing some of the taste, and stumble to the dining table. Ayako took one look at me and said that I looked green. I quickly told everybody I felt sick and wanted to go straight to bed. My father released his hand from the back of my neck, and I walked away as fast as I could. I couldn't have eaten anything anyway.

Another time he erupted while Susan and I were in the middle of a game we had started so we could be like him. We had watched my dad at his desk many times. When we asked him what he was doing he always said, "Important papers." So we invented a game we called "important papers." One evening we carefully moved his papers from one side of the desk to the other, pretending we had "important papers."

I was in the process of moving a stack when he spotted me. His rage burst like the fire department releasing the water from a hydrant on the hottest day of the summer. The burst was uncontrollable and savage. Within a few seconds he had his belt out, my pants pulled down, and he whipped me until I cried, begging him to stop. My bottom had red welts, and for days Ayako applied a cream on it to heal them.

After I was spanked, he ordered me to the corner of the room and grabbed my sister. She was already crying, pleading with him. She couldn't get the words out because her lips were quivering so hard. Her right hand was in her mouth, biting down, and her

47

other hand on her fanny, trying to cover it. Dad put her over his knees, pulled down her panties, and beat her with his belt. He loudly counted as he struck, from one to ten. Then he paused and suddenly hit her again. She was crying and begging him, "Please stop! I promise I will never to do it again!" When another blow fell, she couldn't help herself. Her bladder emptied from fear and she peed on his pants. He sprang to his feet in rage, dumping her on the floor. He looked at his pants and started cursing and stormed out of the room. Susan crawled over to me, hiding her face, trying to pull her underpants up, sobbing uncontrollably. My body twitched as well. Yet I could not console her. She didn't want to be touched or held, even by me.

The evenings were the worst, though. That's because my parents liked to drink. With my father, he might as well have been pouring gasoline on a fire.

When my father came home and my mother was around, Susan and I exchanged glances and slowly retreated upstairs. They liked to start with drinks before dinner. I didn't really know what "drinks" meant, only that they poured a lot of brown, smelly liquid into a glass with ice. I did know that after they had a few drinks, the tenor of the evening would change. The noise level increased, and we did not want to be in sight when the shouting began. We could become a target for anger. Our retreats up the stairs became a game, only in deadly earnest. Reaching the top of the stairs without being noticed was winning. We closed the door to a small crack, then stayed quiet so as not to be heard. They argued, yelled, walked around waving their arms. We easily heard them from our rooms because their voices were filled with meanness and rage. Susan and I did not dare go downstairs until we were called for dinner.

48

When we sat at the table, the air sparked with menace. I felt like a huge electric storm was about to sweep everything off the table and blow everybody into another room. Words weren't spoken; they crackled out of mouths. The cap keeping the dinner discussion civil was loose and wobbling, about to blow off at any time. Susan and I stuffed the food into our mouths, hoping to finish our dinners, excuse ourselves, and escape before any explosions happened. If we didn't get away fast enough, we would have to witness the eruption of wrath and be ready to duck to the nearest corner of the room to keep from getting hurt. One time my father yanked the tablecloth so hard, he pulled all the plates and glasses off the table, right in the middle of our meal. On another occasion he stood up, raised his hands over his head in frustration, and pulled the hanging light out of the ceiling. As the light and ceiling plaster came cascading down, I pushed back my chair so fast, it fell backward with me falling over it. I rolled to the wall and remained frozen, wondering what else he was going to grab and destroy, like me. But he stomped out of the room instead. My mother had her glass of whisky in her hand, and she gulped it down in fear. Once he left the room, I grabbed my sister, ran out toward the kitchen, around the hallway, and up the stairs to my room.

I never talked about this with my sister, but both of us knew that the longer the evening went on without erupting into terror, the closer we were to the explosion. We learned to walk carefully, not making any noise. Our hope was to make it to bedtime without them noticing us. If they did, I could be certain that something scary and painful would happen. This formed such a pattern that I cannot recall an evening inside our house, or outside in the summer time, when my dad wasn't threatening or my parents weren't drinking and yelling at each other.

The terror of those evenings set our family apart, though I

49

wasn't aware of it. I didn't get my first sense of normalcy until I went to visit my friend, Freddy Otto, who lived next door. His garage door was open and Freddy's dad was inside. He told me that Freddy was not home, but I stood and watched him. He was standing in front of a large slanted rack, putting comic books on it in some specific order. He had hundreds of comic books in his garage, some in boxes, some tied together, some in loose stacks. He was taking some out of a box and placing them onto the rack while I stood, grinning at this wonderful sight, wishing they all were mine.

Mr. Otto glanced up at me and asked, "Do you like comic books, Hersch?" I answered yes, that I liked comic books very much.

He said, "There's a box of last month's over there; do you want to take a look?" I nodded my head up and down, excited as could be. At the rear of the garage I saw the box, overflowing with comic books. Mr. Otto said, "Those are going to go back. You can look them over. You can even have two of them."

I inched into the garage, never taking my eyes off Mr. Otto. I was convinced he was setting a trap and that something terrible was going to happen. But I could not resist the lure of the box with the comic books overflowing. Mr. Otto said, "Go ahead, it's okay." I still proceeded carefully, ready to run for the door as soon as the trap was sprung.

Nothing that was happening in Mr. Otto's garage was what I was used to. He paid little attention to me but just kept placing comic books at various places on his rack. He looked over once in a while and asked me what I liked, and I told him what I was reading. He nodded and went back to what he was doing. I remained on alert. I sat cross-legged reading a comic, expecting something ter-rifying to happen at any second. I kept reading and finally asked Mr. Otto where he got all the comic books. He answered me that

50

his job was filling stores with comic books. He put the full rack in his van and drove around and replaced the empty racks at the drug store, the market, and some other places. I thought, "Wow, lucky Freddy. He has all the comic books in the world."

I finally got up to leave. I walked carefully by Mr. Otto, half expecting him to grab me and shake me or something. He just kept on what he was doing, on a new rack. "So long, Hersch. Sure you don't want to take some? They're last month's, just going to throw them out." I was so stunned I just walked blankly out of the garage and across the Ottos' lawn.

When I came into view of my house, I stopped cold in my steps. I felt light headed and a tug in my throat said, "Go no further." The abrupt return of fear made me realize that not all homes, not all families, were like mine. No wonder I didn't know how to act at the Ottos'. I felt totally out of balance. I realized that I could not tell the difference as to when somebody was going to hurt me or not. I was sure my father would try to destroy me, but I had to watch other people very carefully too. Normal to me was what happened with my mom and dad. My body had learned to keep constant vigil, to be as invisible as possible. That was how I survived.

Just how different we were became all too clear one Saturday morning. All the evil forces surrounding me seemed to converge on the same day. My father's abuse, my mother's lack of caring, came at me in a one-two punch that would leave me scarred for the rest of my childhood.

I was outside after breakfast, playing on the front lawn, when my father came out and said, "Hersch, I'm going flying. Want to come along? You're going to be seven pretty soon. It's time you learned."

I listened to the timbre of his voice. He didn't seem to be upset. I was excited but didn't dare show it. "In your plane?"

"Yes, right now. Want to come?"

I wanted to jump up and run into his arms. But I stayed where I was and said, "Are you sure?" I was trying to figure out if he was trapping me in some game. Yet he merely waved for me to come along. I got up immediately and ran over to the car with him. We drove to the Twin Falls airport, where he kept his single-engine Piper Cub, with the cockpit set over the wings.

I sat in one of the cockpit seats facing front, something I'd never done before. Before we started I looked all around. He was busy outside the plane, moving blocks from around the wheels and finding some guys to help pull the plane onto the runway. I could see out the front and down the sides and a little overhead. I couldn't see down to the ground because the wings were in the way. I was fascinated by the hundreds of buttons and knobs in front of me. Dad said I was absolutely not to touch anything, or else. Best of all, there was a steering wheel right in front of me, just for my seat. It was really only half of a steering wheel because the bottom was missing, but I took it in my hands and held it just like I was flying the airplane. I was so excited, I was grinning like mad. My dad's seat also had a steering wheel, exactly like the one in front of me. The plane had dual controls. He was the main pilot and I was his helper.

The plane rocked back and forth on the pavement while Dad and some men pulled it onto the runway. When it came to a rest, the runway stretched off to my right. Dad climbed into the cockpit and buckled a belt across his seat and chest. He reached across and made sure my seat belt was tight. I was too small for the chest belt, so it was behind my back. My feet dangled above the floor of the cockpit. A man in front pulled down hard on the propeller and backed away from the plane while my dad turned a key and the engine roared. The noise was deafening and the wind rushed by my cockpit window like we were already flying.

I immediately grasped the wheel. Dad yelled, "Hands off, don't touch." So I reached down and held onto the edges of my seat. The plane sat still, vibrating, for a while. Dad moved a lot of buttons, revved the engine a few times, and made sure all the flaps could move. Then he pushed on some levers, the engine revved up, and we rolled slowly forward. The plane turned onto the runway and stopped again. Dad looked at his knobs and dials, checked the flaps, and eased one lever forward. The engine roared louder, but we didn't move. He pushed another lever, and we jerked forward. We rolled down the runway faster and faster, bouncing and racing as the runway sped by. Then, almost like magic, everything was smooth and soft. The engine noise seemed farther away. I could only see sky ahead of me as we left the runway and ground below. I was flying with my Dad. It felt so great.

I couldn't see out of the plane very well, so Dad loosened my seat belt. He opened the side windows to feel the rush of air and gauge how fast we were going. He worked us higher and higher, controlling everything by pushing and pulling the steering wheel in front of him in all directions. If he pulled it, we went higher. If he pushed a little to the right, we banked the other way. The wheel in front of me reacted exactly the same way as his. If he pushed forward, mine went forward, or to the side, or downward. He said that this was in case something happened, the co-pilot could take over. I strained to be able to look out and see the ground. The airport was far in the distance behind us, and the buildings below looked like little toys.

Our side windows were still open, and the wind rushing through the cockpit was cold. We were flying level when suddenly he let go of his wheel and said to me, "Take over, co-pilot." At first I didn't know what he meant. The nose of the plane dipped down, and we pointed down and I saw the ground far in front of

53

us. I didn't know what to do. He repeated, "Take over, co-pilot." I grabbed hold of the wheel and pulled it toward me. The plane tilted upward. Dad had his hands clasped behind his head, calling to me, "What are you going to do now?" I couldn't see anything out of the windshield but sky and I didn't know where I was. I lifted myself up higher, but that caused me to push the wheel forward and the plane tilted down. I saw mountains, and we were rushing toward them. I yelled at Dad. I was flustered, trying to do something I had no idea about. When I pulled on the wheel, I saw nothing but sky, and when I pushed, I saw mountains and was scared of crashing into them. I didn't want to crash and die.

I pulled and pushed, and pulled and pushed, trying to stay even. The out-of-control rocking seemed to last forever. All the while I was yelling and pleading with Dad to help me. Finally, the nose headed steeply downward, and I wasn't strong enough to pull the wheel back. We kept plummeting faster, and I tried to pull harder, but the wheel wouldn't move. It was like it had taken over control. Wind swooshing by the window: we were being pulled into a bottomless spinning hole.

Daddy finally took hold of his wheel and pulled with both arms until we were level. I sank into my seat, with no strength left in my arms, and stared up at the sky, afraid to move. He yelled above the engine noise, "What's the matter, Hersch, get scared?"

I just looked at him. He had been toying with me, a feeling I knew so well. He had a grip on his wheel, and we were flying like normal again. I slouched in my seat and gazed straight ahead at my wheel quietly bobbing forward and back. I was in a trance, trying not to be there, but knowing I was a long, long way from the airport. I was hoping more than anything else that we'd turn around and go home.

I felt the plane bank to the right and thought, "Oh good, we're heading back. Thank goodness, it's over." Instead the plane banked more steeply and I looked at Daddy. He glanced at me and yelled, "You're a big boy, Hersch. You like excitement, don't you?"

My hope was shattered. The plane struggled through a steeper and steeper turn. I knew something awful was going to happen, but I was helpless to prepare. Daddy yelled, "Hang on!" He was pulling hard toward himself and to the left. The plane had turned nearly on its side, and I thought for sure he was done with the turn. But he kept going, holding and pulling his wheel. My seat belt was still loose as I slid against the side of the cockpit, even though I was hanging onto my seat with all my might. The engine was making an awful, straining noise and things inside the cockpit were falling against the side.

In the next instant, we were upside down! I was trying to hang onto my seat, and fell, caught by my seat belt. It was cutting across my legs. Yet that didn't register amid my blind panic. I fought to wedge my legs to hold on. I was completely upside down, absolutely terrified, screaming as loud as I could, "Stop, stop, stop!" My window was open and the air rushing through the cockpit was pulling me toward it. I thought for sure I was going to be sucked out of the window and fall through the sky to my death. I hung upside down, frantically holding on. I could see the ground below as it whizzed by in large patches of brown and green. Watching made me dizzy. All I could think was: He is going to let me drop out of the plane and die.

My body was strained and rigid, so I was shocked when I bumped against something. At first I thought I was sucked out of the window, but it was my father's right arm and side. He bumped me back. The plane was quickly rolling back on its side and then into a left bank, and then back to level. When my seat belt strap eased up, I realized it had held me in place. I was so petrified, I

55

thought it had come off and I was loose and going to fall out of the plane. I gasped and curled my body and grabbed the strap with my forearms because my hands wouldn't close. I collapsed in my seat in relief. My head bounced against the hard side, just next to the window. The air rushing by grabbed my hair, but my arms felt too weak to reach up and close the window.

"Is that enough excitement for you, big boy?" My father was laughing, thrilled at the aerial maneuver. He asked the same thing over and over, but I didn't reply. I stared dully at the floor of the cockpit. I was trying to gather myself. I didn't know what else was to come. The longer we bounced along, and I just sat still, the better. Maybe he had gotten enough excitement for one ride.

I could tell by the engine noise that we were slowing down. I hoped fervently we were going to land. I didn't look outside because I was afraid we were still up in the sky and he was turning off the engine for some other thrill. When the nose pointed slightly downward, I peeked out of the windshield. I saw mountaintops higher than we were. I felt so happy, so happy.

It was hard climbing out of the airplane. I crawled out of the cockpit and sat on the wing until my father came over and lowered me to the ground. I ran over to a fence and watched the plane being pulled back into the hangar. When my father came out, I ran over to our car and climbed in. He didn't say anything on the drive home, and I sat silently with my hands folded on my lap. It felt good to hold myself, even in such a small way.

The second shock of that summer's day came right after we got home. I ran into the house, afraid of what my father would do next. I found Mom sitting at the table playing cards with three other women. She had a glass of whisky in one hand and a cigarette in the other. I went up to her, but she instantly shooed me away. "Go on out and play, Hersch. We're busy here." She didn't realize I wanted her protection. When I didn't move, she insisted, "Now, go on out. Close the door too."

I had no choice but to obey. The front door was still open, and I walked slowly through it and down the front steps. I was all alone.

To keep from crying, I shut down inside. I didn't want to feel anything. I wandered aimlessly over the lawn until I spied my special bush at the far edge. I halted when I reached it, my arms at my side. There was no place for me to go, so I just stood there. After a long while, somebody yelled at me. I heard them but pretended to be busy looking at a bug on a leaf. I just wanted no one to bother me.

I noticed my father's car was gone, and I slowly returned to our house. When I reached the front door, I could hear the ladies talking and I went in. One of them said, "Hersch, your mother's in the kitchen, with Betty."

I approached the kitchen carefully and stood quietly outside the door. I recognized Betty McRoberts' voice because of her rasp. She and her husband knew about all the turmoil and stress in our household. She had two daughters and she liked children— Susan, me, and Kit, my brother who was four years younger than me, included.

I heard her say, "Marge, I tell you, and I'm your friend, he's going to drive them into the nut house. They can't move without him throwing a tantrum and torturing them. Did you see the look on little Hersch's face when he came home? He was scared to death."

There was silence. Then my mom's voice: "Betty, I just don't care anymore. I just want out. I want out of this flea-trap town. I want to go back to Los Angeles." Her delivery of the words was sloppy, and I knew that meant she'd been drinking. But what she

57

had said made me freeze inside. My stomach felt sick, because I knew it was true. She didn't care.

Then Betty said, "Marge, they need you. You're their mother."

My mother paused again for a few seconds. Then I heard her say, "They don't care. Just the other day Kit called Ayako 'Mommy.' Did you know that?" She sounded disgusted. "I never wanted them in the first place. He can have them. I just want out of here."

I lurched backward, reeling in shock. I felt empty and numb. Just then Betty and my mom came through the door. My mom walked past me without saying a word.

Betty looked down at me and gasped. "How long have you been standing here?" She must have read the expression on my face because she didn't wait for me to answer. She put her hand gently on my back and walked me toward the front door. I thought she was going to push me outside, but she came out onto the front porch with me.

"Hersch," she leaned down to me and spoke in a low, calm voice, "your mom and dad aren't getting along right now. They may say things, crazy things, but they don't want to hurt you. Tell your sister to call me if you three need help."

Her red lips moved and I heard words come from her mouth, but my mind was filled with what I'd heard my mother say. Betty squeezed my shoulders and returned inside to her card game. My eyes didn't focus too well, but I managed to walk down the steps without falling, continued across the lawn, and stopped next to a huge tree on the parking strip. I put my hand on the tree to steady the shaking that had taken over my entire body. I stood there rigidly, staring at nothing.

My sense of utter hopelessness was broken when my sister skipped up to me and asked what I was doing. I told her what happened and what Betty had said. She crept behind the tree, near the street curb, and looked up and down our street. She said, "There's nowhere for us to go."

The rest of the summer, we became even more careful to keep out of the way of both of them. They drank more than ever, and their arguing became violent. He hit her and she threw things at him. We learned to duck out of the way, crawl out of the dining room, and hide.

Now, as I lay in my bed after my grandfather had come to visit, I was still holding the envelope with the note he'd written to me. I felt once again the determination he'd shown when he saved me from certain harm at the hands of my father. I had been plunged into another bottomless pit of terror when an old man grabbed my father's hand and made him stop. My roly-poly, smiling grandfather had shown me the support that I craved.

Yes, he'd shown his unbending resolve out on that island in the Snake River. No man, no matter how large, would stop him from what he decided to do. As I held that note in my hand, I looked inside myself for something similar. If I could only become determined like my grandfather, I could survive whatever came next.

CHAPTER THREE

The Passing
of Two Sons

By that fall my parents had dropped any pretense of civility. They traded hate-laced jabs between them, fueling the blistering tension with alcohol. Susan and I avoided them, spending as much time as possible in our rooms. I was in first grade at Washington Street School, which became a safe refuge during the day.

The rift between my parents hardened. The rancor and insults spewed back and forth unabated, always edging toward violence. Just after Christmas, my mother moved to Santa Monica, California. I remembered so clearly the conversation I overheard when she told her friend, "I never wanted them in the first place. I just want out of here." Her declaration haunted me for many years afterward. Her departure struck an exclamation point on my memory like a pick ax striking granite.

After my mother's departure, winter snows filled Twin Falls, and my father spent considerable time traveling to Oregon and

60

California. Ayako took care of us while he was gone, and when at home he occupied himself with his business and hunting. He largely ignored Susan, and I received a few spankings for no reason I understood, and remember them because they seemed halfhearted. His mood was short and pouty, but not aggressively violent. He did not make any mention of my mother returning, and Susan told me she was not going to leave Los Angeles.

During my Easter vacation, my mother insisted that I join her. She favored me over my sister and brother and likely sensed that she needed one of us with her so my father would continue to send her money. My father acquiesced, and I finished first grade in Santa Monica. When I joined her, I quickly understood that she did not want to live with my father, but wanted his money.

My father's travels had a purpose. He negotiated the purchase, with the help of my grandfather, of the Coca-Cola Bottling Companies in Bend, Oregon, and Santa Maria, California, and at the beginning of summer, my father moved to Santa Maria, California, a small town on the central coast, taking my sister and brother with him, along with Ayako. He bought a large Spanish-style home at 223 Morrison Street.

My mother had rented a small apartment, and while I was in school, she watched TV. Initially, I felt a reprieve because I'd escaped my father's violent outbursts. I soon realized, though, that I faced an equally pernicious danger. I could be discarded upon her whim.

My mother liked to go out at night and she frequently took me with her. The first time occurred during the early evening, and I thought it was fun to sit in a dimly lit lounge, on a soft leather seat in a booth, and watch my mom talk to men who sat down with us. Soon, she and a man got up, left the booth, and walked away. I waited, expecting them to return, but after a long time passed, the room had emptied out. I scooted out of the booth and made my way to the man behind the bar.

Before I even asked, he said to me, "Here, that woman left this for you, and she wrote an address on this napkin." He pushed a ten-dollar bill toward me, along with a napkin that had our address written on it. "There's a taxi stand right out that door, over there. She said for you to go home." He turned away, wiping the rim of a glass with his bar towel.

When I opened the side door, I was briefly blinded by the setting sun, but I saw an orange-yellow car with the word "Taxi" on the side. I showed the napkin to the driver and asked if he'd take me to that address for ten dollars. The first part of his answer scared me stiff.

He examined the napkin, turned it sideways, and said, "You're a long way from home, kid." Then he paused and said, "But I think this is enough; climb in the back." He smiled creepily as he pulled the bill from between my fingers.

I realized how expendable I was. How could she just leave me in a strange place far from home? From then on I carried a paper with my address on it whenever I went anywhere with my mom.

First grade ended, and by early summer my dad stopped sending money, so my mom was forced to move to Santa Maria, joining my father, sister, and brother in the house on Morrison Street. Neither of them had any thoughts of reconciliation. The bitterness my mother and father felt toward each other reignited the instant we arrived, and it boiled over at the slightest contact between them.

My father became openly violent toward her. Once, they were picked up in front of our house by my Aunt Shirley and her date to attend a jazz concert. My father slapped my mother across the face. Blood poured from her mouth, and she rushed inside for help. Shirley followed and applied a towel as I watched in the front hallway. She was aghast at the violence she had witnessed from her favorite brother, shooed me to my bedroom, and immediately drove away with her date. My dad used the side door, stormed up to his bedroom, and locked the door behind him.

We kids had a buffer in Ayako, who warned us of any danger signs and guided us out of harm's way as often as she could. Susan did her part as well to protect me and Kit. I knew that my mother had effectively taken me, Daddy's first-born son, and favored me, and he was prone to destroy anything she favored.

The atmosphere of terror that we lived in day to day could not last for long. One night I was awakened by rage-filled screaming. I peeked out of my room toward the double door leading into my parents' bedroom. As I watched, my father swung his right hand and hit my mom so hard, her body lifted off the floor and flew through the air. She landed with her legs hanging over the wooden footboard of their king-size bed. In his rage, he looked larger than his six foot, one inch frame with nearly three hundred pounds on it. When my mom raised her head, blood was running from her mouth, dripping on her dress and the bedcover. My father suddenly saw me and slammed the double doors shut. I shuddered uncontrollably, both from fear for my mother and the thought that he'd come and find me next.

The next day she moved out and returned to Los Angeles.

During the day, my dad worked at the Coca-Cola Bottling Co., so daytime was relatively safe. I started the second grade at Miller Street Elementary School, four blocks from my home on Morrison Street. Once again, school was a safe haven. At home, I stayed as close to Ayako as possible.

As weeks passed, Daddy came home later and later from his office. He did not seek us out for punishment. He even seemed

63

even-tempered during the short periods we saw him. Usually we were asleep when he came home. The reason why he was calmer was soon forthcoming. One night I heard voices and crept out of my room. Susan was already on the upstairs landing, listening to them downstairs, laughing and playing jazz music. Her name was Nelda, and it was easy to tell he liked her. Susan knew about Nelda for some time before I became aware of her. When I met her, I liked her too. Susan confided in Ayako, and she concluded that as long as "Mr. Cobb was happy, the rest of us are better off."

He still had many times when he was not happy. Phone calls from my mother would ignite his fuse and an explosion inevitably followed. Susan told me that Mom had hired a lawyer, and I acted like I knew what that meant. Susan liked to show off her superior knowledge of adult ways, and said that they were "officially separated." I didn't know what that meant either.

One day during summer I came home from playing, and Ayako told me my grandfather had written me a letter. I rushed to the chest near the front door and spotted a small envelope with writing in dark green ink on the front. I looked at the envelope and turned it over. On the back, small block type printed in green ink read, "Tyrus R. Cobb, Glenbrook, Douglas County, Nevada." That was it, no street address. Ayako told me he was at Lake Tahoe. I knew the letter was for me, because it was addressed to "Herschel Cobb Jr." He thanked me for writing him, asked me how I liked school, told me to be sure to read a good book, said that he knew I was a good boy and could do anything I set my mind to. He told me he had been at Lake Tahoe for the summer, and that I would like it there, and that he was going to go to Atlanta, Royston, and some other places, and that he missed me. His handwriting was steady, and I especially liked the end, "I am, With Love, Granddaddy."

I read the letter again as I climbed the stairs, and again in my room. I sat on the edge of my bed, looked around the room for a safe place to hide the letter, then returned it to the envelope, sat and looked at it while my body filled with warmth and hope.

He wrote me again in late August, telling me he was leaving Lake Tahoe, had put his boat in dry dock, had locked up his cabin, and was anxious to visit Royston. He didn't know where he would be if I wanted to write a letter back; he wanted me to study hard and told me again I could do anything to which I set my mind.

Susan received letters from him as well, and we shared them. He missed her and said he wanted to see us as soon as he took care of some matters. Neither of us could bring ourselves to write him about the terror we lived with each day.

The months passed toward the holiday season, and I managed to avoid spankings, beatings, confrontations in the bathrooms, and being thrown around. Daddy was very busy with his business, and Nelda held sway over his emotions. The phone calls from my mother, however, were broadcast like an air horn blasting from a large truck. His voice boomed throughout the house from the instant he picked up the receiver. Kit and I scrambled to our room, shut the door, hid, and stayed hidden until Susan found us.

Susan had a special role in our lives. She looked out for us, took care of us, cooked us dinner, made us lunches, baked chocolate chip cookies, made sure we had clean clothes, and acted as our lookout, ally, and protector. My father had grown to love my sister, especially as she matured during the third and fourth grades. Physically, she was built like him, a little plump, with a round face and lovely red hair that hung in large curls to her shoulders, framing the flawless peach complexion of her cheeks. On most occasions she could dampen his fury with her smile and her willingness to stand directly in front of him and tell him what she thought.

We knew he was in a battle with my mother, and we children were barter. She wanted more money or us. She was living a life he was supporting, one dominated by drinking, going out at night, and sleeping all day. He had to pay the bills, and any reminder of that fact made him furious. Susan and I knew his anger would eventually erupt, and we dreaded being within range when it did.

It burst with uncontrolled fury one Saturday. The heavy rains had stopped and early spring was in bloom. Nelda was not around. It was a late afternoon in April 1951 when Ayako called to Daddy, "Mrs. Cobb is on the phone, Mr. Cobb."

The phone was downstairs, and the three of us huddled on the second-floor landing, leaning against the banister, listening intently. Ayako stood midway up the stairs. Susan and I exchanged glances, filled with apprehension. I held Kit's hand, listening as hard as I could. The sounds from downstairs were muffled but loud, sparked with a fury that sent shivers up my spine.

It ended with a final "Damn you!" and a huge slam of the receiver onto the phone. A ripping sound was followed by a crash. We heard Daddy start up the stairs. Susan and I, holding onto Kit, backed up against the wall across from the banister.

Ayako gasped, "Mr. Cobb, you pulled the whole phone right out of the wall." Her voice was filled with terror, but she was only hoping to slow him down. Her hands were in front of her face, half protecting herself.

He bolted past her, up the stairs two at a time, and saw us cowering against the wall. In one powerful swipe he reached down and grabbed Susan. She shouted to us, "Run! Run!" then, "Daddy, don't, that hurts." He picked her up and held her like a football. I heard him shout, "That bitch will never have you," as he threw her against the wall.

I pulled Kit with me as I ran down the hall. I opened the door to the linen closet and looked back as Susan fell to the floor. He turned and started after me, but I was prepared. I pushed Kit into the bottom of the linen closet, into my secret cubbyhole, and crawled in after him as fast as I could.

The closet was narrow and deep. The bottom shelf was a mere foot and a half from the floor and was nailed fast to the side walls of the closet. I had made a secret hiding place under that shelf, way in the back. I had happened upon it during one of our hide and seek games. The rear of the closet was unfinished and opened into a space formed by the thick supporting studs of the house. When I hid there, I piled towels and sheets in front of me. That way I could never be found. The deepest part of my cubbyhole went back probably seven or eight feet from the closet door.

I pushed Kit all the way back and coiled in front of him with my arms braced on each side of the wall. Daddy opened the door and tried to crawl in to grab me, but he was too big to fit through the space between the floor and the first shelf. He was furious, and his voice bellowed into our cave, demanding we come out at once. I was crying by this time, and could only repeat over and over again, "No, no, no." I was so scared, I could not have moved anyway. Kit was crying too, not understanding what was going on, and I was squashing him as I tried to back farther and farther away from my father. I will never forget his face, red and screaming. Sweat was pouring down from his forehead, his under-arms were wet, and his huge hand groped toward me, trying to grab hold. I pushed with all my might against the side wall of my cubbyhole. I sucked in my belly to make myself smaller. This was it. I thought, "If he reaches me, I'm a goner."

He was yelling, "Come here, come here, come here, damn you." His face was twisted by his shouting and squirming to reach

67

farther into my cubbyhole. His hands remained two feet distant, outstretched and grabbing. If the shelf above broke loose, he would have me.

I kept shouting, "No, no, no! Go away, go away!" I pushed harder backward, ignoring Kit pushing at me. I was not going to surrender, even though I was so scared I could feel the warmth between my legs, in my crotch.

Long minutes went by, and suddenly he withdrew. He turned his head as if listening for something, then pulled his wedged body out of the cubbyhole. I saw his knees under him, and then his feet, and then nothing but dim light. I didn't dare move. I knew he was setting a trap. Kit pushed at me, yelling he couldn't breathe, so I shifted a little bit, but kept him pinned far back in the cubbyhole. I waited and waited.

Ayako's face appeared and she motioned for me to come out, saying, "It's all right, Hersch. It's all right to come out."

I could barely move my muscles. I crawled out and stood up with Kit staying right behind me. I heard talking outside and went to a window overlooking the front yard. Daddy was talking with two policemen. Ayako had gone to the neighbor's house and called them. She took Kit and me and led us downstairs to the back door, where Susan was waiting. Ayako put us into her car and drove us to her friend's house, where we stayed overnight.

The next day, we returned home and Ayako had set up beds for us in the downstairs bedroom next to the kitchen. I saw my dad pass on the stairs a couple of times during the next few days, but he didn't look at me. The tension in the house was like walking barefoot through a field of bristles. At school, all I could think about was how he was going to pay me back. I didn't talk to Susan because I knew how much she loved Daddy. She would only say that everything was going to be okay.

I rode my bike home on a Friday and knew I had two days to dodge and hide until I could get back to school on Monday. I walked in the front door and thought nobody was home because it was so quiet. I went to the kitchen for cookies and saw Ayako leaning against the counter, holding Susan in her arms. I stopped short, preparing for whatever it was.

Ayako said, "Hersch, come here. I have to tell you something."

I edged toward her. Tears were streaming down Susan's cheeks. Ayako softly said, "Hersch, your father died today." I instantly felt sick in my stomach. "He had a heart attack."

I asked what a heart attack was, and she answered, "His heart just gave out; it exploded." I couldn't picture this in my mind, but that didn't matter. "It happened this morning, in Paso Robles, while he was working. I called your mother and she'll be here tomorrow."

She then asked if I wanted to be held, and I shook my head a little. Instead I took small steps out of the kitchen. I wanted to be alone.

I felt dazed walking to the front door and outside, where my bike was lying on the grass. All I could hear in my mind was, "He's dead. He's dead. He's dead. He can't hurt me anymore. He can't kill me." I got on my bicycle and took off. I could hardly believe how relieved I felt. I rode for a block and then it struck me like a lightning bolt that I'd wished my father dead before and my wish came true. I had killed him. I instantly felt awful, filled with guilt, and wanted him back alive.

I would never have a father—not the father he was, but the one I wanted in my heart. I stumbled to a stop on my bike, walked across the train tracks, and sat on the cement steps of the old railroad building. I was overwhelmed with a horrible mixture of guilt, remorse, and elation. I felt sick and wanted to throw up,

69

but I was also free of him. I couldn't stop the words in my head or the feelings washing through my body. I looked around and didn't see a single person. I had nobody to talk to or ask for help. I swallowed hard, and as all my feelings and thoughts bubbled up uncontrollably, I sat for a long, long time.

When I got on my bike and started to ride home, I kept looking everywhere, trying to find my dad. I held the idea in my heart that if I found him alive, he would be the father I truly wanted, loving and protective. It was April 13, 1951; he was thirty-three years old, and I was eight.

The next morning, Ayako woke Susan and me early. Nelda had gathered the possessions she had at our house into a suitcase. Crying, she hugged us both and mumbled that though she loved us, she probably would not see us again.

My mother arrived just before noon. She hobbled up the front steps on two crutches, with her left ankle heavily bandaged. She tried to bend down to hug us, but the crutches under her arms interfered, and she settled for patting me on my head. She smelled of whisky. Later, Ayako told us that she had sprained her ankle when she fell down some stairs. I guessed that she had smelled of whisky then too.

The next day was Daddy's funeral. Susan and I dressed in our church clothes and waited in the kitchen. Mom appeared in the middle of the morning and told us that we were not going to see Daddy buried. I looked at Susan, bewildered. She looked at Mom, but she would brook no arguments. We weren't going to see our father buried. Nor would we see any of our aunts or uncles or Granddaddy that day. Mom left by herself, and we were left behind.

Granddaddy called in the afternoon. Susan answered the phone, and I knew it was him by the way she conversed with him. I stood next to her and listened to her part of the conversation, hanging onto each word, whispering into her ear, asking if he was going to come and see us.

Susan asked him, "When are you coming to see us?" Then, "Why not?" And then, "Oh. Why?" and "Well, Hersch wants you to too." Silence for a few seconds, then, "Hersch wants to say hi." She turned to me and said, "He says for me to give you a big hug." Then I heard, "She's not here. We'll be okay. I'll take care of the boys. Ayako is here."

I knew the conversation was nearly over when Susan said, "Yes, if she does anything, I'll call you."

"Bye-bye, Granddaddy, I love you too. So does Hersch." I was nodding my head while she slowly put the receiver back on the cradle, as if she was letting go of our lifeline to safety. She was crying when she gave me my hug from Granddaddy.

I asked her why Granddaddy wasn't coming. "Hersch, he doesn't sound very good. He doesn't want to see Mom, and he doesn't have anything to say to her."

That part I understood. I mumbled, "What's going to happen to us?"

She weakly replied, "I don't know, Hersch. Where could we go?"

I just shook my head.

The rest of the day passed as if nothing had happened, except my father was gone. I was filled with guilt and longing. I hadn't seen my father laid in the ground, and suspected that Mom had lied to me, that he was alive somewhere. I constantly looked at strangers, hoping to find my true father.

My mother expected to inherit all her husband's wealth. The opposite happened. He had spent every penny that his father had given him, and on top of that his business owed creditors a great deal of money. She was stuck with these debts and three children she did not want. The only asset, the Coca-Cola Bottling Co., was in jeopardy of being sold, leaving her nothing. While in Los Angeles, she became close to a powerful lawyer who kept my father's estate open for years and the banks at bay, and permitted my mother to maintain an income. My mother was furious and disgusted. No inheritance, three unwanted children, debts, the faint smell of Nelda's perfume lingering, and only a modest income.

When school ended, she moved us all into an old house on a rundown street in a rundown neighborhood in Santa Monica. Ayako stayed with us, which was fortunate because my mother had no intention of raising her children. She went out nearly every night and slept most of the day. We didn't visit Grandma that summer, and Granddaddy wrote to me only once. I knew how much he disliked my mother, so I wasn't surprised, but still I felt isolated and invisible. Susan and I were anxious that we might never see our grandparents again. We were stranded. Our father was dead, our mother openly resented us, and our grandparents were old and far, far away.

Summer in Los Angeles was hot, and without any friends there wasn't much to do except wait for school to start. In September, I started third grade at a huge school on Wilshire Boulevard, called Wilshire Crest School. During recess I met a bully named Marshall Cohn. The problem for him was, he was close to my own size and I could hit him back. Although he was in the fourth grade, he played tether ball with the third graders so he could win all recess long because he was a little taller and could hit over their heads, then laugh when they couldn't reach the ball. I watched him taunt them for a few days at tether ball and take their candy when they lost. The next day at recess I made up my mind. I got in his line to get my turn to try to "stay in." I grabbed the tether ball on his first serve, while the tether was long, quickly aimed, and hit it as hard as I could right into his face. His nose started to bleed and he stumbled out of the circle, done. With my job done, I handed the tetherball to the next third grader in line and went over to the basketball hoops. Marshall never bothered me again.

That first school year in Los Angeles was miserable. I developed a reserve, feeling that I was alone in the world. That feeling never left me even as the months passed and I gained friends to play with. I had not one whom I actually trusted.

As summer approached, Susan and I dreaded the prospect that Ayako would return to her family in Seattle, leaving us alone with Mom for the entire summer, targets of her caprice and rejection. Fortunately, our mother fervently desired to rid herself of the three of us. On the last day of third grade I came home from school to find Mom waiting at the open front door. Just inside, our suitcases were packed. We would, she announced, spend the entire summer at my grandmother's.

The next morning, she took us to the train station, put the three of us into a train car with bench seats, and waved good-bye. Ayako had fixed us a bag of sandwiches. We headed off to Palo Alto, where my grandmother would pick us up. To Grandma, we were her son's children, and we were always welcome.

The rail journey took all day, but it wasn't boring. I saw all kinds of pretty hills, trees, and animals, a little bit of the Pacific Ocean, and a string of small towns where the train stopped. Susan and I shared an unspoken comfort in knowing that our grandmother would welcome us with open arms.

The old-fashioned train station in Palo Alto looked a dirty pink color in the late afternoon sun, its thick plaster walls and tiled roof barely catching the fading light. We climbed down the railcar's metal steps onto the platform, peered through an arched doorway, and spotted Grandma waving to us. She was smiling, but she looked visibly pale and tired. Susan and I and Kit all started talking at the same time, and Grandma laughed as she tried to sort out our stories. We climbed into the back of her light blue four-door Chrysler. The drive to her house in Menlo Park, on Bay Laurel Drive, took only a few minutes.

As soon as we stopped, I jumped out of the car and ran up to the house. Immediately I saw the reason why Grandma looked so tired and pale. Uncle Ty was there, sitting in a wheelchair, dressed in pajamas and a robe. His hands tightly gripped the side armrests, and I saw his hair had been shaved off the back of his head. He had trouble saying hello, but his smile was as warm and enveloping as ever and he knew our names. By the end of summer, Uncle Ty would change forever, and he would not even remember the names of his own children. The brain tumor diagnosed several months before would steadily follow its irrevocable course.

I had first met Uncle Ty when he visited Twin Falls one summer. He was tall, with a broad smile, scarce of red hair on top of his head, much like his father. He picked me up and looked me over while he held me in outstretched arms. He pronounced me a "strapping young'un," gave me a big kiss, and walked around with me held high in the air, leaving a deep, affectionate first impression on me. He exuded a charm and easy confidence that made me feel like all was right in the world. Now, Uncle Ty was helpless, and my Aunt Mary was pushing his wheelchair over the uneven brick porch at the front of Grandma's house. His children had gathered as well. My cousin Ty III was my age, his brother Charlie a couple of years younger, and their sister Peggy a few years younger yet. Susan, Kit, and I quickly said hello to Uncle Ty, then stood awkwardly before him, not knowing what else to say.

Finally, Aunt Mary turned so her body was between us and Uncle Ty and quietly said, "Ty is sick, very sick. We hope he'll get better, but we don't know." I knew she didn't want Uncle Ty to hear what she said. "You children said hello, but Ty gets tired very easily, so you'll have to understand."

Grandma quickly put in, "Go say hello to your cousins, and then we'll get you settled."

Ty III and Charlie had settled in chairs on the brick porch, and their gloom was so thick it cast a dark pall around them. We had never spent much time with Ty and Charlie, so we didn't know what to say. We all walked out on the front yard and stood looking at each other, silent and uneasy. Susan grasped the situation better than I, and she told Ty and Charlie how sorry she was, but never asked them what was actually wrong with Uncle Ty.

My Aunt Shirley lived with Grandma in the Bay Laurel house, and she soon walked outside to join us. "Susan, Hersch, I'm going to take you over to your Aunt Beverly's house. Aunt Mary and her children are staying here. You'll be fine. You can come back tomorrow and see your cousins."

I had so looked forward to seeing my grandmother's porch, with its white posts, overhanging roof, white painted windows, and planter boxes filled with plants and bright flowers. Yet I found myself riveted on Uncle Ty's profile. Aunt Mary was wiping his mouth, and his knuckles shone white, clinging to the armrests of his wheelchair.

Uncle Ty was the oldest of Ty Cobb's five children, Aunt Shirley was next, and then my father. The three of them had grown up with a special emotional bond. Aunt Beverly and Uncle Jim came later. Aunt Shirley was very close to both Uncle Ty and my father, but especially my father. She felt an affinity with him and reveled in his peevish humor and schoolboy antics that balanced her bookish, proper ways. She missed my father deeply for the rest of her life.

75

He had died just over a year ago, and now she was watching helplessly as her older brother slipped toward his end. The man sitting in the wheelchair was only a shadow of her brother. She grew up with Ty Jr. and knew him as tall and handsome, very athletic, capable, and a bit rebellious. He had been born in 1910, and by the time he was ten years old, he frequently watched his father play professional baseball, the highest paid player in either major league, winning the most batting championships in history. His expectations of himself must have felt like a test over hot coals.

Ty was a good athlete, and at the age of seventeen or eighteen he was an alternate on the United States Davis Cup team. My grandmother told many stories of Granddaddy bringing home famous sports people of the times, athletes, sportswriters, announcers, owners of clubs, businessmen who backed the clubs and, frequently, Uncle Ty's tennis coach, Mr. Bill Tilden. Uncle Ty's interest in competitive tennis turned into sickening revulsion after an improper gesture by Mr. Tilden while they were riding in the back seat of Grandma's car. They were returning from a practice, dressed in tennis shorts and shirts. Grandma tried to convince Uncle Ty to keep playing, but the incident marked his view of what he might come up against off the courts traveling with strangers to tournaments. Grandma was taken aback and wanted to mollify the shock that rocked Uncle Ty. She assumed her gentile Southern manner and tried to describe Mr. Tilden's gesture as a mistake, but years later, Aunt Shirley related an entirely different picture. We nephews and nieces were at her home and asked, "What really happened with Uncle Ty and his tennis?" It was late in an evening of tales and talking, and we didn't really know how famous Bill Tilden was or the place in American sports history he occupied.

She replied, in a sternly restrained voice that could quietly blister the pants off a listener, "Mr. Tilden ran his hand up the bare leg of your uncle, absolutely scared the wits out of him, and totally devastated his confidence in playing tennis ever again." She was nobody to back down from the truth as she saw it, and her loyalty to her older brother was that of a warrior, ready to engage the fieriest foe in defense of her ally. I deeply admired that.

My grandmother was a gardener all her life, finding her joy in nurturing and tending life. Her home was filled with flowers and plants, but now she was entirely focused on her son, sitting helplessly in a wheelchair, waiting to be cared for. It was a somber and haunting sight, watching her make busy movements to comfort him, all the while being closely watched by Aunt Mary, Ty III, and Charlie. Their eyes followed every gesture, their smiles were worn out and wan, and the emotional drain showed in their every movement and expression. Time crept by slowly, as if its feet were stuck in clay. As tired and worn out as Grandma was, she insisted to our mother that we three were not a burden and that she wanted us with her that summer. She knew our plight at the hands of our mother, and her capacity for affection and love was boundless.

We stayed at Aunt Beverly's home, located a short distance away. On the ride to her house, I sat in the back seat with the window rolled down, feeling the evening breeze flow over me, listening to the sounds of birds singing and kids playing and cars driving about. The world was carrying on as though it didn't know that my uncle was dying.

We made short visits to see our cousins, but their focus was on their dying father, emotionally caught in a dark cave of dread, helpless in their knowledge of how it would end. Instead we tagged along with Beverly's children for four days, swimming at the club until she picked us up in the late afternoon, then fed us at night.

77

Granddaddy lived nearby, in Atherton, and I wanted to see him, but Beverly evaded my requests for several days. She finally received a phone call from Aunt Shirley, phrasing the gist of the call in the strangest way, "It's all right now if you go visit your grandfather. Shirley will take you in about an hour."

When Aunt Shirley arrived to take us to Granddaddy's, Susan, Kit, and I were ready to go. Kit and I climbed into the back seat of her DeSoto, and Susan sat in front. The short ride was silent, except when Aunt Shirley told Susan, "Susan, let me go in first and make sure he's all right. Then I'll come and get you children."

Susan cautiously asked, "Is Granddaddy sick?"

"No, hon, he's not sick. I just want to make sure he's okay."

A few turns later, we were on Spencer Lane, a short cul-de-sac, and Shirley slowed down to turn into Granddaddy's drive. The driveway was flanked on each side by a square Spanish-style gatepost, with dark beige plaster, topped with red bricks. The gatepost on the left presented a brass plate, which read, "El Roblar."

"What's that mean, Shirley, 'El Roblar'?" I asked.

"That's the name of this house, 'The Oak,' just like that big ole tree right there in the middle of the front yard." She continued around the curved drive while I gaped at the huge California oak. Yet my mind rapidly shifted to all the conversations between Aunt Beverly and Aunt Shirley about whether Granddaddy was okay or not. I felt a hot, sickening pit inside of me, not knowing what to expect. My dad was dead, my uncle was dying, and my mother floated into whatever relationship pleased her at the moment, openly resentful and destructive toward her children. I stiffened at the thought of losing my grandfather.

As the DeSoto rolled to a halt, I glanced at the scar on my right pinkie finger. I'd gotten that cut escaping into the stubble of razed stalks on that day when my father shot at me with his

BB pistol. I had scrambled up the side of the ditch to hide when I felt pain in my right hand and saw blood dripping. As I landed, I jammed the base joint of my right little finger into the stubble, and a stalk tore through my skin, down to the bone. Blood was everywhere. Somehow, I felt like a warrior with a noble wound. My finger eventually healed up, but left a scar, and it was that scar that I was looking at and rubbing when Aunt Shirley turned off the engine.

That memory in turn shifted to the morning on the Snake River when my grandfather dominated my father through his sheer strength and determination, then the message in green ink saying that he loved me.

When Shirley stopped the car, she told us firmly, "Wait here until I come and get you." We waited for only a few minutes before Shirley reappeared, looking more relaxed. Her summer "spectators" made a clicking sound on the porch tiles as she strode to the car, opened the door for Kit, and told us, "Your grandfather is waiting, hurry up." She liked Kit a lot, and her smile broadened as she watched him run for the front door, grab the doorjamb, and swing himself into the house. As Susan and I followed, Aunt Shirley told us, "I'll be back when Louise calls me. About an hour."

The reason for Shirley's caution was not hard to find. The entry hall and living room were almost dark with thick curtains pulled shut over the glass doors. The only light came from a dim floor lamp behind where Granddaddy was sitting. He was slumped down in his favorite chair, with his left hand languidly hanging over the armrest, scratching the neck of his bulldog, Chudly. He barely raised his right hand toward us. Susan and I stopped at the edge of the oriental carpet, adjusting our eyes and waiting for him to say something. I was gripped with fear that he was sick

79

and dying. I didn't want to look at him and see that he too was leaving me.

"Susan, come here. Granddaddy's a little tired. Come here and let me look at you. It's been two whole years." Susan walked slowly toward him, visibly concerned.

I noticed books strewn everywhere, opened at the binding, lying half read. Four or five were on the floor, one on his armrest, several on the piano behind him, one on the fireplace mantel. I didn't want to ask Granddaddy if he was sick or say anything. He didn't look like the smiling, roly-poly, energetic grandfather of two years ago. There was no twinkle in his eyes, his skin was pallid, and he looked exhausted. I tiptoed through the books lying open on the living room carpet, bending over to look at the names. One book was bound in red leather with the name encrusted in a gold arch across the front. "Who's Winston Churchill?" I blurted out. I avoided looking at him, not wanting to see what I feared.

"Never mind that, Hersch, we'll talk about him later," he said. "Right now I want to see you all." He paused, taking a deep breath, "Susan, come closer." She was dressed in a light pink and green flowered summer dress, with white flat shoes with a strap across her arch; she called them Mary Janes. Her hair was in large ringlets, hanging down the sides of her face, showing off her strawberry blond color, and perfect peach complexion. As he looked at her, his smile broadened, he straightened his posture a little, and his eyes showed some life.

"Granddaddy's had a hard year, honey, and it's so good to see you." He swallowed these words, as if he was talking more to himself than to us. And, as I found out a few years later, he was admitting more to himself than saying something to us. My father had died suddenly of a massive heart attack at age thirty-three. Granddaddy felt my mother was responsible for the stress Daddy was under and his unhappiness, and ultimately, for him losing his son so young.

Now, less than a year and a half later, Granddaddy's oldest son, Ty Jr., was gravely ill from a tumor at the base of his skull. Uncle Ty was a doctor and he had quickly deduced the implications, knowing that no operation would cure him. When the symptoms became severe enough, he flew from his home in Florida to his mother's home. He was only forty-two years old. There was nothing Ty Cobb could do; no amount of fight, determination, or ferocity would save his son.

Granddaddy was especially distraught knowing that he and his son had often fought while Uncle Ty wandered from college to college. The distance between them widened when Uncle Ty went to medical school and set up his own medical practice. Over the years, neither had made a meaningful effort to reconcile. Now, as Uncle Ty sat helplessly in his wheelchair, Granddaddy knew in his heart that the rift between him and his firstborn son would never be healed. Uncle Ty was too sick, and Granddaddy didn't know how to let go of the past and embrace his son. Now all he could do was to visit him at the home of his ex-wife and watch as he fumbled in his wheelchair. Granddaddy had taken to drinking too much and his behavior estranged Aunt Shirley. He was emotionally devastated, isolated from his family, alone, and unable to right what had gone so tragically wrong.

All I knew that day, at his home in Atherton, was that Susan, with a smile on her face, her hands clasped in front of her, her toes pointed slightly inward, calmly came over to the side of his chair so he could wrap his arm around her. In response, she wrapped both her arms around him, pressed her cheek next to his, and whispered, "Granddaddy, it's going to be all right. Just you wait and see."

His eyes closed and his chest heaved raggedly, exhaling a slow, controlled sigh even as he sniffled back a tear. Susan had the biggest heart I've ever known, and in those long seconds, it glowed all over him. It was like she gently smoothed a balm over his wound, helping him retreat from the edge of destructive remorse. Granddaddy adored her, and she had a special way of talking to him, listening to him, suggesting to him, and asking of him what he wanted to be asked, always ready to agree with her. When she said he looked nice, he beamed. When she asked him to put on a tie, he did. When she told him "the boys" needed a kind of food, or something else, he responded as if it was his pleasure to do so. He relished pleasing her, and her effect on him was curative.

Kit and I stood with our feet nudging Chudly, who was sprawled on the left-hand side of the chair. When Chudly moved, we got close enough for a hug. Kit squirmed and Granddaddy let go of us, calmly saying, "Hersch, take Kit out to the backyard and play for awhile, I want to talk with Susan." I could see he wasn't sick, but his skin was pale, he was puffy under his eyes, his beard showed, and he stayed slouched down. Even so, I felt relieved and knew Susan would be with him. I looked around the living room and realized I didn't know how to get to the yard, but I wandered through the dining room, then the pantry, and the kitchen, past the back bedroom and out to the courtyard. From there, we found the gate to the backyard. For me it was exploring a new territory, one where an anchor of safety was right nearby.

We played outside for nearly half an hour. When we returned, they were still talking, and I heard Granddaddy finish what he was saying: ". . . and if it gets bad, Susan, you call me right away. Do you understand?" She was nodding in agreement as they both looked up to see me.

I knew they were talking about our mother, so I didn't say

anything. He was sitting up straighter, and his expression was livelier. He called, "Now, Hersch, come over here and tell me about your school." Susan was sitting on a large ottoman next to him, her hand quietly on top of his. He wanted to know what books I was reading, my arithmetic problems, what my teachers were like, what I did after school, just about everything except for my mother. I liked school, so I couldn't stop chattering. I maneuvered to sit on the right armrest, my feet dangling over the front. I could tell he was really interested and understood everything I was talking about.

I was still unleashing my fill when Louise, Granddaddy's housekeeper and nurse, called from the kitchen that Mrs. Beckworth—that was my Aunt Shirley's married name—was on the phone, ready to pick up the children. In ten minutes, Aunt Shirley's car circled the driveway, and Louise appeared and told us it was time to go. We hurriedly exchanged hugs, and Granddaddy said, "I hope I'll see you all in a few days."

I didn't know if he meant what he said, and I feared that my short visit was all I'd see of him that summer. I held hope in my heart that I could believe him.

On the ride back, I sat in the rear seat with Susan and whispered to her, "Did you tell him what Daddy did?" She knew I was referring to the eruption after our mother's phone call, Daddy throwing her against the wall and chasing Kit and me into my cubbyhole.

Susan did not hesitate. "No, Hersch, I didn't." I instantly understood the finality in her voice. From that day forward it became our pact never to talk about our father's brutality.

I asked, "Well, what did you talk about?"

She pulled me close, cupped her hand to my ear, whispering, "He's sad, awful sad. He said something really strange. He said he'd been too hard on his kids, too hard on Dad, even Shirley. He said he should have been closer to them." She glanced at the back of Aunt Shirley's head and pushed away from me, leaving me sitting in wonderment as another piece of my grandfather's past snapped into place. I felt like I'd crossed over into a different world.

A few days later, Aunt Beverly found us in her backyard and told us, "I think you are going to see your grandfather after lunch." It sounded strange, but I assumed she was really telling us not to get dirty. Sure enough, Aunt Shirley picked us up after lunch and took us to El Roblar.

When we got out of the car, she said to Susan, "I'll pick you up later this afternoon, after I close my store." I knew that meant it'd be close to 5:00. We'd have the whole afternoon to spend with Granddaddy.

The house presented an entirely different impression this visit. The entrance and living room were sunlit, with the curtains pulled apart. The full-length glass doors were opened to both the front porch and rear patio, allowing a mild, warm breeze to blow through.

Granddaddy's greeting to us that day set a pattern, a repartee, a kind of codification of honor and humor that repeated itself at every first greeting for the next eight summers. "Susan," he would say, "come here and give your granddaddy a big hug." And she would. Then he'd say, "Hersch, come over here." I would take a position in front of him. "My," he'd say, "you're getting bigger and bigger. Would you like a beer or something to drink?" I'd answer, "Granddaddy, no, no, I don't want a beer. I don't drink. I play sports." Then he asked, "Well, how about a cigarette, then?" I'd answer, "Granddaddy, I play sports, I don't smoke cigarettes." And finally, he'd flash a devilish smile and say, "Well, you young'uns go in the kitchen and check the freezer, down at the bottom of the fridge, and see what we got. Now, Susan, get along. Show the boys the freezer." And off we ran, through the dining room, the pantry, and into the kitchen. The freezer door was easy to pull open. Then we'd hear, "And bring in some of those great big spoons on the counter."

The freezer was filled with round gallon cartons of ice cream: peach, strawberry, French vanilla, and chocolate. We knew he loved the peach, so that was for him. Each of us grabbed a gallon of our favorite. Kit latched onto the chocolate, so that was always his. Susan and I alternated between strawberry and French vanilla. We sat around him in the living room, eating directly from the round cartons, with huge spoons, larger than soup spoons. For the next half hour we would eat, smile, and catch up between dripping mouthfuls of ice cream. Ty Cobb loved ice cream.

The frost on the outside of the cartons began to melt and run down onto his pants. Granddaddy finally laughed at himself and said, "Susan, I'm making a mess of my pants. Here, take this back and put it away. Kit can help you." Between bites I'd caught his eye, him watching us as much as enjoying his ice cream. His eyes roved over us, absorbing the three children of his son, now deceased, smiling and filling huge spoons with as much sweetness as they could fit into their mouths at one time. His face softened and his eyes, normally sharp and almost piercing, had a mist of tears. Susan left, carrying his gallon carton and her own. Kit followed, still feeding as much chocolate into his mouth as possible while he walked. I was going to go with them, but I instead put down my carton and asked what I had been worried about. "Granddaddy, are you sick? Aunt Shirley—"

Before I could finish, he said, "Hersch, come on over here and give me a big hug." His arms were as strong as ever, and as he pulled me close, I awkwardly leaned over the chair and hugged

85

him back. I was off balance, but he wouldn't let go. His right arm wrapped around me and his hand held me tight. I didn't mind. I worked my right hand down to his and grabbed his fingers tightly, recalling the strength of his grip on the Snake River when he'd forced my father to let go of me.

With my face next to his, he whispered, "Hersch, your Uncle Ty is real sick, and there's nothing I can do. Nothing." I recalled what Susan had said as he went on, "And your dad died too. My boys, my boys; I've lost my boys." His voice fell away until it was practically an echo. He kept me close, his arm wrapped around my shoulders, and I felt his whole body soften, as if he felt the full force of what he just said. His grip on me was steady and I didn't resist; I hugged him as tightly as I could.

I didn't say anything because I knew—his second son, my father, had died suddenly of a heart attack at the age of thirty-three. Now, just seventeen months later, his first son, Uncle Ty, was dying in the most visible and painful way, slowly losing all power to help himself or know his own children's names. These losses stripped him of ever reconciling with either son as grown men. After having lived through all of his disappointment and con-flicts with them, he was emerging in the face of their deaths to realize life was too short to hold onto these differences. When my father died, I felt a crushing mix of emotions, knowing I would never have a good relationship with my father. Granddaddy was just devastated, knowing his two sons were gone. It was a huge, gaping, wrenching wound.

Soon I heard his voice, as from off in the distance, "Susan, we're talking. Come on over here." He unfolded his arm from around my body, with his hand keeping its control over me, pre-venting me from leaving him too quickly. I turned my head just enough to see the side of his face. As Susan rounded the corner from the dining room into the living room, his eyes twinkled, his whole body straightened up in the chair, head upright, and voice firm and full.

"Sweetie," he said, "Hersch and I were just talking about you." The sight of Susan had this effect on him. His life was revived, given a second wind. She looked the same to me, but the nascent bond that had begun a few days before was blossoming right in front of me. She was as comfortable taking care of him as she was caring for Kit and me. He looked at all of us and whispered, almost like a prayer, "You three mean so much to me. I want you near me." He made room for her to sit on the edge of his chair and she nestled in.

She had been with Kit and Louise in the back of the house, looking at old stuff he had saved and collected over the years. The back room was full of porcelain figurines, sets of linens, boxes of silverware, riding crops, boots, hats, pictures and papers, all from a part of his life long past. Bits and pieces of our aunts' histories appeared when we explored his house. Aunt Shirley's riding boots, jodhpurs, crops, hats, riding jackets, an English saddle, and pictures of her as a young horsewoman. Details of a privileged upbringing she abandoned when she decided to be independent and open her bookstore. Aunt Beverly's party dresses and shoes were there, along with makeup brushes and the tools for grooming to attend the fanciest parties in the area. There was nothing of Uncle Ty nor of my father, as if when they married and left home, they took their histories with them.

While we sat together, he talked with Susan, complimenting her and declaring she was a fine young lady. "You watch out for your brothers, and be sure to call me if you need to." He did not dwell on his comment, but what he said stayed with me for many years. Kit and I became "the boys," and Susan watched out for us.

87

His eyes took us in, and I heard a whisper, "I want to see you all, maybe next year—"

Before he finished, Louise walked into the living room and announced, "Mr. Cobb, Miss Beckworth just called and she's on her way over to pick up the children." The afternoon had passed so quickly and so fully. All too soon we heard the sound of a car engine. Louise went to the front door, then motioned for us to gather our things and say our good-byes. Granddaddy said he would see us in a few days, and I couldn't wait to go back.

During the first half of August, we visited Granddaddy every week, and then again when the weather turned cool and breezy. Our visits were much the same, with ice cream, exploration of the yard and house, talking, and playing with Chudly. On our last visit, just before we left, he held Susan and me close to him, telling us, "I want to see more of you; I want you near me." I had hope in my heart. He was smiling, talkative, but in private moments seemed withdrawn and sullen. In between our visits with him, what was happening at Grandma's home occupied his mind and pulled his emotions near an abyss of grief.

Uncle Ty was getting noticeably worse day by day, having difficulty holding his head upright or remembering the names of anybody, including his children. Our grandmother was steady, brave, and ashen-faced. When we visited Bay Laurel, we added a burden she did not complain about, but her heart was breaking at the sight of her once strong son, struggling to make his end as graceful and easy as possible. Parts of our visits at Bay Laurel were just plain scary. Our cousins Charlie and Ty began having horrible, screaming nightmares, awaking in the middle of the night and running out into the street, still asleep. Their eyes were huge, bloodshot disks, focused insistently on the shell of the man they knew in their hearts was their father. Kit was not there, and Susan and I could say nothing that would comfort or distract them.

Our departure to Los Angeles came as a sad relief after being so near to such helplessness and agony. During the last days of August, we didn't visit Granddaddy. I only partly understood when Aunt Shirley told Beverly one day, "The Old Man is not doing well. He's not doing well at all." Her words were not intended for me or Susan to hear, and Beverly's lips pressed together in disapproval. Her annoyance emanated from the disruption of her social schedule and vexation with her father rather than from concern at his sorrow. She wasn't close to Uncle Ty, for he had joined with Shirley and my father in calling Beverly "Miss Prissy," a characterization that she suffered with all her life, but described her perfectly. For her, Uncle Ty's passing was the loss of a distant brother who came to die at his mother's home, took too long in the process, and exposed the family suffering to a public view she would have rather hidden.

Grandma took us to the Palo Alto train station early in the morning. Her face was pale and wan, but her smile and the hug she managed were comforting. She understood the chaotic ways we were returning to better than we did. I sat next to Susan on a hard, padded bench seat and waved my last good-byes to Grandma.

When the train pulled away from the station, I finally asked Susan, "What did Aunt Shirley mean?" She knew what I was talking about and replied softly, "Granddaddy is at home alone, and he has a bottle of whisky near him. He's really sad, Hersch, really sad."

Ty Cobb Jr. died two weeks later, at age forty-two, at his mother's home. Ty Cobb's two oldest sons had passed. The effect on him was wrenching, as we would come to learn in later years.

My fear of losing my grandfather haunted me during that fall. There was nothing I could do to comfort him, to bring him closer to us. I had to muster my resolve and brace myself to face my mother's daily resentment of children given to her by a man she had hated.

During the summer, while we visited Grandma and Granddaddy, and watched Uncle Ty quickly deteriorate in front of us and his own children, Mom bought a large home in a nice section of L.A. She had managed, through her attorney friend Bill S., to convince the bank to hold off selling the assets of my father's estate. The assets were worth less than what was owed, and Bill S. convinced the banks to let her keep the Coca-Cola Bottling Co. in Santa Maria, hire a manager to run it, and use profits to pay them off a little at a time.

Mother also remarried. His name was Dick Branstedder, and he was a would-be architect. We three children didn't know any of this when we left Grandma's at the end of the summer. The house was a grand surprise, with seven bedrooms, a large backyard, two basements, and a playroom off the garage. It had a magnificent library, completely paneled in mahogany, a large fireplace, and a bay window looking out on the backyard. Branstedder did not actually work; he and Mother spent most days, at least from the time I came home from school, in the library, drinking, while Branstedder built model houses out of red and white plastic bricks that locked together. I was often invited in to watch him take down a wing of his model, fiddle around with the plan, and laboriously put the red bricks back up into a small alteration. The site of his creations was the library table, intentionally positioned in front of the bay window so he could pretend there was sunlight beaming down on his latest house. They both easily refilled their glasses from a wet bar built into the wall nearest the entry door.

I usually watched for a while until their speech became slurred and Mother's comments became sarcastic criticisms of Branstedder's work. He was no match for her barbs and ridiculing, so he meekly defended himself, gave up, and then got nasty back. Later, when Ayako had dinner ready, Mother and Branstedder weaved into the dining room. If we three kids were lucky, Ayako had our dinners set up in the breakfast room.

The weather in Los Angeles in late September was warm and just right for eating outdoors. Ayako set the table on the patio so we could eat there. Mother sat at one end of the long table while Branstedder sat at the other. They had spent most of the afternoon in the library, playing with the red bricks and drinking. When dinner was served, their barbs, criticisms, and counter-barbs turned into a slurred, bitter shouting match. Susan and I sat on the inside of the table, while Kit sat on the outside, closest to the yard. I avoided looking at either of them, and Susan did the same. One time while I was taking a bite, my mother stood up from her chair, lifted her full plate of food, and threw it at Branstedder. He managed to duck the plate, but a lot of the food hit him. He rose up, throwing a ceramic glass at her. She started grabbing anything near her—plates, glasses, silverware, the salt shaker—and throwing things at him as fast as she could, all the time calling him foul names. Food, plates, and utensils were flying. I raised my arms to protect myself, grabbed Susan's arm, pulled her under the table, scooted over to Kit, and pulled him out of his chair, and we all ran across the backyard to hide in our play area. We hid behind the bushes, but that didn't matter because they were yelling and throwing things at each other and didn't even notice us. Kit was fascinated by the throwing of food and plates and wanted to sneak back through the bushes on the side of the garage and watch them.

When there was nothing left to throw and the table separated them, Mother cursed at Branstedder, turned on her heel, and walked through the screen door at her end of the patio, slamming it behind her. Branstedder, not to be outdone, cursed back at her, walked through the door on his end of the patio leading to the breakfast room, slammed and broke the door. It was dark by then, and Susan and I decided to creep back and see what the patio looked like. All the dishes and cups were thick ceramic and had a green and pink flower design; at least they did before they were broken. There were shards of ceramic all over the patio tiles, in the seats, and on top of the table, and one piece was stuck in the door frame. Food, milk, drinks, and red wine were mixed in. The patio lights were on and Susan and I didn't want to stay, so we got Kit, crept around to the side door, found Ayako, and stayed in the downstairs rooms until it seemed safe to go to our bedrooms.

That exact dinner was not repeated, but several came close. After a couple of weeks of being home with tension-filled dinners in the dining room, Susan and I figured out that if we asked for dinner early, we got to eat in the breakfast room, avoiding the dining room with Mother and Branstedder. We took care of Kit, and after dinner, we used a stairway in the kitchen wing to go to our rooms, dodging the drama. Mother slept until noon, using a sleep mask to keep out the light. Luckily, we were in school.

We got home from school a little after three in the afternoon. Mother and Branstedder usually had their drinks in hand by that time. Susan and I quickly learned the prelude and signs of impending fury. For some reason, Branstedder could not put the red bricks in a shape or form that met with Mother's approval; she said something critical and caustic no matter what he designed. He took what she gave. He didn't have an actual job, she had the money, and to her that meant she could do or say anything she pleased.

Branstedder's tenure with Mother lasted about a year and a half. Fortunately, during that time he didn't dare touch Susan, Kit, or me. I remember toward the end, when he was essentially a beaten man, on a Saturday afternoon, they had been drinking since lunchtime. Mother was shouting profanities and threatening to call the police. Kit and I listened from the top of the main stairs. I told Kit to stay put and hang onto the banister. I crept downstairs to the entrance hall and peeked around the wall. Branstedder was striding through the living room carrying a black telephone with the wall cord trailing behind him. Mother was shouting about calling the police. I was standing near a table with a telephone on it. Branstedder was rushing by the time he reached where I was standing, his face flushed pink and his eyes shocked. He looked down at me, gathered himself, and said in as calm a tone as he could muster, "Your mother is crazy. She's absolutely nuts." I backed up onto the staircase, ready to run. He stood a few feet in front of me and repeated, "Crazy, absolutely crazy." Then he dropped the telephone he was holding, grabbed the telephone on the entrance table, and yanked the cord out of the wall, throwing that phone down. I followed him into the kitchen, where there was a phone mounted on the wall near the sink. He bashed that phone with his fist, flinched in pain, held his injured right hand, backtracked through the entrance hall, and stormed out the front door, leaving it wide open. My mother staggered across the living room. I zipped upstairs as fast as I could. Kit was still hanging onto the top banister post. He was watching our mother with tears streaming down his cheeks.

She slammed the door shut, turned, and stormed back through the living room. Kit and I did not move or make a sound. We were mostly hidden by the banister post upstairs, lying flat on the carpet, peeking just over the edge of the landing. As soon as she disappeared, I motioned to Kit to follow me, and we crawled to our bedroom, locked the door, and huddled on the floor behind the bed.

Summer was close at hand, but there was no way for Susan or I to call our grandmother and beg her to take us for three months, and we feared our isolation would continue, exposed to the drunken outbursts of our mother. To our good fortune, one afternoon Ayako confided to Susan that our grandmother wanted us with her for the summer and "plans were in place." She was extraordinarily vague about what "plans," but the mystery only increased my hope.

CHAPTER FOUR

Mist and Clarity
at Lake Tahoe

The bow of Granddaddy's Chris-Craft inboard rocked gently from side to side. He had turned off the engine, and we were drifting toward the shore. I gingerly crawled out to the tip of the bow to draw as close as I could to the deer lapping water at the edge of the lake. It was dawn of the first morning of our first trip with Granddaddy to his cabin at Cave Rock, Lake Tahoe, Nevada. He had awoken Susan and me in the dark, hustled us into his boat, wrapped us up in blankets, and cruised north toward Skunk Harbor to look for animals at the lakeshore.

He had stood by his word and brought us to Lake Tahoe. That morning, I could not gauge the resolve of his decision, and was not willing to openly trust that it was not a trick. My uncertainty was like the mist on the lake surface, a veil hiding our boat, only my mist hid my sense of safety and confidence. As our trip unfolded, it became the first of a string of the most meaningful summer vacations in my life.

I was transfixed by the doe and her two fawns, standing with their front hoofs slightly in the lake, lapping and looking, lapping and looking. I had never seen anything like this before. It was nearly dark at lake level, but above me, the cobalt-blue sky had a pinkish hue that marked the beginning of dawn. I knew the mountains surrounding Lake Tahoe would keep the lake dark for a few more minutes and make it less likely the deer would spot me. The mist on the water partially hid the Chris-Craft as well.

"Hersch, get back here. Get back here now." Granddaddy was whispering firmly, worried I would fall in. I heard him but ignored the warning.

The small waves on the Nevada side of the lake were slowly pushing the Chris-Craft toward the shore while I slid as quietly as I could along the bow, reaching with my hand and pulling the rest of my body forward. I knew Granddaddy would not come after me because Susan was with him on the front seat and he wouldn't leave her alone. Besides, he was wearing light beige gabardine slacks and street shoes, neither of which he would risk soiling unless I fell into the cold water.

To improve my view of the doe and her fawns, I gripped each side of the bow and raised myself a little higher. The doe lifted her head and looked straight at me; her brown eyes were huge, moist, and soft. At that exact moment the Chris-Craft rocked with a stiff jerk, my left hand slipped off the edge, and I landed flat on my chest on the bow tie. Ouch! The doe turned her head to her fawns, and off they all bounded, gone in an instant.

I looked back at Susan, who was standing up to wave her hand apologetically. Yet as she gained her feet, she rocked the boat, and I lost my balance. Granddaddy laughed as I bobbled my head back and forth toward them and the shore, watching the deer flee. I wanted to yell at Susan, but I didn't want to scare the deer, even though they were spooked and there was no chance of them returning.

"Now, come on back here, Hersch." His voice had relaxed.

"I wanted to see too," Susan added.

"No, you didn't. You wanted me to fall in," I said crossly.

"Hersch, keep quiet," he commanded. "Look, there are probably some more up by the landing. Scoot on back here, and we'll head up there while it's still a little dark." Granddaddy's voice was low and firm. "Come on now, so I can start the engine."

I crawled back to the windshield of the craft, careful not to scratch the finish on the mahogany foredeck. Granddaddy took a large step toward the middle of the boat, reached over the slanted glass, picked me up, and set me in the middle of the front seat. His hands felt huge and strong, and I could hear a little grunt while he lifted me. The smile on his lips thinned with the effort. He turned on the engine, revved it, and pointed the craft toward the middle of Lake Tahoe.

The inboard retreated quickly from the shore and small cove. The throttle was a chrome lever fixed at the center of the steering wheel, and pulling it downward made the engine accelerate. When we were clear of the cove and I could see the faint blue shoreline in both directions, Granddaddy steadily pulled the throttle farther downward. Through my seat I could feel the engine respond with a strong, rumbling roar, a sound I grew to love. The stern sank low in the water as we sped up. The bow rose so high I couldn't see where we were going, and the waves reached as high as the sides of the boat. He loved the power and speed of his Chris-Craft. I tried to make a remark to Susan, but it was lost in the roar of the engine, the wind rushing by our faces, and the splash of the waves along the sides.

Granddaddy smiled at both of us and yelled, "Faster?"

Practically at the same time, we yelled, "Yes!"

His right arm reached around me, holding me firmly, and his hand held onto Susan.

"Hang on." His voice was jubilant. With his left hand he pushed the throttle lever down, and off we raced. The bow flattened out, and I read the speedometer saying twenty-five miles an hour. I was grinning widely, filled with feelings of excitement and danger.

A two-week stay at his hunting cabin felt like a reprieve after another school year in Los Angeles. The two years since my father died of a heart attack had molded me into a lonely child who distrusted everybody. With my father, what began as fun often turned to pain and terror. I was constantly on guard. At home, in L.A., my mother's excesses with liquor and men continued unabated. As a result, while I was enjoying myself out on that boat, a part of me was sure that the adventure would turn out badly.

An unbidden memory returned, of another time when I had raced on the water, back when we lived in Twin Falls, Idaho. My father had kept several boats on the Snake River, one of which was an outboard runabout. The Snake River has small streams feeding into it, and over time small inlets developed where the water rushes down the hillside. The inlet water is so clear that fish and colored rocks seemed to shimmer and almost jump up and down. My father often invited me to go with him to "check out the new fish," yet the offer sometimes was not as innocent as it seemed. One time, after viewing the fish, he dipped his cup and drank the clear water and then told me to dip my cup. I was stretching my arm over the rail to reach the water when he "bumped" me and I fell overboard, into the river. The water was ice cold, but I was lucky that the inlet was shallow. Nevertheless, when I stood up, I was soaked. Daddy took my outstretched arms, but dropped me twice back into the water. He thought this was hilarious, telling me that this would make me tough, but I was frozen through and through. As we headed back, he piled on the fun by revving up the motor and zigzagging back and forth at top speed, so I was thrown from side to side, my hands too cold to grab the side rails.

When we got near the sandy beach where people gathered, he slowed down and told me to sit way forward, in the tip of the bow. As we passed the beach, he let go of the steering grip on the motor and stepped to the center of the boat, shifting all his weight forward, causing it to level out. Then suddenly he tromped on the rear transom, causing the bow to spring up, flipping me into the air. I flew backward, arms flailing, and yelling for help. Daddy grabbed me out of the air and came down with me in his arms. I was scared out of my wits. He was laughing at his clever trick.

Two women on the beach ran into the water, yelling at my father as he ran the outboard up onto the beach. The women reached into the boat for me. My father, though, climbed out of the boat and told them to leave me alone. "I was just having some fun with my son."

The picture in my mind was suddenly interrupted. "Hersch, is this too fast? You okay? Want to slow down a little?" Granddaddy's voice pulled me back to Lake Tahoe. He sounded genuinely concerned. His arm rested on my shoulders and his hand held Susan, keeping us safely in place.

"Yeah, Granddaddy, I'm okay," I answered.

"Your eyes look a little misty. Still sleepy?" he asked. The Chris-Craft was slowing down, gliding through the smooth water, not making much noise.

"No, Granddaddy, I was just thinking." My voice was light, covering up the nervousness I'd felt. "Can we go over to Glenbrook, please?" I discovered that my eyes were filled with tears and my vision was blurry. I wiped my face with my sleeve and put my arms forward, bracing myself against the dashboard.

Granddaddy's arm was as strong as my father's, I realized. I didn't know what I expected. My entire body was shaking, but he held me firmly in the crick of his elbow. The engine revved a bit, and he turned up the lake toward Glenbrook, cruising at a steady speed. I wondered if Granddaddy knew what I was remembering. In between being terrified, I felt guilt and loss at my father's death. I didn't want to believe he was dead. I remembered in Los Angeles seeing the back of a large man with red hair sitting on a bench, rushing over and touching his shoulder, only to be face to face with a complete stranger. I mistook him. I often looked for my father and sometimes saw a profile or back of a head that looked like him. It was always the wrong face and person. I wanted to find the person I dreaded most.

Now I was sitting next to my grandfather, cruising in his boat out on a huge lake. He acted as though he cared. He treated Susan and me as if we were the most precious things in his life. My dark memories were in complete contrast to being with him and the wondrous sights unfolding around me. I wanted to see through my mist, part the fog, gain some clarity.

I was scared to trust, fearing the empty feeling of being tricked. The rush of cold morning air suddenly chilled me, and I felt like I would never be warm again. I nuzzled into the crick of Granddaddy's arm. He wrapped it around me and held me tight. Susan put her arm around me too, under his, and I was sure she knew exactly what I was going through. After all, she knew what used to happen out in our boat. The leg to Glenbrook did not take too long, and I warmed up along the way. The shoreline between Skunk Harbor and Glenbrook is mostly rocky, and we didn't attempt to drift in to look for animals. We stayed out from the shoreline, the engine roared steadily, and I relished my grandfather's arm around me, imparting a sense of comfort.

Granddaddy received his mail in Glenbrook, Nevada, and he had often talked about the lodge and its owners during our drive from Atherton, along Highway 50, to Lake Tahoe. By the time we arrived at Cave Rock, where his cabin was, I felt I knew about all sorts of places, including Glenbrook. Our intention was to explore Glenbrook Bay, pick up his mail, and perhaps have breakfast at the lodge. As we rounded a last outcropping of huge rocks, the bay opened up, and I looked in awe at how peaceful and beautiful it was. The bay was expansive, more than a half mile across, with huge rock outcroppings on each end and a long sandy beach in the middle. Pine trees filled the spaces between the rocks, which framed the beach like a postcard. As we entered from the lake, the huge meadow behind the resort's buildings came into full view, entirely undeveloped, interspersed with a few stretches of old, worn fences and deer grazing in the far distance.

The buildings were rustic, painted green with white trim around the windows, blending into the grassy landscape and trees. The family who owned Glenbrook was named Bliss, and the place had been in their family for several generations. It had been built as a logging site and ferry terminal for transporting logs from the east side of Lake Tahoe to the west side, and eventually to San Francisco. The bay had the remains of several docks, with huge wooden pilings poking above the water line and old lengths of steel bars and bolts sticking out on all sides. A slight mist lingered on the water, and Granddaddy was careful to avoid any pilings hidden just below the surface as he maneuvered the

Chris-Craft to the lone, long dock that remained to serve guests arriving by boat. As we came up next to the dock, a young man sprinted down from the main lodge.

"Hello there, Mr. Cobb. See you got some help this morning."

"Dennis, you're here again this year?" he greeted the young man, smiling and looking down at Susan and me. "Yes, I do. And pretty good help, if I do say so myself. This is my grandson Hersch and his sister, Susan. Got one more, too, back at the house. It was a little early for him."

"I'll say. It's barely 7:00. Been out on the lake long?" Dennis asked. At the same time he took the line from the bow of the boat and hitched it to a cleat on the dock.

"Awhile. Been over near Skunk Harbor. The deer come down to drink there, and these two have never seen anything like that. A doe and two fawns, right, Hersch?"

I answered promptly, "Right. But they ran before we got close enough." I glanced at my sister.

"Next time," Dennis said to me. His voice sounded certain of that. I thought, "What a neat life he leads." "You staying for breakfast, Mr. Cobb?"

"Not this time, Dennis. Just came for the ride, and to check the mail. Can you watch the boat for me for a few minutes?"

"Sure, it's real quiet this morning. Late sleepers, I guess. Mr. Bliss is up. In his office." Dennis took the stern line and wrapped it around another cleat.

"Thanks, Dennis." Granddaddy stepped out of the Chris-Craft onto the wooden pier. The engine was off and the key was still in the ignition. "Either of you want to come with me?"

"I do. I'll come," I said.

"Susan, how about you? Want to come along? We'll be back in a few minutes."

"Not really, Granddaddy," she replied. "I'll stay here and watch the boat."

I hustled out onto the dock. As I looked down between its huge planks at the lake, the water was so clear I could see the sand on the bottom and lots of little fish swimming around. I was peering through a wide split between the planks, following a good-sized fish, when I felt Granddaddy's hand take mine and give me a little tug. We walked for a little while together, but I kept tugging to look over the edge of the dock, and he let go of my hand.

"It's mighty cold if you fall in, Hersch."

"I won't, Granddaddy, don't worry."

The pier was half the length of a football field, and when we reached the shore, we took a small path leading up to the main lodge, across a small road. The lodge was old but looked well cared for. Its two stories were painted dark green with white-trimmed doors and windows, fronted by an inviting porch with wooden lounge chairs. The front steps were white, the hand railings green, and it was surrounded by a large lawn that faded into the tall grass and meadow at the back and sides of the building. Behind the main lodge, set off thirty or forty yards apart, were several small cabins for guests, all in the same rustic style.

When we reached the base of the steps, Granddaddy took hold of my shoulder and handed me a set of keys. "Here," he said, "go and check my mailbox. It's number twelve, see the number on the key? I want to say hello to some folks. The mailboxes are right inside." He gave me a pat and, eager to help out, I bounded up the steps, two at a time.

I opened the mailbox door, expecting to find lots of envelopes, but only four letters slanted along the side wall. I took them, locked the box, and set out to look around the lodge. The large dining room was immediately behind me, a really old room with the floor made of wide wooden planks, bare wood walls with lots of framed pictures, windows covered in light curtains, and well-worn chairs. The tables had white tablecloths, and one of them was occupied by a young boy sitting with an old man, probably a grandfather too. Both were grinning and chewing on pancakes and eggs and bacon. The food smelled wonderful. And it looked like things hadn't changed in a hundred years.

Granddaddy's mailbox was one of about fifty, located at the rear of the entry area. To the left was a reception desk, with nobody behind it, and to the right were stairs leading up to the second floor. I wanted to follow my nose and go upstairs, but I heard voices laughing behind a partially closed door on the far side of the reception desk. One of the voices was Granddaddy's, so I walked over and peeked inside. He was swaying from side to side with laughter, moving his hands back and forth. I slipped in behind him, trying not to be noticed. But he did see me imme-diately, and in the middle of laughing with the other men, he put his arm around my shoulder and pulled me forward.

"Bill, this is my grandson, Hersch Jr., almost eleven years old now. Hersch, this is Mr. William Bliss, proprietor of this fine place. Shake his hand and show him those muskles." Granddaddy guided me around the desk in the middle of the room, and I squeezed the outstretched hand as hard as I could. I thought I was pretty strong, but the grip from the stringy old arm and hand that caught mine was like an iron vise. It didn't hurt, but the handshake was so firm that I knew it could if he wanted to. His face was filled with deep lines, and he had a mild suntan and pleasant smile. His hair was white as the paint around the windows, cut short on the sides and trimmed flat on top.

"How do you do, Mr. Bliss?" I mustered in as strong a voice as I could.

"Howdy, there, young man. Pleased to meet you," he roared, still laughing at whatever had been said before I entered the room. "So, you're hanging out with this old gent, huh? Well, watch those afternoon naps of his." He winked at me, gave me a little squeeze, and let go of my hand.

"And that's Chip," Granddaddy continued, motioning toward the other man in the room. "He knows what really goes on around here."

I shook another hand. I felt a sheepish smile form on my face as, backing up, I bumped into Granddaddy. I looked up and he was still grinning.

"So, what did you finally do with it, Ty?" Chip asked, continuing their conversation.

Mr. Bliss spoke up, laughing loudly. "He had to throw the whole thing out. Probably the car too. Right, Ty?"

"Not quite, but close. I got pretty used to the smell—used to ignoring it, really. It was rank as anything. Lucky I had it wrapped up good. I left it for the bears, up at the top." His palms were facing outward as he finished.

"And what about that car, you have to give it away?" Chip asked, still laughing.

"Ah, come on, Chip, you know I sold it. Just didn't get much for it." Granddaddy smiled, and then they all laughed again. "You boys laugh all you want, I won't do that again. Now, I've got to get Hersch and his sister home and get them some breakfast."

Mr. Bliss offered, "Ty, stay here. We'll fix them a plate they'll never forget."

"Thanks, Bill. Another time. I've got Kit, his younger brother, 105 at the house, and I've got to get back and make sure everything's okay." Granddaddy was heading out the door as he spoke, waving with one hand and taking my arm with his other. "You boys keep that story to yourselves, now." Their chuckling continued as we crossed the reception area of the lodge and out the front door.

"What were you talking about back there?" I asked.

"Long story, Hersch," he began. "Your granddaddy can be pretty stubborn at times. I'll give you the short version. A few years ago, I'd been hunting in Idaho and bagged a big buck. It was the last day of my trip, and I managed to get the thing into the back of a station wagon I had then. Wrapped it up real tight in a tarp and started the drive back to California, actually headed for the lake. Well, it's a three-day trip straight through, but I got bored driving and stopped to do a little gambling, so it took me a couple of days longer. By the time I got here, my buck was smelling a little gamy."

"What do you mean?" We were outside, walking slowly down the front steps.

"The meat had begun to turn. You know, rot. Ever smell rotting meat? Stinks like the dickens. And the smell was hard to ignore." He made a face. "I drove the last leg down here without a rest and came straight to Glenbrook. I wanted to get my buck gutted, skinned, and dressed up. It was about 2:00 a.m. when I got here and banged on Bill's door. He was mad as the dickens that I woke him up. Anyway, I talked him into taking a look at my buck, but everything went downhill from there. His cook was gone, and when we unwrapped the tarp, the meat had turned. Smelled awful. Just awful. We dragged the thing onto the ground, and I unwrapped a little more and cut the belly. Sure enough, the maggots had started."

"Maggots, what's that?" I squinted as I asked because the very word sounded icky.

"Little worms. Feed on rotting meat. Tens of thousands, crawling all through my buck, just sucking away. Must have been the heat beating through the back window right on my buck that caused it all to happen so fast. It was plenty hot during the drive, but I thought I'd make it. It was a complete loss. Can't eat maggot-filled meat. So Bill and I wrestled the thing back into my wagon. He was still mad, but laughing at me. Told me to get the thing out of here. I wanted him to bury it, but he'd have none of that. So, I left. I was mad and tired. Drove up the hill, round the bend, up a dirt road about a hundred yards, and dumped the thing in the bushes. Good feed for the bears, I figured. I headed back to Cave Rock real quick then, because it wasn't quite square with the law what I'd done. Now, Hersch, I didn't mean any harm, just didn't have any other way to get rid of it. Besides, the coyotes and vultures would have a feast."

Feast? Yuck, I thought. My face scrunched up, nostrils flared, and mouth parted only slightly so nothing could get by my teeth. While I imagined the ghastly picture he described, Granddaddy laughed lightly and put his hand on my shoulder, as if to say everything was okay, and that's just what happens when you're stubborn.

I had the sudden urge to pee. "I have to go to the bathroom," I said, looking back toward the front door of the lodge.

"Fine," he replied. "It's just inside, next to the reception desk, on the right. I'm going down to the boat and check on Susan."

I raced back to the lodge. Once inside, I had to pass Mr. Bliss's office. They were still talking, and their voices carried out to the lobby. I paused because it sounded like they were talking about Granddaddy. I drifted nearer to the half-open door.

"Still stubborn as hell, huh, Bill?" I recognized the voice as the other man, the one named Chip.

"Don't know, Chip. Seems to have mellowed a bit. Taking on three youngsters for a couple of weeks, that's more than I've seen before. Remember last year? He walked around as sullen and touchy as a rattlesnake caught in the open." That was Mr. Bliss's voice.

"Yeah, I stayed way out of his way. So what about the boy? What's his name?"

"Herschel Jr. Same as his dad. The senior died two years ago. Heart attack. Young guy. Thirty-three or so. Getting divorced. Business couldn't have been too good, either, from what I heard. Don't know how the Old Man made it through those two years. He lost the other one too. You know, Ty Jr. died the next year. Brain cancer or something like that. Really went down. Two sons in two years. Really shook him deep." His voice took on a more reflective tone. "Ya know, Chip, he never got along with his children as adults. He made it, they wanted it."

"Whadda you mean?" Chip asked. He didn't seem to understand any more than I did.

"His Coca-Cola stock, lots of it," Mr. Bliss answered. "But the Old Man took their deaths hard. I've known that old coot for a lot of years. It was a real jolt. Sat over there at his place in a snit, alone, moping around. I'm sure he had a bottle. Ya know, Chip, he battled hard all his life. Won everything. But losing his boys, that threw him, that's for sure."

"Yeah," Chip interjected.

Mr. Bliss's voice dropped a tone lower, "But, yeah, that boy— Herschel Jr., that's his name—seemed okay. Nice-looking kid. The Old Man likes him, that's for sure. Held his tongue pretty good. Never seen him put his arm around anybody like that before or laugh like that. Maybe those grandkids will work something his kids never did."

"Yeah, maybe. Well, look here, I got those plans for the dock repair. Let's take a look."

I edged away from the door, as quietly as I could, and slipped into the bathroom. That little bit of conversation started a buzz in my head. Wow, divorce. What was that? Mom and Dad weren't living together when he died. But she had said it was a separation. And what did he make that his sons wanted? Why, Cokes. The questions stuck with me for a while, and then drifted to the back of my mind. They would not be answered for a couple of years to come.

The conversation in the office was still going on when I left. I took the front steps three at a time and raced across the grass, down the long pier, and to the boat. Across Lake Tahoe, the morning sunlight was now shining almost to the base of the mountains on the California side. The blue water undulated without a ripple. I heard the engine of the Chris-Craft rumbling and saw my sister talking to Granddaddy. He was telling her the story of the hunting trip, rotten meat, maggots, and getting rid of the deer. Her head was shaking slowly side to side, with Granddaddy moving his hands as if to convince her that everything was all right. His affection for Susan showed at her slightest disapproval of him. He knew he should never have started telling her about the deer, and he wanted to end the story as soon as possible. I knew this because as soon as I arrived, he quickly said, "Ah, you're here. Climb in and let's go get some breakfast." Just as quickly, he dropped the story of the rotted deer.

"I want to sit in the back," I replied, pointing to the seat at the stern, behind the engine compartment. "Is that okay?"

"Not this time, Hersch. I want you up here with me." His voice brooked no argument. His inboard Chris-Craft was long, about twenty-five feet, with two rows of seats in front, then the engine compartment in the middle and then, at the stern, another set of seats. The rear seat would be out of reach to a helping hand in an emergency. I had looked back there longingly while we were racing toward Glenbrook harbor. The waves splashed high enough to reach out and touch them. That's what I wanted to do.

"Come on, Hersch." Susan's voice was almost lost in the gurgle of the engine, and I slipped into the seat behind them and then climbed over their backrest, settling next to Susan on the outside. Dennis untied the lines, tossed them into the boat, and Granddaddy put her into reverse and eased away from the dock. Then he swung the bow around and headed slowly out of Glenbrook Bay. I expected to hear the engine roar, feel the stern drop deeply into the water, the bow rise up and block my view of where we were going, and feel the pull as we picked up speed. None of that happened. We were barely moving. Granddaddy had his arm around Susan, her right hand on the steering wheel, and his left hand resting on the side. Then he lifted her up, put her on his lap, and looked over at me and winked.

I sighed deeply. Oh, how I wanted to drive the boat. We crept along through the calm water. Nothing special happened to us, except that as I looked around I had the odd sensation of seeing with my whole body what was around me. Lake Tahoe was deep blue, smooth as glass, with not even a ripple to disturb her. The sun was shining like bright yellow honey on the western mountain slopes in California, and the sky was light turquoise in the background. The air was so clear I felt like I could touch the scenic view before me.

Glenbrook Bay was ruffled only by our wake. We were being pulled through blue paint, except that I looked down and could see the bottom of the lake so clearly I thought I could reach down and touch it. As we motored away from shore, the sandy bottom gave way to rocks, and I realized that it was very, very deep. The small rocks then mixed with huge boulders, deep under the sheen of the surface. The boulders spread out, jutting out of Glenbrook Bay on either side.

I put my head back and looked straight up at the big, open sky. Even amid the serenity I could not help past associations with similar scenes from rushing back at me. I recalled the time my father took me flying in his single-engine Piper Cub, nearly turning the plane upside down during an extreme banking maneuver. The same sense of helplessness, feeling that my seat belt was unbuckled, clutched me in its grip.

Granddaddy's hand grabbing my left shoulder startled me out of my bleak daydream. "Hold on, Hersch. Here we go!" With Susan on his lap, he slowly pushed the hand accelerator downward. "Hang onto my belt."

The engine's low roar tightened to a loud, steady, powerful whirl. The rush of air and water spray was exhilarating. His left hand manned the accelerator, and though his right arm was wrapped around Susan, his hand gripped the bottom of the steering wheel. She had both hands on top, trying to turn the boat from side to side. He held it steady, and soon we cleared Glenbrook Bay and sped toward Cave Rock.

He leaned forward to see Susan's face. She smiled brilliantly, proving to him that she could handle the boat. He grinned in response, with the deep lines in his face framing the pleasure that sparkled in his eyes.

"Look up, up there, you two. Tell me what you see." Granddaddy pointed at Cave Rock, his voice barely audible over the engine roar and waves crashing in white foamy wakes on either side of our craft.

I squinted and yelled, "Wow, it's a face." Sure enough, a perfect outline of a face forms on Cave Rock, which you can see best heading south when out from the shoreline a ways. We were speeding along at a pretty good clip, and I braced myself between the backrest and the dashboard, standing with my head above the windshield. The cold wind swept back my hair. Granddaddy worked his right hand around my belt and waistband to grab me tight. I felt pretty brave—and safe from all harm.

I stood the whole way from Glenbrook to Cave Rock. We sped along at twenty or twenty-five miles an hour, and only a few minutes later I spotted the boathouse and pier. I knew it was Granddaddy's because Kit and Louise were standing on the pier, waving at us. On either side were two other piers with boathouses. His pier extended about forty yards out into the water, with the boathouse at the end. It was easy to spot because the rounded metal roof was old-fashioned, standing out from the other boathouses, which were newer, wooden, and painted. I felt a tug that pulled me down into my seat, and I sat obediently while Granddaddy slowed down and maneuvered the Chris-Craft around the lake side of the dock and into the boathouse. During my summers at Cave Rock, the boathouse dock became one of my favorite places to play. I could dive off the huge pilings, either into the late afternoon waves arriving from California or the calm water of the cove side, chasing fish or crawfish that lived in the huge rocks nearby.

Kit's voice echoed off the curved tin ceiling of the boathouse as we entered, but was drowned out by the engine. When Granddaddy turned off the key and the engine died, Kit was shouting the last words of his greeting, ". . . and I'm real hungry."

He was four years younger than me and six years younger than Susan. He was always hungry, loved food, and was a bit roly-poly. He had a cute and mischievous smile, a face full of freckles, and an impish laugh, and got along with everybody. The cold water of Lake Tahoe made him flinch, so he preferred to play with his stuffed animals on the beach and up at the cabin.

"Mr. Cobb, master Kit woke up about an hour after you left, and he has been very patient waiting for you to come back and have breakfast with him. Quite insistent that his sister fix him breakfast." Louise's voice carried a humorous edge that told how "insistent" Kit could be.

I stood up, hurried along the backrest of the front seat, and sprang onto the dock. I felt the sharp dip of the boat as I leaped, and heard, "Whoa, Hersch, not so fast. You'll have us overboard."

Granddaddy quickly shifted his body weight toward the center of the boat to stop the rocking. He continued, "Next time, not so fast. Go slow and keep all the weight in the boat even. I don't want this thing tipped over. We already had that once in this family."

I knew he was referring to the time my father was driving recklessly in his speedboat on the Snake River in Idaho and turned it completely over. A man drowned, and Daddy had to go to court. That's about all I knew about it. I'd heard bits and pieces about the incident, but when I asked questions, I was told I was too young, and the "whole thing was unfortunate." Daddy never went to jail, but the experience sounded like the sort of outsized thing he would do.

Granddaddy and Susan climbed out of the boat, and we filed out of the boathouse through a door that seemed undersized. The sun was brightly shining, sparkling off the water out on Lake Tahoe, and filtering through the shallows at the cove to the sandy bottom. Susan, Kit, and I waited together for Granddaddy to finish tying the lines from the boat. His shape filled the doorway as he emerged.

"Well, just look at you three." His voice had a fullness and gentleness that seemed to wrap around us and pull us toward him. His smile was so broad that all the lines in his face came together. Granddaddy's eyes were sparkling and at the same time looked right through us. He could see farther and notice more than anybody I'd ever met. The slightest motion caught his eye, and he never seemed to doubt what he saw.

Their sparkle that morning was slightly covered with the mist of a tear. He quickly wiped his eye, dropped to one knee, took Susan and Kit in his left arm and me in his right arm. "You three look like you belong here." That's all he said. He stood up and looked down at us standing underneath him. None of us said anything.

Pale turquoise water shimmered between the planks of the dock, and the rocks on the bottom of the cove gleamed vividly. The sand tempered the dark blue of the deeper parts of the lake, and its clarity disguised the actual depth. Granddaddy stood tall, gazing out over the lake toward the golden sunlight on the western mountains. He towered above me, and I could see his broad smile and sense the comfort he felt. Louise had Kit hand in hand, walking with him to the edge of the dock, squeezing lightly in case he leaned too far over the water. Susan stood next to me, holding onto Granddaddy's huge hand.

His chest heaved as he looked down at us and said, "Why don't you two come with me and we'll check and make sure the boat is secure? I'm getting mighty hungry and feel like something extra special for breakfast."

The pier from the beach to the boathouse had been rebuilt many times. Granddaddy told me each winter the storms at the lake created huge waves that pounded relentlessly for the entire season, bashing the planks from the underside, until eventually they sprang loose from their nails. The planks were huge, four inches thick by ten inches wide and twelve feet long, secured on each side by nails longer than railroad ties. Two or three had been ripped completely away and the gaps in the dock were wide enough to fall through, making them exciting to jump over.

The boathouse was a separate structure from the pier. Telephone pole–sized pilings had been sunk deep into the lake bed to form a horseshoe frame running parallel to the shore, and the interior was wide enough to accommodate his Chris-Craft. Thick wire mesh was wrapped around the horseshoe frame and huge boulders were set inside, as if it were a metal basket. Large bolts and wire cable connected the pilings. The boathouse was mounted four feet higher than the pier, and four steps led up to an old wire gate and fence that kept out unwanted visitors. The extra height, the wire frame, bolts, cable, and the massive boulders could withstand the winter storm waves, and the boathouse had survived for years and years. Granddaddy's boat spent the winters in dry dock in Tahoe City, getting serviced and in storage. He respected the power of winter storms and knew the damage the pounding of incessant waves could wreak.

The padlock on the wire gate was small but sufficient to stop anybody from playing around the boathouse, especially from endangering themselves by getting pounded by waves bashing the lakeside wall of the huge boathouse basket. The reason for the pro-digious "U" frame, filled with boulders, stemmed from the fact that the boathouse actually had to be built twice. When Granddaddy bought his cabin in the 1930s, the dock and boathouse didn't exist. He hired a company to construct the boathouse, and they sank large posts into the lake bed and built a U-shaped wooden dock on top. The structure depended solely on the strength of the posts sunk into the lake bed. Furthermore, the metal hut was fixed to the dock.

The firm promised that it would withstand the Lake Tahoe winter, but it failed miserably the very first one. The boathouse was destroyed, and on his initial summer visit, he saw the boat-house was gone, with the wood, metal, and pillars scattered all over the beach and surrounding boulders along the shore. He was furious. He decided to design and guide the project himself. He settled on building a huge wire mesh cage, with pillars sunk deep into the lake bed at twice the depth that was recommended. He hired a barge to haul boulders from the shore and place them in the huge frame he had constructed. The wire mesh was wrapped around the frame twice. With that sort of reinforcement, it had prevailed all these years.

His Chris-Craft swayed gently in the water, all four lines secured to cleats along the catwalk on the inside of the hut. The cover of the boathouse was nothing more than a curved metal roof, like a Quonset hut. Streaks of sunlight shot through the various cracks and bounced off the sandy bottom, making every-thing sparkle in the dark interior of the hut. He checked every knot one more time, and we retraced our steps through the gate, down the four steps, and began the walk along the beat-up pier. I was getting hungry and looked forward to Granddaddy's prom-ised "extra special breakfast."

Sunlight filtered through the tips of the tall pines surrounding the cabin and shone on us. It was still early, a little after 8:00. The waves lapping the beach were no more than a few inches high, and the sand was still cool to my touch. I could hear my stomach growling as we entered the cabin, and Granddaddy told me and Kit where to get place mats and utensils to set the table. The one table in the cabin was huge, twenty feet long and four feet wide, rough-hewn maple. It served multiple purposes: for breakfast, lunch, dinner, playing cards, dominos, board games, drawing, and just sitting and looking out at Lake Tahoe.

Granddaddy went into the kitchen and slipped a soiled red

and white apron over his head. He opened the refrigerator, put bacon on the grill, and lit the propane burners. Then he started rattling through all the drawers and cupboards, looking for pots, skillets, spatulas, and whatever else he needed. It was obvious he was not accustomed to working in the kitchen. Susan and Louise tried to help, but the kitchen was small, and after bumping around for a few minutes, Louise came out and fussed with the place settings at the table, where Kit and I sat in anticipation. The cooking bacon smelled good, and Granddaddy was pleased with whatever else he was cooking because he had a big grin on his face. He cracked some eggs and stirred them around a skillet; he opened a yellow box and whipped up the contents with milk in a pan. I was thinking, "Great, pancakes and syrup." He kept smiling and stirring the contents of the pan around. Then he poured water into the skillet. Susan gave me a look that told me that whatever I thought was for breakfast was not what was being cooked. Kit sat next to me, coloring in a book and looking hungrier every minute.

Granddaddy finally called, "Okay, ready! Grab a plate and get in line. I've got something really special for you." Susan was already in the kitchen, so I handed her a plate and fork. Kit grabbed his plate and dashed in to line up next. When Granddaddy filled Susan's plate, Kit's eyes opened wide. His mouth started to quiver, and his plate shook against his fork and rattled. Granddaddy filled half of Susan's plate with watery scrambled eggs that ran to the edge, and the other half with a ladle full of a runny pale yellow meal that looked like paste.

He topped it off with a couple of strips of bacon and announced, "Now, here's a breakfast that's special in the South, hominy grits and eggs and bacon. Fixed just the way the Cobb family likes 'em. There's butter for the grits on the table and that makes them taste even better. Couldn't be better."

Granddaddy was so pleased he beamed, but he hadn't noticed the expression on Kit's face. It was caught between tears, panic, and the realization that what he saw was his breakfast. When Granddaddy went to fill Kit's plate, it dropped to his side, and he said, "Granddaddy, I'm sorry." Then both his lips quivered. "I guess I'm not really a Cobb, because that looks awful and I think I hate hominy grits."

Kit stood forlornly, freckle-faced, plump, red-haired, his tummy bared between his T-shirt and shorts, waiting for something terrible to happen to him. Granddaddy stopped short, with his skillet of runny eggs extended and a serving spoon in his other hand, clearly baffled. Susan quickly put her plate on the table and returned to Granddaddy's side. Taking a hold of his wrist, she gently guided the skillet back to the stove. She pulled on his apron and he bent down so she could say something into his ear. She touched his cheek while she whispered to him. His expression changed, and he looked over at Kit. He bent over again and said something back to Susan.

He straightened to his full height and said, "Why, Kit, that's all right. That's just fine. I'm extra hungry this morning, anyway. Do you mind if I have yours?" Kit didn't know what to say. He hadn't expected Granddaddy to be so nice about his refusal to eat what he was served. Granddaddy continued, "Susan says you like pancakes and syrup. Is that right?"

Kit blurted out, "That's right, Granddaddy! I really like syrup, and pancakes too."

"Well, she says she can cook 'em up just the way you like them. Can you wait a few minutes?"

Kit's face beamed with happiness. "Yes, sir." Then he handed Granddaddy his plate and fork, as though his sentence of having to eat hominy grits and watered eggs was lifted, and scooted back to the table. Granddaddy stayed in the kitchen with Susan, showing her where things were and cleaning up as she mixed pancakes and cleared the grill. He was a big man and nearly filled the kitchen, and that's where he stayed. His admiration for the way she had deftly handled the situation filled his face, and the easy way he leaned against the counter showed clearly how special she was to him. Her way with him was extraordinary. No matter what the impasse, she formed a kind of beacon that was easy for him to follow. She could ask him anything, make suggestions, and he was happy to please her.

I tried not to be as childish as my younger brother. Still, I merely poked at my plate of hominy grits, added enough butter and syrup to make them edible, and skipped the eggs. My hunch was that Susan would make enough pancakes for everybody, and she did. Granddaddy happily ate his eggs and grits, and somehow the pot of grits on the stove was empty when I went to help clean up. My guess was that the ground squirrels had a special breakfast that morning too.

I'd seen that look of panic on Kit's face before, in Los Angeles at the new house Mom had bought the previous year while we were at Grandma's for the summer. Kit hated lima beans, and so did I. We dreaded having to eat them, and Kit refused to even come to the table when he smelled them cooking. Instead, Kit hid under his bed. My mother, for some reason, thought it was amusing to force him to eat food he hated. She and her new husband, Dick Branstedder, laughed at how picky he was. What they didn't know is that Kit didn't really eat them. He mashed them on his plate, pushed them deep into his cheeks and then excused himself from the table to go spit them out in the garden.

My thoughts of home life in Los Angeles were broken when Susan asked if I wanted more pancakes. She put two more on my plate and two more on Kit's. Life here really was good. Lake Tahoe glistened in front of me, huge and light blue, cradled by majestic mountains and embellished by scattered pure white cumulus clouds.

Granddaddy watched Kit devour his syrup and pancakes, totally absorbed in stuffing more pancakes into his mouth, and Susan, carefully taking one bite at a time. The expression on his face was affectionate and caring, satisfying to himself and to us.

I hurried through the rest of my breakfast, anxious to explore the beach, the dock, and the huge boulders near the water. That's what I did the rest of that first day. I went to bed early, wonderfully spent by the hot sun, ice-cold lake water, rarified air, and constant swimming and exploring. I drifted to sleep in comfort, feeling an unfamiliar conviction that I was right where I belonged.

The next morning, I was awakened very early by a cold breeze gently wafting over my face. I smiled at the realization that I was at Lake Tahoe with Granddaddy. I quietly climbed out of the lower bunk so as not to wake Kit, who was asleep just above me. I discovered Granddaddy and Susan already in the kitchen making hot cereal. I walked in and said, "Susan, how about pancakes?"

Granddaddy answered, "Not yet. Let's have some warm oatmeal to tide us over and get going."

"Where?" I asked, puzzled because it was cold throughout the cabin and probably colder outside.

"To get some of the best water you've ever tasted," he replied with a hint of mystery. Susan was nodding and smiling, in on the secret. I accepted the bowl she handed me, filled the top with brown sugar and cream, and warmed myself with each spoonful.

"Hersch, out on the side porch, grab that aluminum pail and ladle, and meet us in front of the house. Better bring a sweatshirt, it's cold." He was leaving the kitchen with Susan as he spoke.

I didn't know what he was talking about, but I went outside. A narrow porch ran the full length of the north side of the
cabin with a railing and wooden bins attached. That side of the
cabin was always shaded from the sun, and the wooden bins were
used to store fruit and vegetables, taking advantage of the natural
coolness. The icy air gave me shivers, and I quickly put on my
sweatshirt. Looking around the porch, not really knowing what
to expect, I saw a large silver-colored vessel with handles on each
side and a ladle sticking up, and knew it was the large aluminum
pail. I wiped it with the damp towel he had tossed to me, but it
was already clean. I guessed that Louise had already cleaned the
pail. I grabbed one of the handles and went around front to his car.
The pail sat on the back seat, so tall its top was at the same level
as my head, while Susan sat in front with Granddaddy. She turned
on the radio but got nothing but crackling noises. He drove up to
Highway 50, turned right, and headed south, through the tunnel
at Cave Rock. About five miles after that, he pulled over to the
side of the highway and parked behind a couple of cars.

"Well, we're here, I think." He had trouble containing his
laughter as he made a feeble attempt to make his mystery last a
while longer. "Put on your jacket and tie your shoes. We're going
for a hike. Oh, and bring that bucket."

I took the pail by one of the handles and shared carrying
it with Susan. We followed Granddaddy as he started down a
narrow path between scrub pine and small manzanita bushes. The
path was strictly single-file. The bushes came up to my knees and
the branches were stiff and sharp and easily poked through my
pants. Off in the distance, between some pine trees, I could see
Lake Tahoe and cabins near the shore. We hiked for what seemed
like forever, halfway to the lake, when I heard Granddaddy's voice: 121
"Hi, there. Good morning." I looked up and saw adults and some

kids standing together. We had arrived at wherever he was taking us, which was the middle of a meadow, covered in manzanita, shrubs, and rocks. I didn't see anything special about the place. I squeezed past Susan and Granddaddy to get a better look.

Granddaddy put his hand on my shoulder. "Well, Hersch, this is it. Don't look like much, but just you wait."

Three kids, all about my age, and some adults were standing around some rocks with water sputtering out between them, making a small puddle and flowing into a rivulet toward Lake Tahoe. It was a natural spring, snow-fed from the mountains to the east. One of the adults placed a big metal bucket, like the one I was holding, under the spouting water. We all watched the bucket slowly fill up. The kids wore mittens and were slapping them together to warm their hands. Filling the bucket took a few minutes, and after he lugged it away from the spout, another man stepped up and put one of the three buckets he had in place to be filled. A boy about my age stood next to him, watching rapt as water sputtered from between the rocks.

The spring sometimes spurted and sometimes flowed smoothly, so it was slow going for the man filling his first bucket. He struck up a conversation with Granddaddy, asking, "Pretty nice day, I'd say. You from down by the lake?" He motioned with his head toward several small cabins in the distance. "Haven't run into you before." The man's voice was pleasant and friendly, like he was passing the time of day with an old buddy.

"No," Granddaddy answered casually, "we're over past Cave Rock, down that road on the left, down by the lake. In that group of places down there."

The man switched buckets, handing the first one to the boy with him. He remained bent over because he could not find anything except a tiny nubbin on which to set the base of the bucket, so he was holding it while water trickled in. He continued chatting. "These your kids?" I could see him smile and wink at Granddaddy.

"Well, I feel pretty young at heart, but these are my grandchildren," Granddaddy replied, smiling, "here for a week or two." He waited a beat, then asked, "That your boy?" Granddaddy liked kids, I would learn. At the drop of a hat he would buy ice cream for anybody nearby.

"Yup, one of them," was the answer, "too early for the rest. Still in the rack."

"Strapping young'un, I'd say." Granddaddy loved that word, "strapping." And "muskles," for muscles, with a hard "k."

The man switched to his third bucket, got it set, then peered up at Granddaddy. He said, "Say, I think Ty Cobb lives over in that neck of the woods. You anywhere near him?"

I started to say something, but felt a firm squeeze on my shoulder and held my tongue. Granddaddy casually remarked, "Well, pretty close, I think."

I stood bewildered, not understanding. Only later that night, in talking to Susan, would I realize the wisdom of his restraint.

Just then the man's bucket slipped from its fragile perch and spilled. He grabbed to right it, but it emptied in a flash. He rose up, shaking his head, and said, "Back's a little tired. You folks go ahead, and I'll wait till you're done. Go on, now, you just got the one anyway," pointing at our pail.

Granddaddy said he was not in a hurry, that it didn't matter, but I'd already scouted out a way to set our large pail down so I could hold it while it filled. I watched the water dribble and spurt into the wide metal cylinder. Our pail was a lot bigger than his buckets, so filling it took some time. The adults talked, mostly about fishing, what bait was working, what the kids liked to do, and the weather. When the tilted container looked half full, Granddaddy reached down and tipped it so it was standing straight upright. "Hersch, that's enough. Any more and it'll be too heavy to carry." We moved out of everybody's way. "Here, Susan hand me that ladle."

He dipped in the scoop and handed it to me. "Hersch, have some of this." I took a cautious sip and then a big gulp. The taste was simply delicious and invigorating. The mountain stream water was cold, crisp, lively, and the sensation of it flowing down my throat was slightly heavy, and wonderful. I took another gulp, too eagerly, spilling half the ladle over my shirt. I looked up and saw everybody was watching me.

"First time," Granddaddy said through a wide grin. The other folks smiled at each other, nodding with approval. Feeling not too badly for my clumsiness, I quickly handed the ladle to Susan.

We waited around while two other families filled their pails. Granddaddy gabbed a little more about the lake, asked about the fishing at the boat ramp at Cave Rock, what bait was working there, and which stores had the freshest worms. A few small birds darted across the meadow, and after he pointed them out, it seemed time to leave.

Granddaddy waved his hand to the man who winked at him and said, "Well, been nice talking. We've got to head back and fix some breakfast. Maybe we'll see y'all in a few days."

On the way back Susan took the front side, holding onto one of the handles, and we lifted our pail with a heave and stumbled along behind him. I looked back at the man. He was gesturing, saying, "Nice talking with you, Mister . . ." The man's voice tailed off. Granddaddy waved again, but didn't stop and neither did Susan or I. My head was filled with questions about why Granddaddy didn't tell that man his name. But my heart was filled with smiles. And that's what I was paying attention to. This small adventure had tasted just right.

The hike back to the roadside didn't seem half as long as the hike up. Granddaddy helped us the last part of the way, and at the car he wedged the pail on the floor behind the passenger seat. He had brought the lid and told me to keep holding it down tight so our fresh spring water wouldn't slosh out.

Back at the cabin, everybody drank the water out of the pail with the ladle or filled glass canning jars and brought them into the house. The water was always coldest in the morning, but it stayed cool all day in the shadows on the north side of the cabin. Every two or three days, we made the early morning hike down to the rock spring and filled up for the next couple of days. I think I drank more water than I normally ever would, just to empty the pail so I could tell Granddaddy that we needed to go to the spring.

Thereafter, on the first morning of every visit to Lake Tahoe with Granddaddy, I anticipated getting up before dawn, putting on my sweatshirt, and preparing for the hike down the trail to the meadow. We always met families at the spring, and Granddaddy discussed with the other men the fishing, what animals the kids had spotted, how cold the lake was, the weather, where folks lived, and how nice the beach was near them. It surprised me how many people knew Ty Cobb lived over past Cave Rock, and each time this was mentioned, we exchanged a glance. He smiled imperceptibly and carried on the conversation without a break, never introducing himself or mentioning his name.

I never had to ask Granddaddy about why he didn't introduce himself. I found out later that evening on our first visit.

After dinner, I played outside, pretending the moon shadows were Indian spirits and I was part of their dance. I was comfortable in the dark at Cave Rock, and the night sounds in the mountains were enchanting. I played until I was shivering cold and then hurried inside. A huge fire crackled in the granite fireplace, and I practically jumped up and down as I stood in front of it. He occupied his favorite chair, and Susan sat on the red sofa, leaning over the maple armrest, talking to him. He often talked to Susan, particularly in the evenings, and she listened attentively and carried her part of the conversation. Susan was going to be thirteen years old. I warmed myself by the fire and listened.

". . . and your father was a pretty good athlete too—that is, until he got into that rock fight with those hooligans down by the creek. Susan, it was awful. Blood everywhere. A rock hit him right on his eyeball and ruined it." Granddaddy was talking frankly, his voice not revealing any noticeable emotion. Responding to the horrible image, Susan put her hand up and covered her right eye. "No, the left one, he lost it completely," he continued. "He still was a good shot with his bird guns. His right eye even seemed to get stronger."

Susan and I had seen Daddy pop the glass eye out of his left socket. It made me squeamish to see him hold a glass eye in his hand and pretend he was going to open his eyelid. I always wondered, "Where does that hole go?"

Granddaddy looked up at the ceiling and around the room, breathing in small heaves. "I have to admit, I was pretty mad at him. For all the money he spent on boats and airplanes in Twin Falls. What I gave him was supposed to set him up in business."

His face looked pink in the flickering flames from the fireplace. He stopped talking, reflecting back on his second son. When he resumed, his voice dropped lower and lower. "Your father was doing better. Bought the Coca-Cola plant in Santa Maria, was trying to get his business going. But your mother—" He stopped, but then realized he had to finish up with what he started. "If it hadn't been for her . . ." He paused again, "Well, I don't know, it would have been different." He was nearly swallowing his words, not wanting Susan or me to be affected by his intense dislike of my mother. He didn't actually say she caused my father's death, even though he felt certain in his own mind that his son's violent outbursts because of her caused his heart attack. But in all the times we spent with him, he never directly attacked her or talked meanly about her.

"Your father had a part of him that riled easily. Honey, you might know that." He shifted position and leaned toward Susan until I could barely hear him. "There was something inside that ate at him from time to time, but not always. His men loved him, would follow him anywhere and work hard for him. Why, Lester moved down from Twin Falls to Santa Maria. He had a big practical joker inside of him and loved to be the center of things."

A hollow timbre entered his voice as he went on. "When he passed, I know you and Hersch and Kit were alone. I felt terrible." Granddaddy moved his hand onto the table holding the lamp, and I thought he was going to comfort Susan, but he seemed frozen by what he was telling her. "Your daddy was gone. There wasn't anything I could do or say that would change that. Susan," he was looking right at her, "it was a hard time for Granddaddy." She could see the expression on his face much more clearly than I could. She reached over with her hand and put it gently on top of his. He flinched slightly, but not from her touch. No, she had touched something inside him that he wasn't used to. He must have liked the warmth in Susan's touch because he left his hand under hers.

127

He soon gathered himself and continued his monologue quietly. "And then your Uncle Ty passed. Two of my boys in two years. Both gone," he repeated, still sounding stunned. "Just gone." He leaned back in his chair and gazed up at the knotty pine ceiling, ghostly in the amber glow from the fire. I looked up as well, drifting from plank to plank, from knothole to knothole. "Just gone," he said almost to himself.

When Susan looked at me, I knew not to say anything. We both knew what terror our father had rent upon us. We knew pain and fear and burrowing into our own cocoons to protect ourselves from our father's urges. It was the pact we shared. She told me years later that many people who knew our parents thought we'd end up in an institution because no children could endure such constant onslaughts from both parents without, as she said, "cracking up." One reason was because we knew we were safe here, even as our grandfather spilled forth his emotions upon losing his two sons.

Susan got up from the sofa, sat on the armrest of Granddaddy's chair, and put her arms around him. He slowly emerged from that haunting period in his past and hugged her back. "Honey, you and your brothers stay close. Take care of each other. Forgive each other once in a while. Understand me?"

He leaned forward, shifting his balance, and said, quietly, "I think I'll go on to bed." He stood up and awkwardly ambled to the corner bedroom he always used.

I watched him use the doorknob for a brace, enter, and close the door. Susan looked up at me and said, in a voice wise beyond her years, "He's still so very sad. And he's alone."

I moved over to the sofa where Susan was now sitting. We both liked Uncle Ty. We didn't know him well enough to say that we loved him. But our cousins, Ty III and Charlie, loved him deeply, and everybody who knew him did, and that was good enough for us. We knew that when our father died, we would be spared, and terror and pain gone. But, Granddaddy loved him, and Aunt Shirley loved our dad, no matter what anybody said. And that was that. We sat, looking around a room where we had experienced nothing but fun and security.

When we finally stood up to go to bed, I asked Susan, "Why didn't he tell that man at the spring his name?"

"I think I know," she said, sounding tired. "He was talking about his life earlier, and he said something about not wanting us to be bothered because of things he's done, who he is. He knows his kids suffered because of it; people saw them differently, expected things, and he's not going to do that again with us. He said he should have realized all that before," she recounted. "I think that's it, Hersch. He did say he's happy we're here."

Our time at Lake Tahoe passed too fast, and even though we spent many days at the same beach, and around the same boulders or riding in the Chris-Craft, each occasion was a new adventure with Granddaddy. I grew to trust his watchful eye and protective ways, and I realized that he liked the bond that was growing between us. In the evenings I learned how to build a fire in the fireplace and play new card games and board games. I would read on my own or listen to stories my grandfather told about hunting, fishing, Tahoe, and his children.

We returned to Grandma's house, satiated and smiling, eager to share our adventures with her. She listened politely to all our little tales, but she was most interested in how we got along with our grandfather. Our happiness told her everything she wanted to know, and it pleased her immensely. The last weeks of summer at Grandma's were serene ones before we had to return to Los Angeles. Our beginnings of a bond of trust and caring were set during that vacation at Lake Tahoe, and it set the stage for many more visits to come.

CHAPTER FIVE

The North
Shore Club

I hurried through my breakfast, turned to Granddaddy, and said, "I'm ready to go down to the lake." He smiled and said, "Sure, but remember: Wear your shirt. Don't run up the steps. And, oh, we're going out to dinner tonight—the North Shore Club." I didn't pay much attention when he mentioned the club. I was too busy grabbing my stuff and rushing out the kitchen door and across the deck. I hesitated as I looked out over Lake Tahoe. It was 8:30 on the third day of our visit to Lake Tahoe with Granddaddy.

We had arrived three days earlier, late at night, and when I woke up the first morning, Granddaddy was sitting at the huge table in the great room, looking out over the lake. In front of him were two large bowls, a box of Cheerios, a jar of honey, milk, and two large spoons. I ate quickly, stood up, and said, "I'm ready." My memories from last year of rowing around the cove were fresh and exciting.

He reached over and caught my left arm with his hand, saying,

"Hold on a minute. I want you to help me with something. Down on the beach." He gulped a last spoonful of Cheerios and stood up. I followed him across the deck and down the steep steps leading to the beach. He wore an open-collared shirt, nice slacks, and two-tone summer shoes, so I didn't think what he needed help with was going to get him dirty.

On the beach he started picking up pieces of wood, broken, splintered, and bleached gray and white from the constant punishment of the hot sun and beating waves. He was making a small pile and pointed me toward a couple of larger timbers. I picked one up and, even in its ruined state, it looked like the bench seat from the wooden rowboat I used last summer. I looked all around the cove. There was no sign of the small boat I had tied to a tree at the end of last summer.

I cringed but asked anyway, "Granddaddy, what happened to the rowboat?"

He straightened up and said, "Bring those over here."

I gauged the tone of his voice, automatically looking for the edges of anger. I took hold of the plank and another piece that was curved and looked awfully like the keel, and dragged them to add to his pile. I recognized more pieces of the rowboat, all broken or splintered and bleached out. He stood above the pile and didn't say anything. I looked from the pile, then up at him three or four times, expecting at least a scolding.

He didn't say anything, but looked out at Lake Tahoe and back at the pile two or three times, as if deciding what to do next. The lake was smooth as glass. I said, as compliantly as possible, "Is this the boat?"

"Yep."

I waited a moment and asked, "What happened?"

"That." He pointed to the lake. I looked again at the pile of smashed, beaten, ruined timbers and then again at the lake, beautiful and slowly undulating with barely a ripple. "Hersch, that lake is part of nature, and nature doesn't care—been here through all of time. She can be easy, like right now, or harsh, like she will be late this afternoon. And in the winter, with storms and snow and sun, she never gives in. The waves are twice the size you like to play in, and reach all the way up to the steps. I'll bet half the rope you used is still around that tree."

Then, in the same breath, he started chuckling. "But not the other half or your boat!" He indicated the pile and said, "This is what nature can do if you're not careful and don't respect her. Don't forget that, okay?" I nodded, not knowing what to expect next.

"Right now, she's just right for rowing around." He looked again at the lake. "She's taught me an awful lot. You can learn from her."

I looked over the pile of remains of my boat and thought I'd be stuck on the shore for our entire vacation. Granddaddy started walking back toward the steps, and I thought he was leaving me to mope by myself and absorb what he said. I was angry with myself for losing my boat and sorry that I was trapped on the beach with no way to explore the cove and shoreline. When he reached the end of the pier, near the steps, he yelled back at me, "Come on. I told you I needed some help."

On the other side of the pier was a rowboat, about the same size as the one destroyed, resting on the sand but tied firmly to an anchor bolt on the pier. I had expected my grandfather to be angry with me, insist I'd done something irreversibly bad, and teach me a lesson by condemning me to have only the beach to play on. My father's way had been to pound on me until my fear bled throughout my body. I looked at the rowboat in disbelief, wondering if it was a trick.

"Pete noticed what happened. He found this boat for sale at a pretty good price, the oarlocks fit, and it looks worthy enough. What you say we put her in the lake and see?"

I was still cautious but hopped over the pier and pushed on the transom while he pulled the rope. Once we got the boat to his side of the pier, I pulled her down to the edge of the lake. Granddaddy fitted the oarlocks, helped me place the oars, and gave me a slight push into the water, careful not to get his shoes wet. I pulled on the oars with all my might, coasted out a little, and reported that no water was leaking into the boat. I found out later that Pete had thoroughly tested its seaworthiness by filling the boat with water, none of which had leaked out after a full day.

He had his hands on his hips and shouted to me, "Remember the steps. When you get done, remember the steps." His voice echoed around the cove, and I knew he was firm in this. He did not want me to run up the forty-eight steps to the cabin. I shifted the oars into the boat, waved with both hands as if to say yes, and he waved at me and turned toward the hillside leading up to the cabin. When he started climbing the steps, I stopped rowing and watched. Two or three times he paused, put his hand on his raised knee to catch his breath, looked back at me, and then continued on. The rowboat drifted while I watched him. I thought about what he had just done, not quite believing his patience. My sense of closeness mildly thrilled me. His actions spoke loudly, and I learned to watch what people did, and less to what they said.

Granddaddy's rule was to never run up or down the steps from the cabin to the beach below. He told me that's how he "ruined his ticker," thumping on his chest where his heart was. He was on the dock and heard the phone ringing up in the cabin and sprinted up the steps to answer it. He was expecting a call and didn't want to miss it, but when he reached the top and grabbed the phone, the line was dead. His heart was pounding, faster and faster. He sat down in a chair and tried to calm down, but nothing slowed the bursting sensation in his chest. Finally, he passed out, and when he woke up, he was soaking wet. At least he was breathing normally and his heartbeat had slowed down. But ever since that time, he noticed that when he exerted himself, his heartbeat sped up and would not slow down for a long time.

This morning I rushed down the steps, not running but rushing. My "rush" was fast, but not as fast as my "run." The sun glistened hot on my back; I had a towel, a lunch bag with a sandwich and a bottle of juice in it, and the rowboat was waiting. The water in the cove was smooth as blue transparent silk, and I hurriedly checked the oars and oarlocks and pulled the boat across the rough sand toward the cove. I had done this a hundred times; each time brought a new and different world to my senses. Granddaddy wanted me out of the sunshine by 11:30. After that time the sun's rays burned hot, and I had a redhead's skin, which practically fried, no matter how much sun cream I put on. Sometimes I wore a T-shirt, but not until afternoon. My instructions were to keep within the cove, not to venture too far north past Sky Water Lodge, and not to drift to the south. This was fine with me. He bought me a new pair of swim fins and a mask, knowing that I liked to swim under the icy water, chase schools of fish, dive down deep and grab at the crawfish, pretending I lived underwater.

I knew that by 9:00 or 9:30 a dark blue line formed across the lake, on the California side, running from the north to the south. If I watched long enough, I could see it slowly and steadily move across the lake toward Nevada. The moving dark blue line meant that big waves, formed by breezes blowing from California, were headed to the Nevada side; huge. Strong, relentless waves broke the smooth surface of the silky vision that existed from dawn to mid-morning. By late afternoon, the waves would be three to four feet high, pounding on the boathouse piers, beaches, and rocks of the Nevada shore. The change transformed the lake, carrying such power and force that I felt as if I'd been swept away from the mountains and suddenly landed on the beach next to the ocean in the middle of a storm. The winter months were filled with storms, and whatever was left out or caught on the beaches and small coves along the Nevada shore was pounded and beaten and brought under the control of the winter lake so that by spring or summer, all that was left was a reminder of the telling strength and relentless neutrality of nature. I kept my grandfather's words about "learning" from the lake in my mind. At the most unexpected moments, I learned lessons: how to judge the risk of playing in the huge afternoon waves, realizing the timelessness of all nature, growing to love the beauty of the lake, seeing my muscles harden and grow strong the more I rowed and swam. My self-reliance grew, unknown to me at the time, but years later, a comforting force.

The morning sun was positioned just behind the roofline of his cabin. Its brightness made me turn my head, until I put both hands on my forehead to protect my eyes and took another look. There he was, standing, watching, and finally waving his huge hand at me as if to say, "I'm here to make sure you're all right." I knew from past mornings like this that he'd check on me every so often, just to make sure. I would row around for hours, occasionally catching a glimpse of him walking across the deck or slipping back into the cabin. He never said anything, and I never said anything, but his watchfulness and concern filled me with a sense of security that I'd rarely known.

I spent the morning rowing, diving after fish, playing on the huge boulders near the shore, and exploring up and down the outside of the cove. The boathouse and pier were home to schools of fish and hundreds of crawfish, all targets of my interest. I knew it was late morning by the increasing size of the waves breaking against the boathouse and the welcomed heat of the sun each time I pulled myself out of the icy water into the rowboat. My shoulders had been exposed for a couple of hours, and with every additional minute in the sun, I felt the slight burning sensation that warned me I was turning redder. I ate my sandwich, guzzled down my juice, decided to row to shore, and tied up the boat.

The steps from the beach up to the cabin were old railroad ties, with rocks and steel spikes holding them in place. Over the years, the hot, dry summers and wet winters had caused the ties to split and dislodge, so I was careful with each step. When I crossed the rear deck, I peered into the grand room of the cabin and barely made out Granddaddy sprawled out over a chair or heard the radio spitting out what sounded like a baseball game. Radio reception in the mountains was spotty at best, so he turned it up loud, ignoring the crackling of electrical interference. I could tell he was asleep because his mouth was half open, his head slouched onto his shoulder, and his arms flopped over the sides of the chair. I sat down on the sofa across from him and tried to make out what game he was listening to. It didn't really matter to him who was playing, so long as the company of his past was with him.

A small eight-sided coffee table sat between us. It matched the other simple furniture in the room, except the top was copper, held in place with ornamental rivets. On it rested a cigar box, a lighter, some coasters for drinks, and packages of Bicycle playing cards. That was all normal. What was unusual were three white letter-sized envelopes, side by side, open and bulging with money. It was easy to see the edges of the green bills, and make out

137

the number 100 on several corners. I'd never seen such stacks of money, so I slid off my seat and crawled around the coffee table to get a closer look. The envelopes were slightly crumpled, and it looked like all the bills were 100s. The edge of each stack was rough, like they were used bills and someone gathered them together, shuffled them into a neat pile, and stuffed them into the envelopes. The piles looked about the same height, about an inch or so.

My attention was so focused on the contents of the envelopes, I jumped out of my skin when Granddaddy snorted and snored in the same breath. His body lurched a bit and his arms shuffled, but he remained asleep. I settled down and kept peering into the envelopes, wondering what Granddaddy was doing with all this money. After a few minutes, I got bored and went back to the sofa to wait. A loud crackling noise jolted out of the radio, which meant there was a big electrical storm nearby. I looked out the back window toward the lake and sure enough, the sky in the south was filled with a huge black cylinder, nearly touching the surface of the lake. At the same time, it was sunny at Cave Rock. Soon enough, I saw lightning bolts inside the cylinder flash toward the lake, along with huge thunderclaps, and the noise woke up Granddaddy.

He rubbed his eyes, looked at me, and said, "Come over here and let me take a look at your back. Pull your shirt up and let me see if you got too much sun." I did, and I could tell I was a little pink, but not too bad. "Not too much damage." At the same time, he turned the radio volume way down and asked me, "Did you hear any score?" I told him I didn't, and he snapped off the radio.

He looked at his watch. "Let's find Louise, and get you some lunch." I told him I ate my sandwich. He replied, "That's not going to be enough to get you through to dinner. Remember, we're going to the North Shore Club and we'll eat a little late. Now see if you can find Susan and Kit, and you all get some lunch."

He leaned over the white envelopes and contemplated them with his eyes as if he were weighing them. I didn't say anything, but wondered what he was thinking. After a minute or so, he picked up two of them, one in each hand, slightly juggling them up and down like he was deciding which one was heavier. Then he put the one in his right hand down and picked up the third envelope and did the same thing. He repeated this a few times, changing envelopes in each hand, and I watched the edges of his mouth turn up with a satisfied smile. Then he folded the flaps into the envelopes, not sealing them, stacked them, and put a rubber band around all three.

He was still smiling when he looked up at me near the window, saying, "Hersch, get going. Get some lunch." His voice was smooth and factual, just a reminder. But he definitely knew I watched the whole time he was weighing and judging his white envelopes filled with hundred-dollar bills.

I practically sprinted to the front door, shouting for my sister and brother to come in for lunch. They were playing in a level area just across the driveway. I am sure that at one time, perhaps when my dad and aunts and uncles visited, this area was a badminton court. Although the whole property sloped down from Highway 50 toward Lake Tahoe, the badminton court was level, built up on the downside slope with the same railroad-type ties as the steps leading down to the lake. Now it was covered in pinecones, old branches, and leaves, badly neglected on all sides. The stakes holding the railroad ties were loose, and several ties were falling out of place or missing and had not been repaired for years. As far as I was concerned, this was all good. I didn't care about badminton, but the deteriorated railroad ties held all kinds

139

of wonderful bugs. I was particularly impressed with the black beetles, which were huge, and when rolled over on their backs, struggled with tremendous vigor to right themselves. We spent hours digging for those beetles and potato bugs. I found the kind that was yellow and black and a sickly white. They looked creepy, and I never touched one without using a stick.

I played with them for a few minutes and then we all went inside for lunch. Louise fixed peanut butter and jelly sandwiches, juice, fruit, and cold water from the pail on the shady north side, and we ate on the deck overlooking the lake. It was now well past noon and the roar of inboards, pulling their water skiers, was at its height. In another two hours, the waves would be two to three feet high, taking the ease and most of the fun out of skiing. The dark blue line that started on the west side of the lake early in the morning had moved all the way to our side on the east, and with it came the large waves that were formed and pushed along by the breeze from the west.

We finished our lunch, and Susan and Kit went down to the beach. I went inside to find Granddaddy. He was lying on his bed, nearly dozing. The slam of the screen door behind me must have roused him a bit because he lifted himself on one elbow and motioned for me to come into his room. His room was at the rear of the cabin, on the lake side; the windows were open, and I could hear the waves splashing on the shore. The air flowing through was cool and delicious. His room was the same size as the bedroom at the front of the cabin, although he had one full-sized bed and one twin-sized bed. Those bedrooms shared a bathroom in between them that had a door to the outside with steps leading down toward the lake.

He said, "Granddaddy's a little tired. Go on out and play. Come back around five and wake me up and we'll get ready to go out.

Tell Susan to help you boys. Understand?" I didn't have to answer, but I knew to close his door quietly on my way out. He told me many times that he got his best sleep and rest at Lake Tahoe.

The sun settled lower into the western sky and the afternoon faded away. I walked out on the deck and looked out on Lake Tahoe with the sun still above the top of the mountains in California; looking over the lake was like squinting into the midday sun, only broken into a million parts of darting light, each bouncing off the water's surface. It was bright, hot, piercing, and relentless, with part of the intensity the heat and the other part the blinding glare. The heat came directly from the low sun, increased by the reflective glare off the lake, and looking out the huge window of the grand room, I watched the steam rise from the railings around the deck, sucking every bit of moisture out of the wood that had seeped into it during the night and early morning.

The glare was so bright and hot that I couldn't see anything on the lake. My eyes were teased into thinking there were still boats out there, but I knew the waves were too dangerous; only the lost or foolish would be caught on the lake at this time of day. I squinted, trying to imagine a speedboat, slugging it out with five-foot waves. There were none, and I retreated from the glare back into the cool front bedroom, to my bunk bed, sank into the satin comforter, and drifted off to sleep.

When Susan woke me up, the sun had set behind the western mountains and it was noticeably cooler. She reminded me that we were going out to dinner and to hurry up and dress in nice clothes. Kit was standing beside her, already wearing good slacks and a nice shirt. It didn't take me long to get ready, and Granddaddy, Susan, and Kit were waiting in the living room when I walked in. He said jovially, "Well, if I don't say so myself, you're a fine-looking family. Whadda you say we go get some dinner?"

141

He led the way out to his black Chrysler. He wore a sports coat, and I noticed the tops of the white envelopes sticking out of the side pocket, although I couldn't tell if there were two of them or three, and watched him pat them as he slid behind the wheel and started the engine. He always liked big fast cars and the Chrysler was his favorite; he told me he'd bought so much stock in the company, he wondered why they didn't give him a free one every year. I didn't understand, but I agreed they should.

The North Shore Club was on the highway that went around the lake, pretty close to where Nevada ended and California began. I never saw the exact line that separated the two states, and always wondered what it looked like. It took a while to get there, but Granddaddy kept us busy looking for deer on the highway or boats still out on the lake, and the time passed quickly. It was dark when he turned onto a steep driveway, and the North Shore Club announced itself in neon lights. He drove up to the entrance and a young man opened his door and said, "Good evening, Mr. Cobb, welcome to the North Shore Club. We hope you enjoy your evening." The young man also opened the back door, which I didn't expect, and we all climbed out.

Granddaddy shook the young man's hand and gave him a silver dollar. "Park it where it won't get bumped, understand?" The young man nodded and drove the Chrysler slowly away.

We walked up the front steps, and the door opened. Just a few feet inside the entrance stood a man behind a tall podium, making notes and saying hello to everybody who came in. We waited for only a second before he quickly stepped forward, saying in a loud voice, "Mr. Cobb, Mr. Cobb, welcome to the Club. Good to see you. How are you? Oh, and I see you have guests tonight." He gestured toward the three of us. "We have a special table all ready for you." While he was talking, he grabbed Granddaddy's hand

and pumped it up and down and patted his shoulder. Then he turned toward the other people standing nearby and said, "Folks, we have the immortal Ty Cobb as a special guest tonight."

I could feel Granddaddy bristle and he quickly said, "Henry, please, I have my grandchildren tonight. We're here to have a quiet dinner."

The man replied, "Fine, fine, Mr. Cobb, no bother. Just let me check and make sure your table is ready."

We were waiting to be called when another man suddenly appeared and staggered toward Granddaddy. This man didn't walk straight, and I could smell whisky as he approached. I felt Granddaddy's hand nudge my shoulder so that I shifted behind him. Susan and Kit were behind me. The man stopped, barely short of bumping into Granddaddy. The people standing nearby didn't notice. The smiles on their faces remained, and they carried on as if this man was an old friend or something like that. I felt the tension radiating from Granddaddy, and I moved slightly to my right to see what would happen.

The man didn't even look at me or Susan or Kit but stared straight into the face of my grandfather. He was slightly younger than Granddaddy, built full and stocky. "So, you're the great Ty Cobb, huh," he blurted out, "the tough one, huh, the guy who thinks he can give anybody a licking." He drew a big breath and said, "Well, I'll tell you, I've been waiting for a chance, and I'm going to show everybody what a coward and run tail you really are. I watched you play and I think you're a chicken. A chicken, you hear." He took another breath and growled, "You want it here, or outside?" motioning with his thumb toward the front door.

The noise in the room was so loud, no one could really make out what was said. My own body tensed up, and I saw the flush on Granddaddy's cheek. He formed a fist with his right hand,

and I thought, "Oh, my gosh, he's going to hit this guy." I took a step backward, ready to duck or jump out of the way. For me, the lights in the room became brighter, and I noticed Granddaddy shift his body, bend his knees, and put some weight on his back foot. I was sure he was going to knock this guy's lights out. I was scared, but it was exciting.

The man snarled, "Well, you big blowhard, what's its going to be? Get your ass whipped in here or out there?"

Granddaddy was furious. His eyes focused like he was going to drill this guy, and I was sure he was going to bust him in the face. His breathing was quick but steady, and his hand relaxed a little. He knew where I was because his right hand came over and barely brushed against me; I thought he was making sure he had enough room to swing his hardest. The man edged closer, and his smell was just terrible. All of this happened like a quick blurry movie.

Then the strangest thing happened. Granddaddy's shoulders dropped just a little, and his right hand quickly moved across his body. Deliberately, he took the guy's right hand in his in a handshake. The man flinched a little bit, as if he didn't understand what was happening. Granddaddy didn't let go of his hand and held it down at the man's waist, right where I could see both hands, struggling. The man wanted loose, and Granddaddy held tight. Granddaddy moved closer to him, not giving him any room to rip his hand away. I watched him squeeze hard and felt a knowing smile come over my own face. I'd seen that squeeze on the Snake River in Idaho when I was six years old.

As Granddaddy's grip squeezed harder, I heard him whisper in a guttural snarl, probably not meant for my ears, "You lousy bum, you're not going to swing on anybody." His face moved so close to the other man that he edged backward.

The man exclaimed, "Let go of me, you sonofabitch. When I get done with you, you'll be sorry you ever saw me."

Granddaddy, breathing on his face, told him, "I'm not fighting you. You're leaving. Now." His grip tightened on the man's hand. I knew he would never let go; he had taken my hand or arm many times to help me, and just by being helped, I knew his strength.

By this time Henry had returned. He saw right away what was happening, and he whistled and motioned to a big guy who was standing at the entrance to the casino. The big guy came over in an instant, put his arm around the man, and began walking toward the front door, carrying the man along with him.

Henry turned to Granddaddy and started to apologize, gesturing, bending at his waist, and almost pleading, "I'm so sorry Mr. Cobb. Sometimes, this can't be avoided. Please let me show you to your table." Granddaddy put his hand on Henry's chest, slowed him down, and said, "Please, Henry, don't worry. I'm here with my grandchildren. We're here to enjoy ourselves." He was still breathing hard, and I know I had barely missed a fight. I really wanted to see him knock that guy down. I didn't know at the time why this all happened, why the drunk man wanted to fight my grandfather, and how much it meant to Granddaddy to stay out of a fight. He had told me that first summer to stay out of fights, but once in, make the other guy know that I'd never give up.

Henry led us into the dining area where four men on a stage were playing their instruments and singing, but that didn't really matter to me compared to the spectacle next to them, which caught me by surprise and riveted my attention. Eight dancing women, with long legs and beautiful costumes, were moving and flowing together with legs kicking high, singing a song that was lost to me in the flurry of spins, kicks, twists, wiggles, and coy looks; all performing perfectly in unison.

145

Out of the corner of my eye, I watched Granddaddy pause at our table, make sure we were seated, then walk to the smoky doorway of the gambling room, look around, and step inside. No matter how captivating the follies on the stage were, I was grabbed by the mystery of what Granddaddy was up to. He planned this evening to be at the North Shore Club on time, dodged a drunk when we arrived, and was now pursuing his mission. I was determined to witness whatever it turned out to be.

I stood up. Susan and Kit were watching the show, fascinated by the adult entertainment. They didn't even turn their heads as I eased away from the table. A man in a suit stood just past the doorway, watching the room I was in as if he was a guard. I hoped he was watching the long legs on stage and not keeping a lookout to keep some people out of the gambling room. I walked past him like I had business in that room but immediately realized I couldn't have any real business there because it was full of gambling tables, drinking, and cigar smoke. Before me were card tables, roulette tables, a couple of dice tables, and a wall filled with slot machines. I was not yet twelve years old and knew I was not allowed in a casino. It was dimly lit, difficult to see and be seen, so I quickly took up a station on the left wall just past the door and scanned around, looking for my grandfather. Luckily, I recognized the pattern on his sport coat because his back was turned to me and he was leaning over, talking to a man sitting on a straight-backed chair, with hands gripping his knees, his face slightly white with old men's whiskers, thin hair on top, and sorrowful eyes, fixed on Granddaddy. I watched his lips moving now and then, but Granddaddy shifted in front of him and I could only see his left shoulder, arm, and hand.

Just then a tall man with slicked-back wavy dark hair, dressed like a penguin, came up to me and said, "Kid, you're not allowed in here. You'll have to leave." He placed his hand on my shoulder and started to push me toward the door.

I didn't move from the wall. I looked at him as if I knew what I was doing and said, "I'm waiting for my grandfather, that man over there, talking to the guy in the chair."

He turned and spotted whom I meant. "You mean Cobb?" he said, "That guy in the coat, Cobb?"

I quickly replied, "Yeah, my grandfather. I'll only be here a minute, please?"

He looked at Granddaddy again and said, with a lot of hesitation in his voice, "You sure? Cobb. Okay, just one minute and then you're out of here, understand?"

I nodded and said, "Thanks, mister. Yeah, I'm sure. He'll be right over and I'll go with him."

The man's hand covered my shoulder and he squeezed firmly. "Make sure you're not here when I come back." Then he straightened his shoulders and walked toward the roulette table.

Across the room, Granddaddy put his hand on one of the white envelopes in his coat pocket and pulled it out, opening the flap at the same time. He held it open in front of the man sitting in the chair, showing him it was packed with money, lots of money. The man's face looked startled. He began to smile sadly, then cry, then stiffen and look blank for a moment. His eyes lost their faraway stare and moved a dozen times, flitting between the contents of the envelope and Granddaddy's face. He looked both forlorn and giddy with relief. Then Granddaddy stuffed the flap of the envelope over the money, shoved the full envelope into the man's jacket, and put his hand on the man's shoulder. Their hands grasped and shook, almost without moving. I knew that grasp; it was strong and assuring, and said, "Everything will be all right." 147

Granddaddy was walking out and immediately saw me against

the wall. He changed direction and loomed in front of me in no time. "What are you doing?" he asked, his voice level and firm.

I answered, as vaguely as I could, "I came to find you."

"Really," he asked, examining my sheepish smile, "how long have you been here?" His voice exuded a confidence that he knew exactly what I was doing. I didn't say anything. Time stopped as I waited for him to continue. "Well," his response elongated and slightly laughing, "we'll talk about this later, young man. Let's go order something to eat. I'll bet Susan and Kit are hungry." We left the gambling room, his hand gently moving across my shoulders, and I felt the bond of a shared, unspoken secret. I thought, "There are still two more envelopes full of money."

I was scared that I'd done something wrong, which, looking back, was half true, but I didn't have time to worry about it, because before we walked two steps, he moved his hand to my chest stopping me from moving forward.

I thought, "He's angry, I'm in for it." The moment of decision was there—do I run, duck, or scream? I thought of my father and felt a burst of terror pour though my body. I was breathing deeply, hoping, when Granddaddy's voice came through: "Well, I'll be damned, he's here, and it's not midnight. Hersch, come with me."

He took my hand in his and started walking across the dining room toward the club's entrance. A smile formed on his face, really a grin—one that I'd seen so often, wide, toothy, bright eyed, and celebrating something inside that he knew and I wanted to know. He stood straight up, all six-feet-plus of him. Dropping my hand, he walked up to a fellow and grabbed his hand so close to his body that they almost hugged. They greeted each other and said things I could not hear. I was almost within arm's reach, but the music was in full force and blasted out of the walls through speakers. The man regarded Granddaddy like he was a brother he'd not seen in a long time, with a welcoming smile, the nod of acknowledgment, and embrace of warm friendship. They headed, shoulder to shoulder, to a bank of chairs near the entrance to the club. Granddaddy tugged my shirtsleeve to follow. I sat nearby and watched while Granddaddy and his friend gestured back and forth with their hands, punctuating their talk. I only heard scattered words, but was mesmerized, and I understood what was going on just by watching them. They were reliving old times. I could tell that for Ty Cobb, they were still vivid in his mind. His smile was radiant, and his eyes were alive.

He reached over and pulled me toward him, introducing me to his friend amid the loud circus of music, dance, talking, and their own rekindling of shared memories. I could not clearly hear and couldn't make out his name. But the warmth and camaraderie between them spoke loudly, and I, even then, knew the feelings that they shared. I was surprised at how quickly my own teammates popped into my vision. Mike Hermaling, pitching; Larry Flint on third base; Larry Dunn, who wooed me to the Union Sugar team in Little League Baseball. We had a great time, fought hard, won a lot of games, and, like Granddaddy, we then went our separate ways. I didn't really pay attention to my visions, they all occurred so quickly, like a short at the movie theater. But Granddaddy kept his friend chattering, poking, pulling, cajoling, teasing, and recounting what had happened a long time ago. He made their visions last and last. During this almost physical encounter, their only access to the intensity of their past, the level playing field of the baseball diamond was a way they could voice the admiration each had for the other.

I sat back, a little ashamed to admit to hunger and boredom, so I kept my mouth shut. Their faces glowed, various shades of pink and peach. They smiled, laughed, fell into sorrow, arose again to

149

joy, and shifted their bodies into shapes I knew. The shape needed to slide into a base, catch a fly ball on the run, block a runner at home plate, fake a swing and drag a bunt, feign an injury, take the batting stance and mean it, with all your best at the plate, and swing your bat knowing your teammates depended on you. They lived what they knew, a long time ago. Finally, Granddaddy fumbled in his pocket for the envelope—full, fat, and needed. He pulled it out and wrapped the man's hand around it without comment, explanation, or ceremony. I don't think the man expected it right then, but he took it fast, put it in his coat, and abruptly stood up. He shook hands like the end of the world was postponed, and walked toward the front door he'd entered only an hour before.

Granddaddy sat down on the wooden chair next to me. I was glued to my seat and didn't dare move or say anything. He didn't look at me. His eyes wandered around the room, from the floor to the ceiling, to the walls, and to the people standing nearby. He was shaking his head slightly, as if to try to understand something, and I could see his eyes were barely focused. I'd never seen him look quite like this. He created a buffer between himself and the world. After a long while he brought his hands together, fingers interlocked, then reached his arm across my shoulder and said, "We'll talk about this later."

"Later" came late that night, after dinner, after watching the follies show, laughing and being slightly embarrassed when the MC introduced him and he had to speak to the audience, and having ice cream and fancy desserts. He made especially sure that Susan had a good meal and was comfortable. "Later" came at his cabin at Cave Rock, down the road from the North Shore Club.

In the parking lot, the boy ran to the end of the lot to retrieve Granddaddy's Chrysler. When he returned, he climbed out and thrust a piece of paper and a pen toward Granddaddy, saying quietly, "Please, I'd like your autograph."

Granddaddy stepped back, somewhat startled, then brushed aside the offered pen and reached into his inside jacket pocket. He took out his Parker fountain pen, asked the boy his name, and took the paper and put it on his thigh. On it he wrote in large script, "To Bud, Best Wishes, Ty Cobb," and dated it. He signed in permanent green ink, which was his favorite. At the time I didn't know what to think; it had happened in a second or two, while Susan and Kit were climbing into the car on the other side. Granddaddy quickly took the keys and slid behind the wheel. The third envelope was still in his coat pocket and he patted it to make sure. Its recipient did not show up, and the help it contained would have to wait until another time. I jumped in behind him and we drove off.

We turned left onto the two-lane road that circles Lake Tahoe. The lake shone brightly below us, reflecting a partial moon high in the western sky, its cone of pale yellow flowing across the water like an undulating and inviting gate. Kit jabbered about his evening, reliving what the waiter served him—pheasant under glass, how he played with the hundred silver dollars Granddaddy left him, and mostly, about the show with the dancing girls and fancy-dressed musicians. Soon, we started up the hill, and a little inland, took the road around the huge property that was Glenbrook, Nevada. As soon as we passed the small sign that was all the indication that Glenbrook was there, our road was next. The road down to the cabin is unmarked, and you just have to know it's there. Granddaddy pulled in front of the cabin with the small, bare light glowing above the front door; we jumped out, shivered in the cold night air, and rushed to get inside.

Susan and Kit were using the bunk bed room, just to the right of the front door, on the driveway side of the cabin. It was small and cramped, but Kit wanted to sleep on the top, so Susan stayed below to make sure he kept the guard up to keep him from rolling out of bed. Granddaddy's room was on the other side of the large living room, on the lake side of the cabin. Two small windows on the wall faced the lake, and when I stood on the twin bed in that room, I could see a view of the water filtered through the pine trees. In the dark, the shadows cast a magical picture on the hill leading down to the lake. It was a hunting cabin designed to keep the warmth inside during the winter, hence the small bedroom windows; the only large window was in the living room, looking out on Lake Tahoe. Keeping the heat inside during the winter was important, and small windows did the trick.

My room was next to Granddaddy's, separated by a bathroom. I changed into my PJs and, hearing water running and shuffling in the bathroom, knocked loudly. The door opened, and Granddaddy stood brushing his teeth in striped pajamas. He looked funny, and I laughed a little.

He asked me if I was sleepy, and I told him I was not. Then he said, "It's late. Brush your teeth and we'll talk."

He was a big man, sitting in his pajamas on the side of an extra-long full bed, feet bare, hair scuffed and showing that there wasn't much of it, with a tired twinkle in his eye. The only light was the small lamp on the bedside table between us, and only one of the bulbs was on, so it was dim in the room. The sound of the small night waves, gently splashing on the lakeshore, was one of the most relaxing sounds I've ever heard.

"Well, Hersch, I told you we'd discuss things. Sit down so we're not here all night. Did you get dessert?" I knew he wanted some ice cream, but we didn't have any in the cabin because I'd finished it off earlier that afternoon.

"No, sir," I answered, "I don't want anything." Then I just blurted out, "Granddaddy, you looked so happy and so sad."

"Those men haven't done so well since . . ." and he stopped, hesitated like he didn't want to say more, but then continued, "since . . . we worked together. I knew them a long time ago."

"Granddaddy, we don't have to talk about this if you don't want to. That's okay." Part of me wanted to know, because what I'd seen in the smoke-filled room was so intense between him and those men, but part of me knew I didn't want to pry.

"No, Hersch," he continued, "you were there, you saw everything, and that's why we went to the North Shore Club. I've been doing this for quite a few years. This year, you happened to be with me." He paused. "The guy by the door, Eddie, knew me from a long time ago. I fought hard to play the best I could and didn't let anything stand in my way. Some players hated me for it, maybe didn't see what I wanted. Eddie and I played together for a few years, and then he moved on to another team. But we crossed paths, and he was friendly in a way my other teammates were not. I remembered that."

I interjected, "He looked so old, and his clothes were beat up." I remembered how expectantly the man waited for Granddaddy to reach him. The expression on his face was mixed elation and embarrassment, and I could tell he sure didn't want to meet me or Susan or Kit. He moved so close to Granddaddy when they greeted that their faces almost touched. Only when they talked about their time together did he look at ease. And when Granddaddy handed him the envelope full of money, it was almost a ghost scene from a movie. I saw it in slow motion, two blurry figures moving together as if they were connected by a huge rubber band and kept apart by a short stick. After Granddaddy locked the stuffed envelope into his hand, Eddie moved away and disappeared into the smoky mist. He held the envelope like there was gold in it.

"He wasn't always that way," Granddaddy said, defending him. "He played hard. I was lucky."

"Why were you lucky? You told me you worked as hard as you could and fought and fought to get to the top." I was really puzzled. "That's not luck."

"No, no, that's not what I meant. It's not luck. But looking back at it now, I was lucky. I worked hard at playing ball; and I met some people. Not everybody met people who helped them."

I had no idea what he was talking about.

"Hersch, look here, you see, when you're young, when you're just starting, it's hard, and lots of things happen, some things not so nice. Some folks push against you, they might want you to quit, get out. They might do things to you. Things that make you mad. Things you never forget. It sticks with you for a long time, maybe forever." He was watching me as if I were going to give a sign that I understood what he was talking about.

I felt more lost than ever. "Granddaddy, what did that man want?"

"Hersch, he missed out." His voice dropped lower. "It was all there, in Detroit, all the factories, the cars, the industry, and in Atlanta."

I still didn't understand. "What about the man at the front door and the man in the gambling room? What about them?" I heard my voice waver between asking and insisting.

154   "Yes, the two friends of mine. Yes, about them, yes." He straightened, sitting on the edge of the bed, looking at me like I was

exactly eleven and a half years old, and it was the first time he'd realized that.

Then he continued, "The fellow at the front door, I played ball with him. I saw him over the years, and then in 1941, I played in an old timers game and saw him again. He was behind the crowd, which were mainly a lot of kids. They really wanted the Babe's autograph, mostly, but some wanted mine. But I saw Eddie, and we waved, and I knew he wanted to get down to talk to me. We met later, and I noticed his clothes and shoes and knew he could use some help. You know what I mean? He needed some money.

"When I was playing ball, it was all in Detroit. And some in Atlanta. I saw it happening all around me. Businessmen were building factories, making cars and parts for cars, and everything they needed. Texas had oil, and Detroit had car factories. The city was growing; electricity was being put in homes." He looked at me like he wanted me to understand, but knew I probably didn't. "Like I said, I was lucky. I was introduced to businessmen. Of course, they wanted to meet me, but they talked about what they were doing, told me to buy stock in their companies. I did."

He stopped talking, shifted around, and said, "You don't know what 'stock' is, do you?"

"I've never seen one, Granddaddy."

"No, no, Hersch." He held back a small laugh, and it came out with his smile, going clear across his face. "No, stock is a piece of paper that says you own part of a company. If the company does really well, it becomes more and more valuable and you have more money." He paused to make sure I understood. I nodded my head. And my expression no longer looked like I was lost in the woods in the dark.

He went on, "Well, I spent a lot of time with these businessmen and went to their offices and saw their factories. It was amazing

155

to me. And I wanted to make money. So, I bought some stock in an automobile company that is now called General Motors. It became very profitable. And I did the same thing in Atlanta with Coca-Cola."

I immediately figured this out and asked him, "Does this mean you get free Cokes?"

"Hersch, that's not important." He didn't like me drinking Cokes and sodas because they had too much sugar in them. "I was lucky. Businessmen invited me into their meetings and clubs. These companies grew bigger and bigger, and what I bought grew too. Lots of ball players never had anything and left the game with nothing."

"Why?" I asked. "Didn't they play like you?" I realized that I didn't really know anything about Granddaddy and baseball, only that he played, and he was my grandfather. I was more interested in him being my grandfather.

"Sure, they played. But those business guys helped me a lot. The game was new, and they liked being seen at the ballpark, next to the players. After games finished, I was mostly by myself, so I went to the places they went, talked with them, and listened to them." He was looking at me, knowing that only a bit was soaking in. I reached over to the end of the bed and grabbed a couple of pillows and rested my head on them.

"Getting sleepy? Let me finish and then we can turn in."

I recalled the looks on those men's faces when they talked with Granddaddy, and the look when he gave them the fat envelopes. I pushed myself up and sat again on the edge of the bed, and said to him, "No, I'm okay, just a little tired. Tell me the rest of what happened."

"So I took some of the money I earned and bought stock in these men's companies. I did pretty good and later had some jingle in my pockets. You know what I mean? Jingle?" He waited and watched. I nodded my head, and he continued, "When I saw them, especially after that old timers' game, I had cash in my pocket and gave some to them. The last few years they've gotten older and, well, it's been sort of regular. You know what I mean, Hersch?" I'd rested my head again and mumbled that I did. "So we meet, up here at the lake, at the North Shore Club, just briefly, usually longer than tonight, and I help them out. Not at the same time, though. Sometimes we sit and have a drink and talk about the old days and enjoy a few stories and laughs about folks we knew. I know they need the help. I don't really know what else they do." He paused, "It's something I can do. Understand?"

I was resting on the pillows, my eyes half closed, but my mind was whirling with pictures and images of Granddaddy and how he might have looked with these men years ago, and how he now sounded like he wanted to tell us stories about himself when he was young.

I liked his voice and the way he told a story, especially about himself, because he moved his arms, hands, and face with the rhythm of the story. It was like being there. He had a force about him that filled the room with what he was remembering.

My eyes were fading, and I knew I was falling asleep. I felt Granddaddy's arms slip under me and pick me up. He carried me through the bathroom door, which was narrow, and I was just awake enough to shift my head and keep from bumping on the door frames. He laid me down in my bed and tucked me under the covers. His hand gently stroked my forehead, and I barely heard, "You and Susan and Kit, you mean so much to me." Then I heard the door close, and the light in the bathroom went out.

The window above my head was open, and I felt the cold air drift over my face like a gentle hand, and I heard the sound of the lake waves rhythmically lap up on the beach. The moon, now positioned in the west, gave my room just enough light so I could see outlines of shadows and shapes. I wasn't falling asleep anymore. Granddaddy's last words and the cool air had awakened my spirits, and my mind whirled like a kid's kaleidoscope, each section filled with fragments of the scenes, sounds, and impressions of the evening at the North Shore Club and listening to my granddaddy, imagining his life long ago.

When I thought about listening to him in the other room, I realized that he didn't have to tell me about those men. It was late for me, and it had been a long evening. He told me about his life because it was important to him to share that with me. Our presence, and especially Susan's, had opened a door for him to connect with his grandchildren in a way he never had with his children. It was new for him to have someone listen to what had happened in his life. It was awkward, but I sensed that he was determined to continue, and I sensed he'd been in this beginning position before. As the years went on, and we spent part of our summers with him, more of these changes would appear. His world with us grew larger, and ours with him deepened. My sense of trust was growing, and I felt a sense of well-being that actually warmed my body. The cold air flowing over me provided the perfect balance with the warm snuggling feeling that lulled me to sleep.

A few days later, I spent the day rowing around the cove and returned to the cabin in the early afternoon. I expected to find Granddaddy sleeping in his chair with a ballgame on the radio. The radio was playing, but the crackling sound was just noise, impossible to tell what it was, and he wasn't sitting where he usually sat. I spotted him hunched over the small writing desk on the side of the living room. He didn't notice me until I walked over and asked what he was doing. I was eager to tell him about all the crawfish I had caught.

He swung his chair around like it should have been on swivels and nearly tipped it over. His voice was excited as he said, "Hersch, come over here. Let me take a look at your back." He pulled me around and lifted up my shirt to check my back for sunburn. "Ah, you look okay. Go and get yourself some fruit and come on back here."

His mood was almost jovial, which was unusual. I had learned how to gauge his moods, and this afternoon he was visibly animated. When I returned, he closed his fountain pen, leaned back, and gazed over the freshly written letter with a big smile. "While you were rowing around, I went over to Glenbrook and picked up my mail. I think I'm making some real progress on something I've wanted to do for a long time. And I think now is the time."

I asked him, "Can I help?"

"Well, I'd like you to, but it's not like that." He was grinning. "I want to start a fund to help youngsters pay for their college education, and I've been writing to some folks I know in Georgia to help me. And they wrote to tell me that they will."

"College, what's that? Why does somebody want a fund, what's that? Why can't I help?" My questions bubbled out quickly, more because he wasn't going to let me help than because I didn't know what he was doing and had to ask.

He began his answer by explaining about himself. "Well, I never went to college. And that's where an educated man goes. You didn't know this about your grandfather, did you?" He started talking again before I could say anything. "College is where you go after high school. You've seen the high school in Los Angeles, haven't you?"

"Yeah, but it's a long way from our house," I answered, remembering that I'd only seen it once.

"Well," he said as if to correct me, "maybe not that far. You'll go to high school in a couple of years, and then, I hope, to college."

I was following him so far.

"Hersch, colleges cost money to go there, so I want to give some money to help any youngster in Georgia pay for going to college. That's what I'm writing all these letters for. To get some help. I can't do all the details myself. These fellows will help me set things up, choose who gets helped and that stuff."

"Who?" I asked, not knowing what else to ask.

"Well, I hope mostly Georgia kids. Any kid who works hard and has the stuff to make a success of himself."

"How many kids?" I wondered out loud.

"I hope a lot. I'm giving some money, and I hope it helps a lot of kids. I want it to last a long time, way after I'm gone."

"Is this like at the North Shore Club, with those two men?"

"No, no, no." He shook his head, realizing that I wasn't getting his idea. "No, no, not like that." He leaned forward, resting his elbows on his knees, holding his hands together. "You don't know this, but my father was a teacher. He wanted me to go to school, but I didn't. So, now I can do something."

I was curious about what he just said and blurted, "Where's your dad?"

My question startled him. He leaned back in his chair and his smile disappeared. Twice he started to say something, but didn't.

Then he quietly said, "He died." I nodded, realizing that of course he would have, because Granddaddy was old himself. "But that's not what I want to tell you about. I want you to know about what I'm doing. I want these kids who work hard to go to college. So, that's what I'm doing, helping them out."

"How come?" I queried.

"Hersch, remember after we went to the North Shore Club, and we were talking, and I told you I'd been pretty fortunate and had met some businessmen who helped me out early on?" I nodded my head.

"That's what I'm doing. Helping. I want to give back. I've done okay, and now it's time to help some youngsters with their lives. When you're older and you've done well, I want you to do this too. That's what you do, understand?"

He was looking directly at me, telling what he expected, which sounded right with me, so I nodded.

"Good." He was smiling again. "Now let me finish one more letter, and then we'll see how the fish are biting."

Before I went to get the poles, I stopped to watch him. He was so focused on his letter that he didn't realize I hadn't left. I liked what I saw, pleased that Granddaddy was so pleased. I realized how much I liked being with him.

When I got older, I learned that the two ball players at the North Shore Club were not the only men who received help from Granddaddy; there were several others. Not only that, his Educational Foundation was established, has flourished, and has distributed millions of dollars to recipients in Georgia and elsewhere.

We finished the summer at Grandma's, and she took us to the train station in Palo Alto early one morning. She bought tickets for us, and we hugged and said our good-byes. When she handed the tickets to Susan, she exclaimed, "Grandma, these are for Santa Maria, not Los Angeles. We have to go all the way to Los Angeles."

Grandma replied, in a rare somber voice, "Susan, your mother moved back to Santa Maria this summer, while all of you were up here with me. She'll explain. I think she will pick you up." The conductor was calling for passengers to board, so we all kissed Grandma, took the package of sandwiches she made for us, and jumped on the train.

The train ride took most of the day, and we had nothing to do except look out the window, play cards, and wonder where our new house would be.

In Santa Maria, our mom didn't pick us up at the station, Ayako did. As we climbed into the car, Ayako greeted us but didn't say anything during the ride. Susan and I looked at each other and knew something was wrong.

Ayako drove through a tract of one-story homes and parked in front of a small ranch house. She quickly said, "Your mom's inside, but she doesn't feel well, so we have to be very quiet."

I walked to the front door with my bag and saw all the shades for the windows were drawn. When Ayako unlocked the front door and I walked inside, it was nearly dark with all the windows covered. The house was small, and the front door opened directly into the living room. I put my bag down and looked around. Everything was green. Green rug, green walls, and the light green sofa that I remembered from our house in Los Angeles.

Ayako could see the questions written all over our faces. Finally, almost apologetically, she explained, "Your mom doesn't feel well, and Dr. Dunn will be here any minute. He will explain." Almost as soon as she finished, there was a knock on the front door. She opened it and Dr. Dunn came in, carrying his black bag. We all knew him; he was our family doctor when we lived in Santa Maria two years ago, when I was in the second grade. He had a son my age and a daughter Susan's age.

The three of us were sitting on the edge of the sofa, with our suitcases still at our feet, waiting with puzzled expressions on our faces. He greeted us, saying how nice it was to see us again, and then cleared his throat with a slight cough. He proceeded like we were patients. "Your mom is quite ill, and I need to visit her twice every day, morning and evening. The house needs to be quiet and kept dark and cool." He took a deep breath. "Can you three do this for your mom?"

We all nodded, like toys at the end of a string. Susan had the presence to ask, "How long is Mom going to be sick? Where is she?"

Dr. Dunn looked over at Ayako, expecting her to say something, but she declined. "Susan, I'm not sure how long. Maybe a few weeks. I don't really know. She's in her bedroom, down that hall, and the door is locked. She has to stay there. You can't visit her. She needs to be by herself."

I didn't say anything, but I felt my stomach twinge with a familiar nausea.

"Ayako will take care of you. And Susan, maybe you can help. Right now I have to see your mom and take care of her." Dr. Dunn's voice was flat and final. He fixed his left hand on his black bag, jingled some keys in his right pocket, and walked down the hallway.

Dr. Dunn appeared every morning and every evening for two months to give her a shot. Maybe for him it was routine, because he barely said anything to Ayako or to us after his visits. During that time a large lock guarded the room where my mother was staying. Dr. Dunn had a key, and Ayako had a key. I also saw that the outside windows had been nailed shut and the inside curtains were drawn closed. We went to school during the day, and at night the room where my mother was kept was usually quiet. Occasionally, we heard moaning and low, rumbling howling. We kept quiet, practically tiptoeing around the house; not ever knowing what would happen if we made a noise. Susan helped Ayako with our meals, and Kit and I more than ever were "the boys."

My mother had become addicted to uppers and downers. She used the uppers to go out at night to clubs, and the downers to get to sleep when she came home. During the two months that she was locked in that room, I found pink pills, blue pills, and yellow pills hidden everywhere in the house. The first time I was looking for more toothpaste and reached in the back of the cabinet in our bathroom. Behind everything I came upon a plastic bag filled with blue or pink pills. Susan found pink pills in the flour tin in the kitchen. Pills were hidden everywhere: under a throw rug, behind record holders, in a music box, under a flower pot, all through our bathroom, and deep behind stuff stored on the top shelves in the closets.

She had divorced Dick Branstedder, and then discovered that the manager she had hired to run the Coca-Cola Bottling Co. in Santa Maria had stolen from the business. She could not afford another mistake like this and returned to Santa Maria to run it herself. Once in Santa Maria, she started drinking more than ever, staying out late, knowing that we three were with our grandmother and grandfather. The pills came after the liquor, compounding her dissipation.

Late in the fall, I returned home on a sunny Saturday afternoon from playing with my friends. Ayako was waiting at the front door with Susan. As soon as I reached the front door, she told me it was all right now for us to see our mother. She took Susan and me down the hall and opened the door. My mother's room was bright and cheery, and Mom was sitting on the floor.

Her face was made up with eye shadow and bright red lipstick, and she held a deck of cards in her hand. The first thing she said was, "Let's play some cards," then she motioned for us to come over to her. She didn't say anything else. No other greeting, no hug. I looked around her room, which I hadn't seen before. It was the garage converted into a bedroom and bath. She was motioning with her hand for me to sit down on the rug with her. The scene was scary-strange and I didn't like it. I told her hello and left. I took my bicycle and rode over to Miller Street School.

Mom traded her uppers and downers for a nightly quart of Old Crow. Susan continued to help with meals and take care of us "boys." The tension in the evenings depended on how the Old Crow affected Mom or what her plans were for going out. School became more and more of a refuge for me. The old sad cycle had started up again.

CHAPTER SIX

My First Visit
to His Office

On my first visit that summer, I rushed through his front door at 48 Spencer Lane, rounded the corner into the living room, and found him. Even as I sat down, I adamantly asked him, "Granddaddy, what did you do? Who are you, really?"

I saw the familiar twinkle in his eye. He knew exactly what I was asking about. He sat across from me in the same easy chair he always used, dull brown with a faded yellow floral design; wide, rounded arms; and a low back with a seat cushion soft and worn from use. He wore dark brown slacks and a light beige gabardine shirt, pockets on each side, buttons up the middle, with long sleeves. It looked freshly pressed, like something Randolph Scott would wear, except the buttons were not on a slant. His shoes looked funny to me with white woven tops and light brown leather sides. The look around his eyes softened as he took me in, almost slowing me down in my rush. I heard Susan whispering to me, but I didn't pay attention to what she was saying because I was so focused on Granddaddy.

The three of us had arrived a few minutes before, and he didn't consider my question until we all said our hellos, hugged him, and then sat on chairs facing him. His questions to me after a long hug were the same as last year, and the same as the year before that. My answers were the same too.

"Now, Hersch, do you want a smoke?" he asked. Even though he smoked a cigar now and then, he wanted to know if I smoked cigarettes.

"No, Granddaddy," I answered dutifully. "I don't smoke."

"Well, how about a drink, beer or something?"

"No thanks, Granddaddy, I don't drink either," I replied. I felt like giggling, but I knew from years past that these were things he wanted to know.

The next question was always about what books I had been reading. He asked the details of every story, about the characters, what I thought, what I liked best, what book was next on my list, and so on. Yet this year I cut short his inquiry; I'd jumped to the heart of what was important to me.

My question lingered in the air. I waited. Susan sat quietly.

"Hersch, come over here," he said at last, his voice quiet and firm. "Sit down here," he added, patting the right armrest of his chair.

"Tell me, what's been going on?" The question came out slowly and deliberately. He gave me a soft, broad smile. His right arm reached around my back, and he shifted me forward a little bit. "Susan, take Kit out to the kitchen and see what you can find in the freezer. Bring a couple of extra big spoons." As he spoke, his left hand brushed the air upward, as if helping Susan move toward the kitchen. I knew what he had out there—ice cream—and a part of me wanted to go with them, but I felt his arm around me and his huge hand holding me close. It was like being cradled in a large basket, and I carefully watched his face out of the corner of my eye. His patience calmed me down, and he seemed to know where this path led.

Susan and Kit rounded the corner into the dining room and disappeared. He said, "Well, tell me a little bit about what's been going on. How was your baseball season?" There was a knowing inflection in his voice.

My mind jumped at the mention of baseball. How did he know?

I didn't really know how to start, but I'd thought about it all the previous night and on the ride over from Grandma's house. I wanted to know who my grandfather really was and exactly what he did. I had good reason, because of what happened during my Middle League baseball season at home, in Santa Maria. The season started a few weeks before the end of my eighth-grade year and would continue until the middle of summer. Each boy was supposed to try out for each of the teams, and the coaches checked out all the players and prepared to "buy" a team. Each coach was given "points" to "spend" on players, and they bid for the players they wanted and "spent their points" to build a team. I don't think they spent a lot of points on me because I didn't show up for tryouts for every team, so most of the coaches didn't even know I was around.

The previous year, in Little League, I had known all my teammates. We all tried out for the same team so we could play together. Of course that was against the rules. We were supposed to try out for each of four teams and be bid on by the coaches. I knew I would make a team. It was easy because I was the only kid who could throw the ball all the way to home plate from straightaway center field. Now, in Middle League, there were a lot of bigger, stronger kids.

I didn't like the idea of playing for somebody I didn't know, so I only tried out for two teams. I was lucky one of them picked me. I never mentioned that I would not be around for the full season, that I would leave soon after school was out for the year. I felt badly about this, but I wanted to play in some games and knew that I wasn't the best player anyway.

My first game I started in center field, and things were pretty quiet until I got up to bat. This was my first time at bat in Middle League baseball. The kid throwing the ball was tall and bigger than anybody I had played against in Little League. I'd seen him before from the first base side and knew how hard he threw the ball, so when I stepped up to the plate, I was excited, nervous, and a little scared. I watched him throw a strike right by me, and then the yelling began. At first I heard just a lot of noise. Then I recognized my name, being called over and over again. "Cobb, come on . . . hit it, go after him, swing. Come on, kid, show your stuff. Swing, swing." All of the yelling blurred together, but I knew they were hollering at me, and I didn't know why. My teammates weren't yelled at the same way. The shrieking was loud, from the stands, both sides of the baselines, and the infield. The calls were jeering, derisive, and demanding, like everybody screeching at me. I felt as if I had done something wrong or was about to. I looked at the pitcher and knew the screaming bothered him too because he stepped off the rubber, walked around the mound, rubbed the ball, put his glove hand on his knee, and took a long look at me and his catcher. I took a couple of practice swings and could feel my body tense up to defend itself. I didn't like this at all. When I glanced toward our dugout, I saw my coach waving his arms furiously, as if to swing a bat. The thought that kept repeating itself was, "What is going on?" I looked past my coach to my bicycle. I came alone to the field, and I saw my way out. Half of me wanted to leave.

The pitcher peered down at me and began his windup. His left arm went back and came at me. I saw the white ball roll off his fingers and spin toward me. It looked as big as a grapefruit, the seams spinning in a blur, the white brilliant in the sunlight. I swung as hard as I could. I heard a crack. I'd hit the ball, and I ran like hell for first base. When I got there, the first base coach was yelling, "Go, go, go, Cobb! Take second!" Yet I watched the ball come in from left-center, and by the time I'd completed my turn, the shortstop had it and was waiting for me to try. I stayed put. I was on first base with a hit. I felt great and excited. I touched the base under my left foot, took a couple of steps off and looked down the line toward the home plate. My senses were revved. Everything I looked at was vivid, colors standing out brighter than usual. The grass, dirt, hitter, backstop, every bit looked gigantic. The white chalk line running to home plate was wiggly, but followed a straight course, and I could see the bumps along its edges running over the dirt. I glanced at the pitcher, then down at the second base bag. It looked like a small, dirty white island sitting on a scuffed-up sea of dirt. I was ready to go.

The yelling turned to taunting, didn't stop. It got louder and louder. "Steal, steal! Go, go, go, you chicken, steal!" I heard a lot of names, like "chicken," "bum," and calls like "use your spikes, kid." I didn't know why I was the focus, but it felt awful. The fathers behind the fences along first and third, the other players, my own teammates, and my coach, all yelling at me. I saw open mouths, strained necks, waving arms. The kid guarding me at first base said mockingly, "Go ahead, Cobb, try it. You'll never make it."

I could feel the voices as much as hear the words. It felt like a challenge to fight. Something was the matter because it was not encouragement but derision. I glanced over at my Schwinn, leaning against the fence. Oh, I didn't want to be there, and I didn't want to leave. Second base began to look like it was across the entire sports field. My teammate at the plate struck out on four pitches, and he was the third out. The inning over, I went back out to center field. The yelling calmed down, but when I came in for our team's next at-bat, my coach started yelling at me.

"Why didn't you try to steal? Your name is Cobb," he cried in front of my teammates. "Next time, go. Just go. I want you to steal second base." His strident voice was full of disappointment. I knew he meant it, but I didn't really know what he meant. My next at-bats were like the first. Each time I stepped into the batter's box, my ears filled with jeers, taunts, demands, and loud disappointment. That day I grounded out, got another single, and flied out to deep left-center. Two for four for my first game. I was pleased with myself and knew I could do this Middle League stuff. But nobody said anything that confirmed what I felt.

Something else was expected. I could see the disappointment in the faces of the adults and kids watching me, and hear it in the voices of my teammates. I walked to my bike, put my glove on my handlebar, and rode home alone.

At our house, I sat in my uniform at the breakfast table. My mom walked in the front door and asked, "What's the matter with you?" Her voice was slurred, and as she came closer I smelled whisky.

"My game," I started, "it was awful. Everybody screamed at me."

I didn't have to explain any more. She stood in front of me, looked down at me in my uniform, and said, "Your grandfather." The look on her face and her voice were full of contempt. She turned on her heel, heading toward her bedroom. She never said

171

anything more. I knew she resented him intensely, and I knew he disliked her. I didn't mention the heckling at my games again.

My mother never mentioned baseball in our house, and only referred to Granddaddy in contemptuous terms, usually when she was intoxicated. She refused to have baseball books around and never attended a game of mine. I'd signed up for Little League on my own, encouraged by two school buddies, and did the same in Middle League. I rode my bike to my games and liked the idea of being on a "team."

After a dozen and a half games with screeching, yelling, and mocking taunts aimed at me, I was not sad to board the train to Palo Alto. I'd spend the rest of the summer at my grandmother's and leave the rest of the Middle League season in center field to someone else. Neither my coach nor my teammates talked to me about what had happened or why, and by the end of the second game, I decided not to ask. I knew there was something I wanted and needed to know, but in Santa Maria, there was no adult I trusted to ask.

Now, sitting next to him in his living room, I said, "Oh, Granddaddy, please, just tell me. What did you do? Who are you, really?" I felt his hand grip my whole waist.

He was smiling broadly as he asked me, "Go on, tell me what's been going on. How did your season go?"

"Everybody yelled at me, Granddaddy, they just keep yelling. A lot of names. My first base coach never stopped yelling at me to steal. They wanted bigger hits. Wanted me to steal every time I got on base. It happened every game. They want me to get a hit every time. I can't do that." I blurted all this out without knowing exactly what to say, feeling frustrated, a little teary; I wanted comfort and an answer.

Granddaddy shifted starting to get out of his chair, and his right hand nudged me to stand up. "Well," he said, "let's see what we can do. Come with me."

He stood up beside me, appearing huge. He took my hand as we walked across the living room, toward the hallway that went to the back of the house. Once again, I realized how large his hand was as it wrapped around mine, and I felt his flesh gently squeeze mine, hold on for a moment, and then let go. Directly across from the archway that led in and out of the living room was a closed door. He looked down at me as he opened that door, and said simply, "Come on in and you can help me for a while."

Susan and Kit returned from the kitchen with four large bowls of peach ice cream and spoons. He saw her before she could speak and told her, "Susan, take care of your brother. We're going to be busy in here for a while. Let Kit have Hersch's share, and save mine in the freezer. Thanks, sweetie."

His office was a modest-sized room, probably a bedroom at one time. Every wall was lined with shelves, and a large desk occupied the right wall and filing cabinets filled the left. On the shelves sat baseball trophies, award plaques, signed baseballs, a bat lying lengthwise, framed pictures with autographs, a pair of cleated shoes, caps, and a couple of baseball gloves. In one corner were dirty, used bats leaning in a clump. Between the shelves and where they ended were large framed photographs of Granddaddy. Most were old action pictures of him playing baseball, some with other ball players, some showed him with men in business suits. His uniform was old-fashioned, had a big "D" on the chest and a stand-up collar. I studied several of the pictures and just stared for a moment, my mind taking in that all this was really him. Granddaddy sprinting around third base to home, hitting left-handed, stealing second base, sliding into third base, catching a ball in the outfield. I remember saying to myself, "He's really trying

173

hard. Look at his face." In several photos he appeared with groups of other baseball players, another with Babe Ruth, and another in front of an old-fashioned radio microphone with a crowd behind, yet another in which he wore a funny square hat with a fringe hanging down, and others with his family. I saw pictures of my father when he was a kid, of Uncle Ty playing tennis, and Aunt Shirley riding horses. I was stunned by all the pictures, telling the story of a long life. I was so curious, I forgot he was there with me.

I heard him say, "Hersch, pull up that chair and give me a hand."

I sat down beside him, and he pushed a small cardboard box into my lap, just right for holding a baseball, and handed me a pen. "Now, you need to tape this shut and put the address on it," he told me. "Just a minute."

He reached into a huge barrel placed next to his desk and pulled out a new white baseball. Settling it in his left hand, he held a fountain pen poised in his right. He leaned over his desk reading something, then said, "This boy's name is Peter, lives in Pennsylvania. He plays ball there, second year in Middle League. Must be about a year older than you. Wants a signed baseball. Didn't send one with his letter. Asks which way to hit. So, we'll do it this way." I stood up and saw he was reading a handwritten letter.

On the ball he pulled from the barrel, he wrote the first line, "To Peter," then under that, "Hit Left-handed," then "Ty Cobb," then the date, "7/23/56." Green ink, large scripted letters, and a curlicue under his name.

"Here," he said as he handed me the ball. "That might help him out. Let this dry for a second. There's some tissue in that box to put around the ball. Here's Peter's address. Print in big letters so the post guy won't have a problem."

I reread the signed baseball while I fumbled for the tissue paper to wrap it in. I glanced up, and right in front of me was a large poster framed in dark brown wood. In a large center oval was a picture of Granddaddy's face, and then four action shots in pie shapes filling the corners of the poster. At the bottom, in white, slanted capital letters, it read, "Ty Cobb, World's Greatest Baseball Player." I was transfixed. His picture in the oval was just like he looked now when he smiled, only he was younger. His eyes were looking off to the left, and the collar on his uniform stood up, close to his neck. I felt a tingling rush through my whole body, finishing in my head. This was no joke, this was my grandfather.

I looked more closely at the other pictures of him, on each side, this time reading the print within each picture. At the top, a picture showed him batting left-handed, but it was a different photo than the single picture on his wall. The grandstands were full of fans and distinct, and his swing looked stronger. I read the words at the bottom three times because I couldn't believe what they said: "Lifetime batting average, .367 over 24 years," on the first line, then, under that "4,191 lifetime hits." Oh my. I read it again. I felt like I'd stepped into a dream, where everything I'd known about myself suddenly changed. I knew I was good at baseball and basketball, and could run faster than most of my friends, but what I was reading amazed me. I felt awestruck, proud, and a little afraid of not doing as well as him. What did he really think about me?

I was leaning far forward, starting to read another pie-shaped picture on the poster, when Granddaddy swung around. His elbow caught me by accident and rocked me back into my chair.

"Sorry," he said, "where are you going?"

I quickly answered, "Nowhere, Granddaddy." I felt embar-rassed, but at the same time giddy and elated. I knew in an instant that all the razzing I'd taken was because those people expected that I'd do the same things on the diamond as my grandfather. Here was the full story of who he was. Only it was bigger, way

175

bigger, than I'd ever suspected. I struggled to catch my breath. Now, what was I supposed to do?

"Hersch, can you read this handwriting? It's terrible." He thrust a piece of paper in front of me. It was signed, "your best fan, Terry Ragel," and the letter began, "I play third base in Little League and would like a baseball from you." The sentences began straight across the page, but then slanted down more and more, so that by the end of the page, they were almost vertical.

"His name is Terry, and he's in Little League, so maybe he's only in the fourth or fifth grade. He wants a baseball too," I said.

"How does he bat?" Granddaddy asked. I reread the letter, but it didn't say anything about which side of the plate he hit from. "He only says he loves third base, and is that the right position for him?" Granddaddy laughed, which led into a cough. Then he cleared his throat and grinned at me.

"I had a hell of a time stealing on Baker."

I thought, "Who is Baker?" I'd find out later he was talking about Home Run Baker, the famous third baseman. One of the most famous baseball pictures of all time was taken of Ty Cobb stealing third base on Baker. The picture was taken almost by accident and settled a long-running argument and accusation about whether Granddaddy intentionally used his spikes to gain third base. The photo is clear: the steal was clean.

"Well, tell him 'Good Luck,' then," I suggested. And that's what he did. "To Terry, Good Luck, Ty Cobb," dated "7/23/56." He handed the ball to me to pack and put the address on the box.

He took another letter from the stack on his desk. As my hands worked, I again leaned far forward to inspect another pie-shaped picture in the poster. This showed Granddaddy standing in front of an old-fashioned radio microphone. He is grinning, and his hair is thin on top. The uniform has an elephant on the left side of the chest, not a "D." Another player stood next to Granddaddy.

"That's Tris Speaker," I heard him say, "one of the best ball players there ever was. Connie Mack brought us together. Ever hear of him? He was a great friend of mine. Our last year."

He was talking over his shoulder, and I saw him turn his head back to his desk. I mumbled, "I don't think so, Granddaddy."

I learned later that Tris Speaker was famous too. Granddaddy always spoke highly of him and said that Speaker and Rogers Hornsby were the best hitters ever in baseball.

I examined Granddaddy in that picture. He was old, with the lines on his face etched deeply and very little hair on his head. His nose had changed a little, and the collar on his uniform lay flat. But one thing really caught me: even in a picture, his eyes possessed the twinkle and clarity that I knew so well. Within the picture, in smallish white print, it read, "12 Times American League Batting Champion, Batted over .400 Three Times, 23 Years Over .300." I thought, "Could an old guy really do that? Over .400, three times. That's four hits in ten at bats, all season. Did he really do that?" I wanted to ask something, but I couldn't think of how to have it come out right.

He put another baseball in my lap. I had been almost standing up, gawking at the poster, and the movement of his hand pulled me back down into my chair. "Here," he said. "This one goes with this letter. Take a look at it."

The letter read, "Dear Mr. Cobb, I love baseball, and I play outfield, just like you did. I can throw pretty far. My dad said you were the greatest ever. He died last year. Please autograph a baseball for him and me. His name was Jim." It was signed, "Thank you, Charlie."

He signed that ball, "To Charlie & Jim, from Ty Cobb" and under that, "7/23/56." Granddaddy hesitated but in the end didn't write anything else. He leaned over his desk and began reading another letter. I stared at the letter in my hand and wondered what Granddaddy was thinking. He seldom mentioned my father, who had been dead for nearly five years now, nor my uncle, Ty Jr. Thoughts swarmed in my head, landing near my heart, where I was afraid to go. I liked my grandfather, and I wanted him to like me. I was still searching for something of the father I did not have.

I looked up again at the poster in front of me, at the pie-shaped picture that showed him sliding into second base. The slide was called a "swing slide" or "hook slide." The idea was to slide to the outside of second base, hooking the corner of the bag with your left toe, thereby sliding under the tag.

While I was reading and imagining, I heard his voice, very soft and close to my ear: "When I was a young boy, I built a sliding pit in my backyard and practiced that slide hour after hour, just to perfect my timing and technique. I wanted it perfect. I wanted to be the best." He had leaned over, his head level with mine, looking a little at that picture and a little at me. His voice sounded almost sad, and he slowly withdrew as he turned back to his desk. I looked closely at the picture, and at the statistics underneath. It read, "96 Stolen Bases Single Season, 892 During 24 Seasons. Stole Home Plate 54 Times." I was amazed and a little bewildered. Granddaddy never mentioned any of this during the past three years while we visited him in the summer. He never said one thing about baseball. I was like every boy who played baseball. I knew statistics and averages for lots of current players. These statistics were truly astounding to read, especially while sitting next to the man who created them.

Many of the letters asked for an autographed picture. He had stacks of different action photos of himself on the shelf in front of him and tried to pick a picture that matched the request of the writer. He showed me pictures of himself racing around third base, sliding into home plate, standing at home plate with a bat, catching a fly ball in the outfield, and other action photos, asking me which seemed best for the request. He was careful to sign them across the bottom, with a message and the date. Anybody who wrote received an autographed baseball or photograph.

I packed the signed baseballs into the small boxes, careful to wrap them in tissue. Granddaddy's green ink looked splendid, with his signature carefully measured between the two converging seams on the ball. I made a little room between the tissue and the ball to make sure the ink wouldn't smear. He handed me one ball after another, and I reveled at reading a personal tip or salutation now and then. I finished packing a ball addressed to a boy in Bakersfield, a town I knew of, and waited for him to hand me another. Yet he didn't budge for a long time, and I rose up and looked over his shoulder. He kept reading and rereading a letter. It was written on school paper, wide-lined, like the kind I used. It was a short note, and I wondered why he was taking so long. His head moved slightly from side to side, and his hand quivered a bit, making the edge of the letter flutter.

He let out a long, soft sigh, rocked back in his chair, handed me the sheet of paper, and said, "Hersch, read this."

Dear Mr. Cobb,

I'm 13 and this is my first year. The other boys tease me a lot. They hid my bat when it was my turn and I had

179

to use the wrong one. My glove is old. I want them to stop. Please sign me a ball, so I can show them that you're on my side. I want to be better.

Please, yours truly,
James

The handwriting was wobbly, but the message was so very clear. I too couldn't help but read it again. Granddaddy reached in the barrel for a baseball and swung his chair back to his desk. When he turned to me, he held a ball carefully between his middle finger and thumb. I took it the same way, blew on the green ink, and read, "To James, from his good friend, Ty Cobb," and underneath, "7/23/56." His signature and writing were a little larger than on the other baseballs. I knew that this letter affected him in a personal way, and he meant what he wrote.

Granddaddy didn't take as long to hand me the next baseball. On it he had written, "To Mike, Ty Cobb, 7/23/56." As he did, he said, "That's enough for now. I hear Susan and Kit rustling around. Let's go see."

I wrapped the ball and put it into a baseball box, put the address on it, and set it down on Granddaddy's desk. He had already gotten up and left the room. He had signed two dozen baseballs and as many action photographs. In a little less than an hour, an entire lifetime had opened up before my eyes. Before I followed him out of the office, I looked around again at the trophies, awards, and pictures, sorting out in my mind what I saw. I now knew what he'd done, who he was in baseball, yet by the way he acted, he still was my grandfather. That's what I wanted. I held lingering fears of people expecting accomplishments I could probably not meet. Nevertheless, after my first visit, the office was always open to me to walk in, explore, and revel in amazement.

He didn't say anything more about his career in baseball that day. He never spoke of any of the ninety major league records he held when he retired, other than an occasional nod. I realized this was an intentional decision. That morning when he didn't introduce himself to the other families at Sky Meadow while we filled our pail with spring water came to mind, and I remembered what Susan had told me: "He doesn't want us bothered by who he is and what he's done. He saw what happened to his children, and he didn't want what he accomplished to affect us."

When I left the office, I immediately asked Susan, "Where's my ice cream?" knowing she wanted to talk about my visit, but I was not going to, and that was that.

"In the fridge. Well, what did you ask him?" she asked. She repeated the question, but I didn't answer. I walked past her and into the kitchen without saying another word.

I was bubbling, carrying on three or four conversations in my head. I ended up in the kitchen but didn't remember walking through the dining room, the butler's pantry, or the preparation room, but there I was, in front of the freezer. I pulled out the bottom door of the refrigerator and stood there for a minute, just breathing and staring. Everything looked familiar, just as I'd seen it dozens of times before, but I felt as if part of me were back in another time, back in those pictures in the office. I was standing in a ballpark, watching Ty Cobb round first base, streak for second, go into his hook slide, touch the bag, and rise instantly to his feet, poised to take third. I felt the intensity of his effort and determination to succeed. I saw dirt kicked up, dust in the air, and heard the shouts and cheers coming from the grandstands.

I was living in two places at the same time, and my body felt it. I took out the remaining bowl of ice cream and opened the drawer to get a spoon. They all were oversized soupspoons, huge and fun. I grabbed one, plunged it into the ice cream, and put a big, cold glob into my mouth. Somehow, the ice-cold sensation shifted me out of my daydream. I left Ty Cobb at the ballpark and settled into the old kitchen in Granddaddy's house, knowing my grandfather was nearby. I started walking back to the living room and noticed my body felt slightly off balance. By the time I'd eaten two more big, cold bites, though, my balance returned, and I was smiling as I listened to the laughter and chatter coming from the sofa.

Kit wanted to go outside and play catch. Granddaddy said, "What with? I don't think I have any balls or stuff around here." He had his left arm around Kit and was holding him in the sofa as he wiggled to get up. Granddaddy was tickling him around his waist.

I said, "What about the barrel in your office?" Instantly I sensed the change in his mood. It was as if a veil of reluctance lifted. His eyes focused on me, and then he looked at Susan.

"I want to play too, Granddaddy," she insisted. "Not just you and the boys. I can do every bit as good as them, just try me."

I was smiling, inside and out. I didn't say anything about what happened in the office. I stood there, feeling full, watching.

"Well, it must be time," he muttered, more to himself than to us. "Hersch, go and get some balls, a bunch of them, and there're some bats in the corner. Get the ones with my name on them, they're better."

"What about gloves?" I asked.

"Oh." He stopped, having risen halfway out of the deep cushions of the sofa, a line on his forehead wrinkled. "That's a problem. Well, what the . . . Can you kids use those old flat pancakes?" he said as he looked directly at Susan.

"Old gloves, Susan," I said. "Really old. No padding, nothing, flat as a pancake."

"Is that all there is?" she asked.

"Yup, that's it, I didn't see anything else," I said.

Granddaddy said, "Herschel looked around a mite. I think that's it. It's okay, I've played with all of them. They used to work."

Susan had already gotten off the sofa and walked into Granddaddy's office. She came out holding her skirt pulled up, full of baseballs, with a bat over her shoulder and three mitts pulled on it. She stopped next to the piano and asked, in a concerned voice, "Granddaddy, there's only three mitts. What about you?"

"Oh, Susan, these old hands are pretty tough. Let's go out on the front yard, it's the biggest." His voice sounded a little resigned. "Hersch, you and Kit, roll up your slacks and take off your shoes. Susan's okay as long as none of you get stains from the grass. Your grandmother would be very upset."

It was the first time I remember that he ever mentioned my grandmother. His voice was so even, like he had spoken from a different part of his life, long ago when he was head of a family. The four of us paraded out to the front yard of El Roblar, bat, balls, and mitts in hand. Three of us ran around while the Old Man walked slowly, watching as if he was living a life he never really had.

At first he spent most of the time with Susan, showing her how to hold her hands on the bat while waiting for the pitch. I ran out to the part of the lawn closest to the street and looked back on Granddaddy. He looked tall, big at the waist, slow to bend down in his good slacks and shoes, and framed by his wonderfully shaped Spanish house. He held the bat for Susan in just the right position, waiting for the pitch. I went into the same windup I'd seen facing me a few weeks before in my first Middle League game. Only now I knew just a little more than I knew then. Kit was next to me, playing, waiting for something to happen. I had a dozen baseballs at my feet.

"Who's catcher?" I yelled.

"Don't worry. Just throw the ball," he answered. "It's okay."

As I threw, he easily guided her arms and her hands. They hit the ball cleanly, and it sailed over my head! It looked so easy. So I threw again. And this one went right to Kit, rolling sharply through his legs. I kept throwing until the dozen or so baseballs at my feet were scattered all over the grass. Some ended up behind Susan and Granddaddy, but most were hit out past Kit and me.

Susan's turn was over, and Kit was next because he was loudest. Susan and I collected all the baseballs, and I remained the pitcher. Kit was four years younger than I was and much shorter. He swung the bat right away, and Granddaddy dodged his head to avoid being hit. He grabbed Kit with one hand and the middle of the bat with the other hand. He positioned my younger brother just as he had Susan.

"Herschel, go ahead and throw. Now!"

I moved closer and closer until I could place the ball right where Kit could swing for it. He swung at every pitch, whether it was near him or not. Granddaddy ducked and dodged and guided the bat as much as he could, but Kit took full swings, wrapping the bat around himself. The technique didn't work too well, but he was excited and the big, old man hovering over him continued to smile, talking in his ear while looking out at us, his eyes alive and twinkling. A few balls were hit, a lot were missed. Kit would have stayed there all afternoon if Granddaddy had not made the rule of "one round apiece." So I was next.

184   He asked, "Hersch, how do you hit, left or right?"

"Right," I answered.

"Left is better, you know," he responded almost imperceptibly, "two steps closer to first base, better for a drag bunt. But we'll do it righty if that's how you do it. Show me how you stand."

I took my stance and he stood behind me, checking my feet, adjusting their distance apart, his hands on my waist, tugging a little to check my balance. Then he put one hand on each shoulder, leveling me out. "There," he said, "let's start this way." He had rolled up his sleeves, and I was startled at the size of his wrists. Huge. He was old, but I always remember that about him: muscular, strong forearms, huge wrists, and strong hands. He was ready to show me a proper swing, with his hands placing my waist and shoulders in the correct position.

The feeling of being helped was entirely unfamiliar. Almost everything I did in my life I'd taught myself. I had learned not to rely on my father. It was scary to ask him about stuff, because he yelled, criticized, and made fun of mistakes. He rarely showed how to do something. Rather, he expected me to learn something almost immediately.

Granddaddy's hands guided my arms, shoulders, waist, and feet through the correct way to prepare and swing the bat a dozen times. No criticism, no ridicule, just guided firmness through the correct motion. He was stooped over me, with his head and eyes aligned with mine, keeping my shoulders and head steady and level with his left hand, and whispered in my ear, "Watch the ball all through the motion. Keep your eyes glued to the seams. Let it come to you. Shift your hip straight forward, off your back foot, then your arms. Head still." His left hand moved to the small of his back, and he pushed in to help lift his body to stand up straight.

"Okay, Susan, let her fly," he called as he took a step back.

Susan had learned underhand pitching in the girls' PE classes, and throwing overhand at a target was new to her. Her pitches went everywhere. I swung at a couple of pitches, but when I had to reach for one that was over my head, I turned and looked at Granddaddy. He didn't say anything, just watched.

When another pitch bounced uselessly into the grass, though, he called to her, "Hold it just a second, sweetie."

He stepped up right against me, took hold of the bat, and placed it just where he wanted it. Once again he ran his hands over my shoulders, touched my waist, and made it level, and quietly said, "Hold this stance, get ready. Move your weight from the back side, turn your hips, head steady, go through the pitch, and carry your swing all the way through the strike zone, then finish." He guided my arms, shoulders, and body three or four times. At the end of my swing, he had moved his face in front of mine.

"That's it," he said gently, looking straight into my eyes. "That's it. You've got it. Now, do that slowly a few times."

Then he walked out to where Susan was standing. "Susan, sweetie, let Granddaddy try out this old arm. Get behind Hersch and stop the ball if it gets past him."

"I just need practice, Granddaddy," she complained.

"I know. We'll do that in just a minute. Let Hersch have his turn at bat. Go along, now. Tell you what, you be the catcher." He nodded with his head toward me, and he swung his right arm around a few times. Susan got behind me. She looked pretty funny in her good dress, with that old flat baseball glove on.

I did exactly what he said. I glued my eyes on the seams of the ball, followed it from the time he brought it with both hands to his waist and lifted his arms above his head. He didn't have a glove on, but his hands hid the ball pretty well. I could barely see it as he started his motion toward me. I sensed my weight on the right side of my body as I saw him release the ball. It looked so big; it was impossible not to hit it. I shifted my weight, held my head still, used my hips and legs, and swung with all my might. My eyes saw the ball as big as a balloon. I connected.

"Ouch, ouch!" I heard him blurt out. I looked up. He was holding the ball in his right hand, shaking his left arm and hand. "Hurts like the devil," he groaned. Granddaddy had caught my line drive in his bare left hand. Susan started cheering. Kit was standing next to Granddaddy, looking up at him with the sweetest, most puzzled look on his face. He tucked the ball in the pocket of his slacks and rubbed his hand.

"Susan, bring me that glove on the grass over there," he requested.

He put it on, and for the next twenty minutes, he coached, corrected, guided, encouraged, and cheered my efforts to balance myself, watch the ball, and swing the bat as he had told me.

After a while, he took my bat and laid it on the ground. He took off the glove and asked, not really a question, "Hersch, remember that slide I mentioned?"

I carefully replied, "Yeah."

He walked about thirty feet over the grass, positioned the flat glove on the ground, and came back. Gesturing to me to come with him, he walked another few paces back so that he was about forty feet from the glove. "Now," he said, "suppose that's second base, and the pitcher is over there and the catcher is over there." He pointed and at the same time he rolled up the cuffs on his slacks, unlaced his shoes, put them aside, and stood in his stocking feet.

Then he bent his knees and whispered, "This is how it goes." He sounded thrilled.

I thought in a full rush of huge excitement, "Oh my gosh, here he is. This is Ty Cobb, and he's going to steal second base!"

Just at that moment Louise came out the front door and gasped at what she was seeing. She called out, almost yelling, in a panic, "Mr. Cobb, Mr. Cobb, what are you doing? What are you doing?" She paused, as if she expected an answer, but none was forthcoming, and she continued, "Mr. Cobb, you shouldn't do that, please. Mr. Cobb, it's the telephone," as if her urgent message would save him, and maybe it did. "Mr. Cobb," she called out, "Mr. Cobb, it's your daughter." She caught his attention, and he straightened up and stopped.

He didn't show me his slide, and I understood. Instead, he picked up his shoes, walked carefully over the pebbles of the driveway to the house, smiling the whole way, still wonderfully animated. He looked back and said, "Susan, take a turn. Hersch can pitch to you. I'll be right back." The call was probably my Aunt Shirley. She would be calling to check on how things were going.

I walked over to Susan and said, "Well, what do you think? Do you think we'll go to Lake Tahoe? I want to. So does Kit. Last year was so much fun. Maybe we can drive the boat again."

"I don't know," she answered. "Grandma thinks it's okay, but Aunt Shirley doesn't. I'll bet they've been talking about it all afternoon."

Grandma had told us that Granddaddy wanted to take us to Lake Tahoe with him. We had gone with him to the lake the past two years. There was always a lot of discussion between Grandma and Aunt Shirley about visiting and traveling with him. Grandma thought it was fine, but Shirley had lots of things to say about what kind of shape "The Old Man" was in, as she referred to him. I never heard her call him anything but "The Old Man" or "Your Grandfather."

Kit wanted to continue playing, but Susan and I were busy piecing together bits and parts of conversations we overheard about us going to Tahoe with Granddaddy.

After a few minutes, Granddaddy reappeared. I couldn't tell

anything from the look on his face. When he reached us, he said, "You are going to be picked up in a few minutes. You can wait here or on the front porch with Louise."

He spied a glove on the ground in front of Susan and knelt down with his knee on the glove. He put his arms around the two of us and called to Kit. When he scrambled over, Granddaddy hugged us all at the same time. "Now," he said, "I want to go up to Lake Tahoe. Would you all like to come with me? Wouldn't be until next Friday. Louise will go too. So, I think it's all right with everybody."

Susan and I shouted in glee and grabbed him around the neck, almost toppling him over. "Good, then," he said, relieved as he disentangled us from his neck. "We'll leave from here on Friday morning, before traffic starts. I'll talk with your aunt about what you'll need."

I was leaning against him, with his arm around me. I could see the whiskers on his chin and my eyes met his. They were slightly moist. He said, "Give me a kiss now before you go. I've got some things to do inside."

He used the bat to help him stand up straight. He touched Susan and me on the head as he turned and started to walk away. His stride was slow and for a moment he glanced over his shoulder, and then walked purposefully toward the house. He didn't want to be in sight when Grandma arrived to pick us up.

Her blue Chrysler arrived in a few minutes. We were still excited, and Grandma knew why. "Well, did you children behave yourselves and have a good time? What have you got to tell me?" she asked, smiling and practically singing, knowing how excited we were to be going to Lake Tahoe with Granddaddy.

I thought next Friday was a long time to wait, and I wanted to visit Granddaddy and see some more autographed pictures.

189

I told Aunt Shirley about seeing his office and all the baseball stuff, and she casually mentioned that last time she looked, he had lots of large baseball memorabilia in the side room of his garage. Later that evening, while I was helping Grandma with the dinner dishes, I asked her, "Can we go see Granddaddy this week before we go up to Tahoe?"

"Well, I don't know, rightly. Let me talk with your aunt when we're done here and see what she thinks." This reply was a good first step. I stayed around to help dry the very last pot, took out the trash, and grabbed the broom to sweep the kitchen floor.

Grandma looked almost startled when I appeared with the broom in my hand. "My, my, you are certainly helpful this evening." I started sweeping while she took off her apron and stepped over my pile of crumbs to leave the kitchen. I peeked around the door and saw her follow the usual route to Aunt Shirley's part of the house. I swept fast, going over the floor a second time, and wiped the counters again, just in case they both came back into the kitchen.

The conversation must have been short, because when I sauntered back to visit Aunt Shirley, Grandma was already gone. Shirley was sitting at her desk in her library, listening to old jazz records on her record player, puffing on a cigarette with the silliest grin on her face, her eyes closed and her head swaying to the music. The voice coming from the machine was as sweet and sorrowful as any I'd ever heard.

I coughed, and Shirley responded in a dreamy smile, "Hersch, may I present to you, Miss Billie Holiday." And she swept her hand over the record machine in a grand gesture of introduction. "Sit down and enjoy, my young adventurer." I took one of the soft chairs next to the small fireplace and settled in to listen to Billie Holiday's haunting voice. All the shelves were filled with books.

Next to me were some Japanese vases and oriental metal plates, and on a lower bookshelf was an artillery shell Shirley had fired in World War II. While it was hot, she signed it and the soldiers gave it to her as a gift of thanks for all the things she gave them while she was in the service in Italy. She had refined tastes but stayed firmly grounded.

When the record ended, I asked, "Let's play the guy with the great voice." She knew exactly who I was talking about.

"Mr. Louis Armstrong, 'Satchmo,' coming up, young man." She changed 78s, and we listened to the voice that could sing, rasp, lilt, talk, and impart rapture all at the same time.

When the record was finished, I started to speak, but she interrupted me. "You three must have gotten along fine today. That Old Goat already called and said you're welcome anytime. So, maybe the day after tomorrow. I'll check in the morning. Okay, bub?" Aunt Shirley was in a buoyant and playful mood, and this was her way of balancing things out. She held no exalted notions of people, but had her father's instincts to see people exactly as they were. If she could call her own father an "Old Goat," she could call me "Bub."

I nodded enthusiastically and then asked, "Who else you got?" I was ready to hear more music, very pleased with myself, anticipating a second visit to Granddaddy in two days.

Grandma was ready to go at mid-morning on Wednesday. The drive from her home in Portola Valley to Atherton took fifteen minutes. I noticed that she changed into a pretty blue summer dress and white gloves, and applied a spray of lavender scent. She looked like she was going to an afternoon tea party. Her light blue Chrysler slowly rolled into the drive at 48 Spencer Lane with tires grinding over the pebble driveway, creating a distinctive crunching sound. She pulled past the front door and stopped her car, but left the engine running. She would not look at the front door, and he would not come outside until she left. We knew this, so we leaned over, kissed Grandma, and hopped out.

Granddaddy was inside, and Kit and I told him what we wanted to do. He gave the okay, and we set out to explore the side room of the garage. Susan stayed behind to chat with him and that was fine with us. We rummaged around for a while, finding huge posters, old pictures of people we didn't know, game score cards, some trophies, magazine covers, and old bats and equipment. Things had been just put here and there in no particular order. After a while, I decided he might tell us about some of this stuff, so Kit and I went back into the house.

When I walked into the living room, he was standing by the bookcase, showing Susan some of his books. "Oh, Hersch, there you are. Did you get enough of a gander at all that old stuff in the garage?" He didn't wait for a reply, but continued, "Susan, see if you can find Louise and take Kit, and you three run over to Edy's Ice Cream Shop and see if they have some of this rocky road ice cream I've been hearing about. I think I should have a taste before I give up chocolate." He leaned down and said something private to Susan, and she smiled at him and then at me and left. In a minute, I heard the car tires roll over the pebbles in the driveway, crunching their way out to Spencer Lane.

Granddaddy fiddled with a book as he walked over to his chair. "Hersch," he said, "I've been thinking . . ." and then he didn't finish his thought. "Have a seat, over here," pointing to the ottoman next to his chair. "You know, about what you were saying the other day . . . about your season and all, and the other people at your game?"

192   I replied, "That's okay, Granddaddy. I kind of get it now." I knew he was referring to the heckling and jeering I suffered

through in Middle League baseball. I still didn't like it, but I didn't think I could do much about it either, knowing what I now knew.

"No, Hersch, I want to say," he went on, "you can't stop them from yelling and razzing you—maybe even your own teammates razz you. But that's just part of it."

The heckling was what really bothered me. I thought he was going to tell me I just had to take it. That's what my dad would have said.

"It looks to me like you like to compete, and you're strong and fast, so you're probably pretty good. That's what I'm getting at." I could tell he wasn't going to tell me I had to just take it, so I sat up and looked squarely at him.

I told him, "Yeah, I'm the fastest in my class."

"Good. That's good." He squinted and looked squarely at me. "If you're going to compete, you need to prepare yourself. Some things you can control and some you can't. You can practice hard, but you can't stop razzing from the fans or even your teammates. You know, maybe another fellow wants your position."

I'd never thought about that, but quickly remembered that I'd beat out a lot of guys to play center field.

"To compete, you have to prepare to win." He was focused now. "You have to prepare and practice every detail, over and over. Running, hitting, sliding, all that. That's your body. You have to prepare your mind to win too, and then when you go to play, play your hardest. Make the other guy know that you're prepared and will never quit, that you'll never give up."

I had moved to the edge of the ottoman, caught up in what he was saying.

He continued, "After a while, you'll have successes, but you have to keep preparing because sometimes there's a slump, know what I mean?"

193

I heard myself say, "Yes, sir."

"Okay. And after some successes, your confidence will build and you'll know how to work out of a slump. But with the heckling, you can't control those things. So, work on not listening. Don't pay attention to it. Pay attention to everything you need to do to come out on top. Train your mind. Hear me, every little detail?"

I nodded again.

He shifted gears and said, "Oh, and Hersch, be your own person. Be able to stand up for yourself. Know what I mean?"

"Not really," I said, and I meant it. I thought of getting shot with BBs by my dad and never feeling like I could trust anybody again, but really wanting somebody I could trust.

Granddaddy seemed to read my mind because he continued, "Sometimes kids get hurt, maybe by their own parents, and they want to hide so they don't get hurt again. If you're your own person, no matter what, you can accomplish what you set out to do. It'll be there when you prepare yourself, have some success, and get your confidence going a bit. You'll notice something."

I was perplexed and asked, "Like what?" The advice sounded slippery and a little over my head.

His voice had gained a distinct rhythm. "You remember the oars on the rowboat up at Tahoe, and the rudder?" I must have looked as puzzled as I felt. "Remember all the hours you spent out there on the lake, rowing around, steering exactly where you wanted to go?"

"Yeah, I remember."

"Well, it's a little like that. You're the guy who gets you around, and you're the guy who steers your own rudder. You choose, you decide, nobody else." He looked at me. "You're your own person. Only as you get a little older, it's bigger than just that."

He went on, "Make the other guy know you're your own person and that you'll never give up. You'll do just fine, and the razzing won't matter a bit. Understand me, Hersch? You'll be just fine." His voiced sounded certain and reassuring, and I could tell he was done.

I understood the basic point and I said, "Yes, sir, I think so."

I turned my head toward the front of the house at the same time Granddaddy said, "I think I hear them coming in the drive. Let's go have some of this rocky road." Susan and Kit had brought the new ice cream, along with double chocolate. We all tasted the rocky road. I liked the double chocolate best, and Granddaddy tasted them both and left for the kitchen to get some peach ice cream out of the freezer and some large spoons. We sat around, talked about Lake Tahoe, planned our trip, and ate lots of ice cream.

We spent three weeks at Lake Tahoe with Granddaddy, and returned to Portola Valley to spend the rest of the summer at Grandma's house. The three of us returned to Santa Maria late in August, about a week before school started. While we were at Grandma's, Mom bought a larger house, with two stories and a nice backyard. Also, Ayako had returned to her family in Seattle. I would be attending a different school.

On the Saturday before school started, I was in the kitchen in the late morning, and Mom came in. She sat at the kitchen table and said, "Hersch, sit down, I want to talk to you." Her voice was business-like, as if she had rehearsed what she had to say over and over.

She continued, "I don't want to take care of you anymore, so I don't want you to live here. You'll have to live somewhere else.

Your sister and brother will remain here with me, so you won't see them anymore."

I could tell she was serious. I sat, stunned and speechless. I felt a little sick to my stomach, and I'm sure the blood drained from my face. I hadn't done anything wrong; nothing had happened. My eyesight became fuzzy, my mind blank, and I just sat there.

She took a breath and said, "I'm sure you can find some place to live. Maybe a foster home, maybe with another family."

I sat listening, motionless, speechless, my mind whirling. I felt almost dizzy.

Then she asked me, "Do you want to say anything?"

I said, shocked at what I'd just heard, "You mean, leave?"

"Yes, leave. You'll have to live somewhere else." And she repeated, speaking very slowly, "I don't want you here."

I had nothing to say. I sat, looking past her, out the window, wondering what was going to happen to me.

She didn't wait for me to say anything else, but pushed her chair away from the table and left.

I sat for a long time. Nobody came into the kitchen and I could not hear any sounds from other parts of the house. I had to gather myself. I looked out the window at the street, and the sidewalk, and the gutter. It all looked so forlorn.

I had to stop looking outside. My gaze settled on the telephone attached to the wall between the kitchen counter and breakfast table where I was sitting. I took the phone off the hook and dialed my grandmother. I felt awful because Grandma was old. But she answered on the second ring, and I told her what had just happened. The phone was quiet for a few seconds and then she said, "She's your mother, Hersch." I couldn't understand what that really meant.

196

The following silence on the other end of the line lasted for what seemed like forever. Then my Aunt Shirley came on, asking me to tell her what had just happened. She listened as I repeated it all over again.

Shirley said, as if giving me drill orders in the army, "Hersch, you stay at that house. Don't go anywhere, don't leave." She repeated all this and asked me three times if I understood her. She must have heard the fear in my voice. I told her that I did, and she said she had to hang up and make a phone call right away.

Nothing else was said that weekend. Not by my mother, at least. When Monday came, I dressed, got my stuff together, and rode my bike the two miles to my new school.

A day later, I came in from playing and Susan greeted me. She took my arm and pulled me toward her, saying in a low tone, "Granddaddy called while you were outside. He told me to give you a big hug and tell you, 'Don't worry, everything is okay.'" Then she let go of me and asked, "What does that mean? What happened?"

I didn't answer, but smiled weakly, relieved, took my hug, and went back outside. I wanted to be by myself. My mother never said anything more, but I stayed on, knowing more than I ever wanted to about her. I did not know the difference between resentment and jealously, but she blistered with both. I'd made some friends through sports and liked school such that my grades were good. Also, I did not hide that I learned valuable lessons from Granddaddy. She saw the world through a lens of spite and envy. When others had accomplishments, she felt slighted; when she did something, she wanted others to feel diminished. She held that any good would be met by an equal amount of pain. If I was pleased or succeeded she felt cheated. If she was pleased, then I must feel left out. Strange. She had few friends, resented other's accomplishments, disliked academics, and despised my

197

grandfather. She resented all that I was developing. Also, I knew that my grandfather would stand by me no matter what, and his steadfastness comforted me greatly.

She continued with her quart of Old Crow in the evenings. Ayako never came back from Seattle, and my mother expected Susan to take up the role of maid, which she did, at least as to "us boys." She never complained about fixing us breakfast, lunch bags for school, dinner, and chocolate chip cookies, or acting as the buffer between Mom's outbursts and us.

By the time the spring arrived, I was looking forward to the end of the school year, certain my mom would ship us to Grandma's for the summer. When we arrived at Grandma and Aunt Shirley's home in Portola Valley, I cornered Aunt Shirley in her office and insisted she tell me what happened. She didn't say a lot, except, "I told the Old Man about you and your mom. He called her bank and her lawyers. That took care of that. Go have some fun, bub."

CHAPTER SEVEN

A Chance
Meeting in
the Night

The door to the bedroom that had been used by Granddaddy and Grandma when they were married was always closed. Whenever I visited El Roblar, I wandered and explored throughout most of the house and the grounds, but I knew the front bedroom was off limits. It was next to the room he used as an office, so whenever I went into the office to look around, I glanced to my left to see if that door would be ajar, allowing me to peek inside. It never was, and each year that I visited Granddaddy, my curiosity grew.

Susan was even more curious than I was, and we often talked about "that bedroom." It was as if "that bedroom" contained precious secrets. Secrets, not only about Granddaddy and Grandma, but about my father, Uncle Ty, Aunt Shirley, Aunt Beverly, and Uncle Jim, and us, meaning me, my sister, and brother. They were raised at 48 Spencer Lane from 1932 until they started life on their own.

"What do you think?" my sister once asked me.

"I don't know." I fidgeted with my fingers, avoiding Susan's eyes. "I want to go in and look around. You remember what Shirley said."

"No, what did she say?" She tugged on my arm, practically jumping into my lap with excitement.

"About all the babies. You know." I pulled away from her, knowing I was now stuck, trying to explain something I didn't know anything about. I was at the age when my body was changing, and what I saw in the world and heard in conversations had new meanings. I didn't understand them all, and it seemed like secrets and forbidden knowledge flitted just beyond my grasp. In particular, nobody had explained what occurs when a young boy enters puberty.

"That bedroom," located at the front left corner, is set forward from the rest of the house; it forms the left border of the wide patio of earthen-colored tiles that spans the front. The right corner of the house is the dining room, which is also set forward. Whenever I entered the driveway of El Roblar, the front door was slightly hidden by the walls of the protruding dining room, and the master bedroom was the first thing that caught my eye. On the patio side, it has a slender iron-framed glass door and double windows looking out to the front yard. On the north side is a small window, which looks out on the scrubs and bushes next to the house.

I continued explaining what I knew about the bedroom to Susan. "You remember," I began, "when we were in Aunt Shirley's bedroom and she was talking to Dixie, her husband, about Grandma. She told Dixie, 'Charlie was pregnant thirteen times. Eight miscarriages or stillborns. She was with child practically every year.'" Shirley always referred to her mother as Charlie; we grandchildren called her Grandma. Her official name was

Charlotte Lombard Cobb, but she preferred to be called Charlie, and that's what people called her all her life.

I looked at Susan, barely putting any air into my words, feeling like I wanted to hold them inside of me, not wanting to show my naïveté. I didn't know what a "miscarriage" was, and when I heard the word "stillborn" spoken during that conversation I was not supposed to hear, the image in my mind was of a small, white, soft pile of flesh, with pink veins showing easily, and sunken, closed eyes. I blurted out, "What does that mean? Stillborn?"

"Oh," she replied, very quietly, "I think that means they were already dead when born."

"Ugh," I murmured. "You mean, in that room?"

"No, no. Wherever they were living a long time ago. Atlanta, Detroit. I don't know." Her voice had changed from softly insisting on answers from me to sharply cutting off the conversation. I knew this meant that Susan was piecing together what she knew, and what she had overheard in conversations at Grandma's house. There were lots of conversations to pick and choose from and piece together a story. Aunt Shirley and Dixie talked, Grandma and Shirley talked, Aunt Beverly and Grandma talked. One of us was always in earshot, so sooner or later we pieced things together. Right now I could only wait.

Earlier that day, we had been sitting outside in Grandma's backyard, perched on the long brick retaining wall that separated the sloping hillside from the lawn. It was just after lunch and the sun was warm, with the flowers around the edge of the yard bountiful and full of color. We huddled together like two kids playing tic-tac-toe on a small piece of paper, bent over each other, nearly touching noses. Only, there were no giggles or gestures of triumph or defeat. We compared notes, looking for clues, filling the book of our lives, and the lives of Grandma and Granddaddy

201

from forty years ago. We knew we were going to go to Lake Tahoe with Granddaddy this day or the next, and our attention was focused on filling in parts to our puzzle. We both jumped with surprise when we heard Grandma's voice; she was practically next to us. I didn't even hear her walk up.

"Susan, Herschel, have you finished packing? We can go down to Atherton now." Grandma's tone conveyed a little urgency. "I just put some things in a bag for Kit. Susan, please make sure the boys have their swim things for the lake. And take something nice to wear in case you go out to dinner." She was smiling as she sat down beside us and looked out over her gardens. "You are fine children. I think you're going to have a special time with your granddaddy."

I quickly asked, "What do you mean?"

"Oh, nothing. Just run along and get ready." And she smiled as she gave me a little push off the brick wall, which only made me more curious about what she meant by a special time.

We packed most of the stuff we had brought for the summer, loaded our suitcases in the trunk of Grandma's car, and climbed into the back seat. None of us knew where Kit was, and she called for him down the hill from her house. Soon he came running up from the neighbor's house at the bottom of the hill. He was smiling with some teeth missing, his red hair flopping and his freckles more evident than ever thanks to the summer sun. His jeans were covered with mud, so we waited some more while Grandma took him inside and helped him change. I bounced on the back seat for a while, impatient to get going. It seemed like forever before they came out of the house, with Kit cleaned up.

The fifteen-minute ride to Atherton was quiet, except for the radio, which Grandma always kept on the oldies station, number sixty-one on the dial. Bing Crosby sang a song, then the Mills

Brothers, then three sisters. The music was mild and old-timey. I had made that ride often enough to let my eyes roll over the familiar hillsides, landmarks, turns, stop signs, trees, and winding streets without really thinking about anything, until we finally turned onto Spencer Lane, drove past one house, and turned into El Roblar. Granddaddy's black Chrysler Imperial was parked in the garage as Grandma pulled up past the patio and stopped her car. The front door was open, but nobody was standing nearby.

Grandma looked in her rearview mirror and said, "Herschel, take all your bags out of the trunk and put them on the patio. Somebody will come on out and help you." She meant Granddaddy but was not going to say his name. I got out and went around to the front, kissed her through the open window, then opened the trunk and took out our bags. In the meantime, Susan and Kit kissed her good-bye and headed toward the front door. I returned to Grandma's open window with a question.

"Are you going to call later?" I asked. "It's late to be heading up to the lake now. It'll be dark by the time we get to Cave Rock."

"Don't worry. I think everything is going to be fine. Give me a kiss and go on inside."

I leaned inside her window and kissed her again. She drove away, waving her familiar hand, which only barely reached out of the window. I grabbed the lightest of the bags and carried it into the house. The front room was empty, but I heard voices coming from the kitchen, so I put the bag down and hurried back to the kitchen to find Susan and Kit sitting while Louise was on the phone.

I said, "Want me to put the bags in Granddaddy's car?"

"Hush, Herschel. Just a minute." Susan motioned with her hand to keep quiet and pointed to Louise on the phone. She was speaking with our Aunt Shirley. I listened to her part of the conversation.

"Yes, Mrs. Beckworth. Yes, all of them. And his shot too. No. Just fine. Been getting up early, 6:00 or 7:00. Regular. Talked with the doctor yesterday. Fine. Did all the shopping yesterday too. The boys like eggs, bacon, pancakes, or toast; Susan likes toast and jelly. Yes, plenty." All of this said in response to questions my Aunt Shirley was asking about Granddaddy. I knew he took pills for his heart and an insulin shot every day for diabetes, but I could not understand why Aunt Shirley was asking about eggs and stuff.

"Everything is just fine. Okay, I'll tell Mr. Cobb, and he can talk to the children. Thank you, Mrs. Beckworth. Yes, I'll call if I need to. Yes, ma'am. Thank you, good-bye." She hung up the receiver and turned and looked at us. "Well, well, look how tall you all are. My, my. Stronger every year. Go on into the living room, and I'll tell Mr. Cobb you're here."

When I entered the living room, Granddaddy was already seated in his favorite chair, holding a book, with his fingers between the pages to mark his spot. I said to him, "Let's go, Granddaddy, we're all packed. It's getting late, and we'll be stuck in all the traffic."

"Come on in, Hersch. Hi, Susan, Kit. Come on over here and give me a hug." He put his book on the floor next to his chair, and we all squeezed onto his lap, with his arms finding their way around all of us. "We needn't worry about the traffic. You all can stay here tonight, and we'll leave first thing in the morning. How about that? Do you want to?"

I looked at Susan, and we both grabbed him and hugged him by his neck. We probably surprised him at how hard we hugged, but we were excited because we had always wanted to spend the night at El Roblar. He had to pull us away so he could breathe. We were so excited we wouldn't let go.

Now I knew why Grandma had given me that funny fare-well in the driveway. I had asked Grandma many times why we couldn't spend some nights at Granddaddy's house, and she always answered, "Hersch, when the time is right." This was the time. I never really considered her feelings about the question. We spent every summer with her, and she filled our days and evenings with love, understanding, room to grow and explore; with toys, adventures, stories, and smiling, laughing humor. We were her "redheads." In some of the most important parts of our lives, she was raising us, providing guidance, care, and love, knowing that my mother's days were filled with alcohol, pills, late nights, resent-ment, and anger. I never asked what she felt about giving us over to the man with whom she had shared her life for so many years, whose children she bore and raised, whose whims and outbursts she managed to endure and straighten, and who still held that place in her heart that would never be touched by another. While I was hugging my grandfather that moment, I thought of all of this. That sense of affection and trust stayed with me as though it were alive, and later that night it would be with me while I was discovering another aspect of my grandfather's life.

"Herschel, put your suitcase and Kit's by the door to the front bedroom; you two can sleep there. Put Susan's in the one down the hall, across from mine. She'll have a bathroom to herself, and you two can share." He nudged me off his chair, and I stood up with a grin like I'd reached into a big box of chocolate. "Do it now, so Louise won't have to do it. Then check out the fridge, or play outside, or whatever you want. I want to read some of this book to Kit."

I carried the suitcases through the arch and put them next to the door to the front bedroom. Susan knew what I was anticipating, and I knew she was thinking the same thing. Now was the time. We were going to find out everything! As things turned out, our discoveries would really wait until the morning.

It was now late in the afternoon, so we checked out the freezer and found two gallon cartons of peach ice cream, one of chocolate, and one of strawberry. Susan fixed a bowl of peach for Granddaddy and strawberry for Kit, while she and I had chocolate.

Louise's phone conversation in the kitchen with my aunt now made sense. Aunt Shirley was double-checking to make sure everything with "The Old Man" was all right. This really meant that she wanted to be sure he hadn't had anything to drink and was not on a tear about something. In all the years I spent with Granddaddy, with all of the evenings out at restaurants and talking to his friends, I never saw him drink more than a sip of whisky.

He never hid anything from us, and Susan and I knew enough to check. We lived with a mother who hid bottles of liquor and all kinds of pills. We had learned to spot what we called "danger" and "to duck." We kept out of her way. She took uppers, which she called "goofballs," to keep her going during parties at night, and downers to be able to sleep. It was impossible for me not to have heard stories about Granddaddy and his various escapades. Some were told and embellished as funny stories, and some revealed that he had a temper and sometimes lost control of it.

Aunt Shirley subdued her disapproval and mild envy that we spent so much time with him, and sometimes argued vigorously with Grandma it was "too much" for Granddaddy or he would behave badly. Grandma had a way of treating people so that their behavior became appropriate. If someone failed enough times, they just disappeared from the rolls of her contacts. She knew Granddaddy better than anyone, knew what he valued in his heart. She saw that he wanted his grandchildren near him, and she knew how to accomplish that by combining his wishes with hers. She realized that his relationship with his grandchildren was different from that with his own children, both the salutary effect on him and the benefit to his grandchildren. He had changed, and each of Susan's accounts to Grandma of our times with Granddaddy gave her more reason to foster our bond with him.

For the rest of the afternoon, Susan and I played, explored the backyard, and stuck close to Louise in the kitchen while she fixed dinner. Granddaddy read to Kit for over an hour, and that was enough for him. When he found us, we were sitting at the kitchen table, splitting peas and munching on carrots. He told us he was going to nap for an hour or so and told Louise that we children could eat early or wait for him. He was still southern and liked to eat dinner when it was dark; this meant nearly 9:00 in July. We wanted to wait, because we'd been eating nonstop since mid-afternoon. Plus, we had never eaten at his huge dining room table.

When Granddaddy returned to the living room after his nap, it was past 6:00, and I was examining the books behind the glass of the bookcase next to the fireplace. Most were beautifully bound in leather with the name and author embossed in gold. He walked across the entrance hall and surveyed the dining room, then sat down and asked me, once again, "You like books, Hersch?"

"Yeah, I like some of them. I get one from Aunt Shirley every Christmas. She never gives me toys."

"Doesn't surprise me," he declared, "she gives them to me too. And I read them, most of them, anyway. You know, she loves that bookstore of hers."

I could tell he hadn't quite woken up because before I could say anything, he said, "Say, why don't you help out and clear off

207

the table in the dining room? Put the papers over on a chair so we can use the whole table for dinner."

The table was filled with old newspapers, magazines, envelopes, some old junk mail, and a few small boxes that hadn't been opened. I put all the newspapers on one side chair and the magazines on another, with the boxes on top. I was stacking the junk mail and envelopes when I spotted a check with a familiar name on it. In the upper left, in red script, was written "Coca-Cola Co., Atlanta, Georgia," with an address underneath in black type. On the right-hand side were numbers typed in after a dollar sign: 83,164.00. The signature below the numbers flowed lavishly and didn't look like junk mail. I'd seen a check before, and this was one big check. I was careful with all the mail and put the whole stack on another side chair. I walked over to Granddaddy with the check delicately held between my thumb and first finger. "Granddaddy, here's this." I handed him the check.

The startled look on his face was almost comical. "My, my, Hersch, thanks very much. I've been wondering about this. Where'd you find it?"

"In a pile of letters and junk mail. What is it?" My curiosity was rising.

"See the date?" He pointed to the upper right corner. "June 30, that's the end of the first half of the year. It's my quarterly dividend check from the Coca-Cola Company." He handed the check to me, and I looked it over and handed it back. "Do you know what a dividend is?"

I shook my head.

"It's the money they pay me on my shares. Do it every three months." Then he smiled wryly. "Helps me keep going." He shook the check slightly. "This has been sitting around almost a month. Got to put this in the bank."

"What's a share?" I asked.

"A share means I own a little bit of the company. Like when I told you about stock? When they make money, they pay a little bit to me for each of my shares. That's my dividend. 'Course, with Coke, I bought a lot of shares a long, long time ago. Still buy 'em. First shares I bought, Mr. Woodruff loaned me the money. Told me he and his associates just purchased a soda pop company and they were going to make it the biggest in the country and I should be a part of it. So he loaned me some money and I bought some shares."

"I thought you played baseball to make money." He had my full attention.

"Hersch, when I started out, they didn't pay me much. Had to work hard and prove myself. I remember battling with my boss for a raise—that was something. Fought with Nevin every year."

He could see the inquiring expression on my face. "When I was your age, I worked tilling a cotton field, behind a mule. Me and a Negro boy, we plowed row upon row behind that mule, stuck in a hot, dusty field. Took turns. We weren't paid much, didn't have any extra money. Never had any 'jingle' in our pocket, and I didn't like it much." He reached into his pocket and showed me a wad of bills: his "jingle."

I started smiling at the image of him working behind a big ole mule. He continued, his voice rising with excitement, "No, it's true. But I loved baseball. That's what I really wanted to do. And I was determined. Yep, baseball had what I wanted. It was fast, and I could outsmart the other guy."

I thought he was done talking, but he went on, calm again. "Hersch, when you get old enough to work for a living, find something you love to do, then do it as best you can. It'll all work out for you."

Then he said what sounded like the strangest advice. "Don't wait for somebody to give you any money. Go out and do what you love and make your own." He paused and then mumbled to himself, "I don't think I did your dad any good by giving him all that money." He shook his head. "Nope, I don't think I helped him at all." Then he folded the check just like it was any other piece of paper and shoved it in his pants pocket.

I thought I had an idea of what he was talking about. My dad never took up something he really liked to do except, maybe, boxing. All the money he was given and spent had blurred his vision, what he wanted to accomplish on his own.

When dinnertime came, we all sat down and listened to Granddaddy tell stories about nearly everybody. We heard about Bobby Jones and golfing, Babe Ruth and the crazy "has-beens" golf match, about Bill Tilden and Uncle Ty, Jack Dempsey, and more about battling over his contracts with his Detroit Tigers boss. He knew a lot of people, famous and not famous, all guests at this very dinner table in past years. Most important to me, he told tales about our dad when he was a little boy. I hung on every word, absorbing the images of my freckle-faced father as a little rascal pursuing his adventures, both forbidden and approved of. He had two billy goats that ate anything they could, so my dad opened the gates to neighbors' homes, watched them rummage around, and laughed and ran when the neighbors saw what was going on. Granddaddy smoothed things over by signing a couple of baseballs for them. My father had played on his high school football team, earning his letter and receiving mention in the local newspaper for outstanding games. Aunt Shirley's and Beverly's bedrooms were on the second floor, accessed only by an outside stair. When they wanted to stay late at a party without Grandma and Granddaddy knowing, Shirley would have my dad go up to her room and stomp around so it sounded like they came home. Granddaddy let us know that he wasn't fooled—my dad made too much noise, so he slyly checked—but decided it wasn't worth arguing with Grandma about. Normally he wanted strict discipline and she was lax, and this became a continuing conflict. Letting it go was unusual for him.

When dinner and the stories were finished, it was late, and Louise had long since cleaned up the dishes and retired to her room. It was easy to talk Granddaddy out of having to take a bath, and Susan did not resist his suggestion that she get ready for bed, and he would take care of "the boys." I took our suitcases into the front bedroom. I wanted to explore, but Granddaddy was standing there, and I was so tired, I happily crawled into one of the huge single beds. By the time Granddaddy kissed Kit, he was asleep.

He pulled the sheet and covers up to my chin, put his left hand gently on the nape of my neck, and kissed my cheek. He didn't say anything, but brushed my hair back from my forehead and looked for a moment straight into me. On his way out he stood in the doorway, looked back over Kit and me, switched off the light, and pulled the door so that it was slightly ajar. I felt the warmth of the covers envelop my body, nuzzled into the pillow, and fell asleep.

Sometime in the middle of the night I woke up with a start at a loud thud down the hall. I opened my eyes but didn't move a muscle. That created the strangest sensation of being there and not being there. The room was softly illuminated by moonlight coming in through the windows. Swinging my legs out of bed broke the floating sensation, and I realized I wanted to go to the bathroom. I opened the bedroom door and peered down the hallway. It was dark, and I couldn't see anything, so I started walking with my left hand against the wall as a guide.

"Who's that?" a voice asked sharply, grabbing the strength out of my legs. I really wanted to pee.

"It's me, Hersch." My voice came out sounding much calmer than I felt.

"Hersch, what are you doing up at this hour? It's nearly three in the morning."

"Granddaddy!" That's all I said, because at that instant he turned on the hallway light.

I looked at him and gasped. "What happened to your legs?" He was wearing a short, faded blue and brownish-red robe he'd bought years ago, and both of his legs, from the middle of his thighs to his ankles, were exposed to the light. They were marked all over by huge scars that looked violet-red, with large ridges crisscrossing over other ridges. There was almost no skin left. Scars on top of scars. On his right leg was a huge red ridge that ran all the way down his thigh, across the inside of his knee, down his calf. Another long, wide ridge covered the inside of his left leg, disappearing up into his robe. More scars pocked the outside of his left leg, and one of them went from his left thigh, down the outside of his knee and halfway down the rear of his calf. His ankles looked like somebody had taken a knife and hacked away without stopping to leave any tissue untouched. Some scars were so red, they looked fresh, as if they might start bleeding right then and there. Some were so large, his flesh must have been gashed open time after time. The horrible sight was seared on my eyeballs. I was repulsed and shocked and worried at what I saw.

The look on my face must have said it all. He stood there in front of me, motionless.

"I couldn't sleep either. Don't sleep well anymore, it seems."

"I have to go to the bathroom, right away, Granddaddy," I said, with more than a little urgency.

"Right here," he said as he motioned toward a door. He reached in and turned on the light. "Quiet, now, everybody's asleep. It's too late for you to be up."

"What happened to your legs?"

He glanced down at himself and replied slowly in a voice he never used, as though he saw the used, beaten legs of a spent warrior. "Hersch, that's a long story. Want some milk or something to eat?"

He was standing behind me, filling the doorway, and when I finished I said, "Yeah, I'm hungry. Do you have any Ritz?" He looked puzzled, so I repeated, "You know, Ritz crackers."

"Oh, I don't know. I guess we can go and see." His voice was resigned, but he was smiling again. I followed him down the hall, and when we went through the arch into the living room, he put his hand on my shoulder. "Hungry, huh? Does this happen every night? Ritz crackers?"

"Yup," I said, very sure of myself, a little more at ease with some words spoken. "Grandma always has lots of Ritz around."

His slippers scratched along the carpet in the living room, but his walk was steady. His hand on my shoulder felt heavy, and I wondered if he was using me for balance. I was concerned, especially after I'd seen his legs. But halfway through the living room, he squeezed my shoulders next to my neck and worked his hand over toward my left arm. "You've got some muskles there, young man." His silly pronunciation of muscles broke the tension. His balance was fine, and I felt my body relaxing.

The moonlight coming through the living room windows provided just enough light that we didn't turn on any lights until we reached the kitchen. When I clicked the overhead light on, it was dim, just bright enough that we wouldn't bump into anything. His kitchen was old with soap-board countertops, an ancient sink, and cupboards showing flaking paint, not like

213

Grandma's, whose kitchen was newer and brighter. Granddaddy started opening cabinets, looking for crackers. I went to the fridge and took out a bottle of milk.

The light from the fridge shone on his robe, and I looked over my shoulder at him. His robe stood out like a cartoon costume with its geometric design and red, turquoise, and brownish-yellow colors. It was practically worn out, with threads hanging here and there, and tufts of material where the weave had caught on something and pulled out.

"Where'd you get the robe?" I immediately realized I didn't know what I was asking, but I'd opened my mouth and that's what came out, and I was stuck with it.

The look on his face was a mix of mild disapproval and squeamishness. "Got it in Nevada, at an Indian trading post. Supposed to bring good luck." He changed the subject. "Here are the crackers. You want the whole box?"

"Sure," I replied. "You want some milk?"

"No, don't drink milk. Doesn't agree with me anymore."

We sat at the table in the kitchen. In the dull light, glancing at each other, munching away. I enjoyed being with Granddaddy, alone, eating Ritz crackers, late at night. I didn't want it to end, so I kept eating crackers and sipping milk. Then he stood up and went to the sink to get a glass of water, and I saw his legs again.

"Granddaddy, what happened to your legs?" I was hesitant to pry, but shocked and couldn't imagine how much they must hurt. I wanted to know what had happened to him.

He looked down at himself, almost as if he were discovering something new. "Oh, that."

"Do they hurt?" I asked.

"They ache a little. More at night." His voice was withdrawn, having to talk about a pain that would never go away. I continued eating crackers, waiting for him to say more. The questions on my face were unavoidable, and so was the silence that began to build up.

Finally, he broke it. "When I first started, you know, broke into the majors, I was pretty fast. I figured when I got to first base, the base path to second and third belonged to me. That's the rule. I liked to steal second, and third. It really rattled the pitcher and his infield. And I was pretty good at it. You know, I told you about the sliding pit in my backyard. I started practicing before I was fifteen. So I stole as often as I could."

He sipped his water before he went on. "I guess, at first, they figured I was lucky, but my hook slide worked nearly every time. In my second year, I started stealing again, as often as I could. They had to try to stop me, so they used their spikes on me. They wanted to scare me." He wasn't embellishing a tale; he was reporting the facts as they happened to him.

"What do you mean?"

"Well, their spikes. They jumped up in the air as I came into second base and came down with their spikes digging into my thigh. Cut the hell out of me. I was using my hook slide just fine, but I was laid out like a fish in a frying pan. Wide open. The first guy who did it, I remember his face as he climbed off of me and said, 'That's what you're going to get every time you come down to my base, got it?' That was supposed to scare me, stop me from stealing, but it didn't. Just made me mad as hell. Hurt like hell too. Blood was all over my pants, but the ump didn't even say boo. I was safe at second, and mad as a bee. So, I stole third on the next pitch!" His eyes now had that special twinkle.

I had stopped chewing, and my hand held my milk glass in midair while he spoke. "Couldn't you do something?"

"Not really. The game was young and played pretty rough.

215

That was 1906. The players had to be tough. And the spikes were a little longer than today. It happened a lot. Some teams had bastards—excuse me, Hersch—that were worse than others. I was nineteen my second year in the majors. They had a mind to stop me right then and there. When I went in with my hook, my arms were back, and I was keeping my body as long and low as I could. Only problem was, I couldn't defend myself."

He was only nineteen. I thought, "I'm going to be fourteen in a few months and nineteen in five years—just five years from now." I imagined spikes gouging into my thighs and blood spurting out of the cleat tracks. I felt a burst of anger at this deliberate attack. "What did you do?" I thought back to my Middle League game, when everybody was yelling at me to steal second base. I could see in my mind some guy getting ready to dig his spikes into my leg.

"I was bloody a lot. Your grandmother took care of my legs at night. Used everything she knew—some salves, compounds, ointments. Wrapped them up pretty tight. But I busted open the scabs sliding. Then she thought of hanging towels down the inside of my pants, to protect my legs. I tied them onto my belt. When I tried it and it worked, I ruined most of the towels in the house. That was in Detroit. So, that's what I did on both legs. It saved my legs when I slid, and helped when the spikes came down on me."

"Grandma fixed you up?" My voice was timid, but I had to get into it. It was an unspoken rule in his house, but as noticeable as if it were in neon lights in every room: Nobody mentions her. And "her" was Charlie Lombard Cobb, my grandmother, his ex-wife, mother of his children, including my dad, griever for the lost children, survivor, and still taking care of him in important ways. She was the one who made sure that Susan, Kit, and I spent two or three weeks every summer with him. He had brought her name up, broken his imposed silence, and I wasn't going to let it slip away. I bit my lip and continued. "Grandma took care of your legs?"

"Well, yeah. Nobody else to. I wasn't making any money as a ball player. Pitiful. First time I got into a bath, the bleeding started again. Damn." He paused, catching himself. "Don't use that word, Hersch. There was bright red blood everywhere. So we stopped that, and just used towels and sponges. Then iodine, and then all these compresses, with powders inside. She got some mixes and herbs from the country people back in Augusta. Amazing people, really. Knew a lot about healing without going to the doctor. Guess they had to, being way out in the country."

He took a breath, as if reminding himself he was in the kitchen with me and not on the base paths in Detroit's Bennet Park, and went on. "The bleeding stopped okay. And I could still play hard. It happened a lot, I guess she fixed me up a lot. Sliding was rough on these old legs. The spikes were worse." He trailed off a little, his eyes drifting around the old kitchen, probably unchanged since he bought the house in 1932.

"All the time you played? You got spiked all the time?" I asked. "What about the other players?"

"Not every guy at second or third tried to spike me. But there were a lot over the years. Guys wanted to stop me. Then, later on, young players, new ones, wanted to make a name for themselves."

"Granddaddy," I interrupted, blurting out, "did you spike a guy on purpose? They told me you did. Did you?" I swallowed hard. I didn't plan to ask that way, but all of a sudden, after two years of wondering about all the tales I'd heard, it came out. I could see the accusation caught him unexpectedly. He withdrew a little from the table, and then leaned way over toward me.

"Hersch, we were in the middle of a series. I was having a terrific year. The second baseman had told everybody to tell me that

217

if I came down, you know, tried to steal second, he was going to put his spikes through me and stop me for good. I wanted him to know I was coming down if I had the chance, and I'd be ready for him. I was ready to give what I was going to get."

Now the old tales took on a new aspect. He placed them in the context of the punishment he endured all those years. My eyes were huge and my mouth was open. He continued, "Well, I got my chance and broke good, and I was heated up. I went in, intending to catch the corner of the bag with my right toe, and my left leg was free. I was ready and probably would have. No doubt, Hersch, I was ready. The throw was late, and he made the catch, but I was already there. He didn't even jump in the air or try to get me. I guess it was bluff, or maybe he knew I was never going to quit. He never made the threat again.

"I never spiked anyone on purpose. My purpose—and I was determined—was to get my foot to the bag. That was it."

"What about in the picture? In the office," I said. "Is that Home Run Baker?"

"That's not Baker," he told me. "That's a different player. Jimmy Austin." He quickly got back on track. "But, oh, yeah. Yep. I was accused by Baker. Baker was furious. But a camera guy was there and snapped one. A lot of heat and yelling. And when he finally developed his picture and showed it around, it was a clean steal. My spikes were low, practically in the dirt. But by that time, what was said was said. In and out of the sports pages. I got a pretty raw deal in the newspapers, but I kept on playing hard. Hersch, I knocked over my share of guys. That's for sure. And I got my bumps and cuts. Didn't cry about it, though. I'm not ashamed. I wanted to win. And nobody was going to stop me."

I wanted him to reach over and touch me. That didn't happen. He was no longer the gentle grandfather who showed me how to bat and throw, who held me on his lap and asked me if I wanted a cigar, or ate peach ice cream with me. His voice was not angry but absolutely firm in its conviction. The fierceness opened a distance between us. Yet I thought I knew how he felt. I got out of my chair and climbed into his lap and buried my face in his chest. His arms wound around me, and his squeeze nearly took my breath away. I felt his chin on the top of my head and heard his heart pounding under my ear. I did not want to move.

When he relaxed a bit, I kept my head low and asked a muffled question, "What about Ruth?"

He pushed me apart so he could see my face. "Hersch Cobb, what have you been reading?"

"The book Aunt Shirley gave me. The one about you by Mr. McCallum," I said.

"Oh, is that right?" I could feel the chuckle in his chest. "Well, I'll be. Now, this is the end, young man, no more questions tonight."

I thought he was going to put me off his lap and run me off to bed. But, no, in a voice that sounded like it came from deep inside, he explained, "Hersch, Ruth came along, hit home runs, and the fans loved it. The more he hit, the more they loved it. My style of play was passing. I could see it. That was hard on me, and I didn't like it one bit. Not one bit. Oh, I hit those five in two games, but I knew that wasn't my game." He smiled at this admission and pulled me close. In a minute I slid off, thinking he might keep talking.

"I liked Ruth, but while we were competing, I gave him a rough time. He was sensitive and I could say things that got to him, under his skin. Know what I mean?" He paused.

"I think so; those other kids in Middle League got to me," I quietly replied.

"I was a little personal on the Babe, maybe too much. It was the only way with him; he was a great hitter and only slumped when he was bothered. So I razzed him about the way he looked, and he was sensitive to that and it worked." His voice had become reticent, as if he didn't like admitting this part of his past.

"Afterward, after baseball, we saw each other more and I liked him. We played that crazy 'has-beens' golf match. I grew to admire him, had a little affection for him too. Boy, could he eat! I felt sorry at the way he ended. Sick, very sick, and without much. One time I told him to buy Coke, but I don't think he understood."

"Mr. McCallum says you played for twenty-four years. You did better than anybody."

"Hersch, I love baseball. It was my life. I played hard every game."

Somehow, I slipped and said, "How come you quit?"

I'd made a mistake and instantly knew it. He bristled, sat straight up, and began in a tone that shook me, "I never quit! I stopped playing!"

I swallowed hard, the moment tinged by the briefest thought of my dad.

"Sorry, Hersch, I know what you're getting at." He collected himself, remembering exactly what it felt like to say good-bye to a life he wished would last forever. "I knew if I played another year, it would be miserable. I only hit .323 in 1928 and knew I'd drop below .300 if I had another go. I wanted to go out on top. I think I did. Tris was going too, two old dogs headed for a rest. I miss 'em. Ruth, Tris, the others." He finished in almost a mumble, carrying a sadness that flowed over when he told me, "Hersch, make a bunch of friends in your life, ones that stick with you." I understood.

Our conversation about his baseball career came to an end. "Come on," he said. "I've got to get you to bed. We've got a big day ahead of us."

His hand found my shoulder and used it to help him stand. He gave me a pat on my back, told me to put the milk in the fridge and to follow him. I grabbed his hand as we left the kitchen. His hand shifted to my shoulder as we ambled through the living room, with him both guiding me and being supported by me. His legs were still violet-red and horrifying. The short old robe looked as funny as ever.

The next morning, I opened the bedroom door and found Susan standing outside, eager to hear what I'd uncovered in the front bedroom. We looked around together, but the passing of time had removed all but the barest remnants of our family's history. The curtains had turned yellow and stiff with age, the doilies on the dresser were pressed and clean, its drawers were empty, and the closet had hangers but no clothes. Still, the two single beds told a story: the large four-poster bed frames were elegantly carved, the linens and pillow covers were smooth as silk, but the beds were separated by a wide space.

Susan said, "I don't think Granddaddy ever comes in here. I think he really prefers to live at Tahoe."

Reminded of what we were doing today, I responded, anxious to get going, "Yeah, so let's have some breakfast and get going to Lake Tahoe."

Although the master bedroom did not give up any secrets, my chance meeting in the night added immensely to my sense of trust and assurance with my grandfather. He'd confided in me, enlarging and strengthening our bond, and my outlook on my own life. He had opened up an entirely new dimension to my

221

understanding. With me he wasn't a legend. He was a man who battled and suffered because he wanted to be the best at what he did. Those scars up and down his legs told a different story than the ones in the books that had dismayed me. I knew my grandfather couldn't be cruel like that. I knew all too well what true cruelty was. The man who was teaching me that it was all right to trust people was another type of legend altogether. I needed to learn how to shoot straight in this life. He knew I didn't have a father who could teach me. So he was making sure he provided those lessons himself.

When summer ended, we returned home to Santa Maria. Our mother's behavior continued the same patterns: she consumed a quart of Old Crow each evening, mixed to make Manhattans, seldom ate dinner with us, preferred to go out in the evenings or lie in bed in her room watching TV with a tumbler of milk and bourbon. On weekends, she slept until noon. Susan was careful to close all the doors leading from the kitchen because Mother became furious at the smell of bacon cooking.

Our house was a block from the high school, an easy walk that allowed me to come home for lunch, which Susan always fixed. I went out for the basketball team in the fall and the tennis team in the spring, spending my afternoons at school playing sports. By the time I arrived home, it was near dinnertime. One afternoon on a Thursday in early winter, basketball practice was canceled and I went to visit a buddy, Griff McClelland, who lived a couple of blocks away. When I headed home, around 4:00, I saw a new black Oldsmobile 88 parked directly in front of our house. I'd seen it before, at the Coca-Cola plant, when its owner was in my mom's office. His name was Jerry, and he was a "manufacturer's representative." Susan usually met Kit after school and took him with her to a girlfriend's home where they studied and he played. The side door to our house was locked, as was the patio door and front door, although I heard music playing when I knocked. Mom answered, asked me why I was home, and when I told her, she instructed me to go play at a friend's house and come back at dinnertime.

I went to where Susan was, asked her what was going on, and she said, "Mom has boyfriends. This is Thursday, it must be Jerry."

I responded, "How did you know?"

"I made the same mistake, only on a Tuesday, and it was a man named Ward, from Los Angeles. They each don't know the other exists. Stay here and take Kit outside."

On those evenings, we didn't see her; she stayed in her room, door locked, and we took care of ourselves. The same thing went on all winter and spring. Susan fixed our breakfast and dinner. Most days, she also fixed my quick lunch, so I could gobble it down and run back to school to play sports.

The following year, after our visit to Grandma and Granddaddy, was the same, except for a real stunt, which would be repeated, but the first time was a shocker. We'd grown used to Mom's drinking and being late; Susan was raising us, in any case. We avoided contact, ate dinner, and I did homework. On a Wednesday night, I got home from school at the same time as Susan, and we found a bag of groceries on the kitchen counter. We didn't think anything of it. Susan fixed us dinner, and we anticipated Mom would come home. She didn't. Not that night or the next. When Saturday night arrived and Mom still had not come home, Kit and I took our sleep blankets and made a camp in Susan's room. We were all in this together.

Sometime in the middle of the night, the bedroom door burst

open, the light went on, and there was Mom with a strange man. She wobbled near us. "Meet your new father . . ." and she said the guy's name. I blinked a few times and stared. They were both drunk. Mom slurred, "We were married in Mexico last night. Aren't you happy to have a father?" None of us said anything. She spit, "Ungrateful little . . . ," mumbling, taking his arm, and leaving. Susan immediately locked the door.

On Monday evening, Mom emerged from her room. The guy was gone. She fixed herself a drink and returned upstairs. The same thing happened two other times that year, only different men each time. In between, Susan and I were careful on Tuesdays and Thursdays, having our dinner quickly and finding something to do. We also avoided cooking bacon on weekends, or making noise inside the house before noon.

CHAPTER EIGHT

Spencer Lane
to Cave Rock,
Through Lodi

T he next summer, I was more excited than normal as I anticipated our trip: two incredible weeks at Lake Tahoe in August, the warmest and best month of the summer. The water would be slightly less icy than in July. Sky Water Lodge, the vacation spot next to Granddaddy's property, would be full, and hopefully I'd meet other teenagers to join up with. At age fifteen, I had my driver's permit and I was hoping he'd let me use the old Plymouth station wagon stored at his cabin.

While we discussed our plans, Granddaddy mentioned to Susan he might have a surprise for her on this trip. We tried to guess, and he allowed us three apiece, but we didn't get anywhere. On the morning of our departure, a heavy fog was blowing through his oak tree and over the roofline, bringing with it a chilling breeze, so we quickly set our bags next to his Chrysler Imperial, said good-bye to Grandma, watched her wave her small glove-covered hand as she departed 48 Spencer Lane, then rushed inside to see him.

Susan's surprise was waiting for us. She had often asked Granddaddy why he never dressed up, and this morning her request was answered. He stood before her, arms open, elegantly attired. Dressed up would be too casual a description. He wore a freshly pressed pale beige gabardine suit with an eggshell blue vest, white shirt with cuff links, blue silk tie, and his best summer shoes with white-laced tops and brown leather sides. He held a wide-brimmed Panama hat in his outstretched hand. Susan beamed in approval, and he laughed warmly as he hugged her.

Granddaddy sat in the passenger seat while Louise drove, and we three barely filled half the huge backseat. We would take the Dumbarton Bridge over the south end of San Francisco Bay and proceed east. As we neared the entrance to the bridge, the fog was thick and blowing hard, the windshield wipers were on, and visibility was poor. It was cold, and the car heater whirled. The bridge was old; concrete pillars held up huge wooden beams and side rails, and the driving surface consisted of wide wooden planks covered by asphalt sheets, so the pounding of the tires rolling across sounded like we were slapping back at the waves splashing against the underside of the planks. The bridge ran only a few feet above the turbulent bay, and the white-capped waves easily splashed through the side rails onto the surface. I thought it was exciting watching waves made by our tires splash by my window, almost as if we were at sea in the Chrysler. Granddaddy was visibly concerned, saying he didn't like this at all, cautioning Louise to drive slowly and take care. The eight miles across the bridge seemed like its own dangerous adventure, and we were all relieved when we returned to solid ground on the other side of the bay.

Soon we began to ascend toward Livermore and the Altamont

Pass, thirty miles away. When we passed over that first mountain ridge, the fog dissipated, the wind blew warm, and the sun shone. As we neared Tracy, the heat of the Central Valley began to bear down on us.

Granddaddy, getting hot, took off his shoes. Sitting more comfortably in silk socks, he chatted about how rough his hunting trips in Wyoming on packhorses had been, and this was not much in comparison. Nearing Stockton, via the two-lane roads that were the norm at the time, it was broiling hot. Rolling down the windows didn't help. He unbuttoned his vest, loosened up his tie, and told us he wanted to go through Lodi and pick up some fresh fruit. Along Highway 99, we passed through Stockton, and when we stopped for gas, the outside thermometer read one hundred degrees! It was only noon and I knew the severe heat would arrive toward 2:00. Lodi, half an hour up the road, was a farming area, and if there was a town, we never saw it. His route was along the back roads where he knew the fresh fruit stands, supplied and operated by local farmers. By this time Granddaddy had his tie very loose, the top two buttons of his shirt unbuttoned, his sleeves rolled up, cuff links dangling, his suit jacket back with us, and his hanky in hand mopping his brow.

He directed Louise to stop at a makeshift shack, set back from the intersection of two country roads near some fruit trees. The open front of the shack had a counter filled with flats of fruit, mostly apricots, with stacks of flats of fruit in the back. He got out in his stocking feet, shed his vest and tie, and made directly for an ice cooler next to the shack. He pulled out a Coke and guzzled it down. Mopping his face, he began talking animatedly to a gentleman with sun-soaked skin. At first I thought the man was angry that Granddaddy took a Coke without paying, but as they talked the man patted him on the shoulder like they were old buddies. He grabbed a Coke himself and pointed to some flats of apricots and the nearby trees. I got out, went over to them, and Granddaddy handed me a Coke, saying, "Just one."

It was hot, dusty, with no breeze or shade cover. Granddaddy and the man wandered toward the trees, then back to the apricot flats, jabbering away. He looked ridiculous in his stocking feet, dusty pant cuffs, two shirt buttons open, sleeves rolled up, the back of his shirt moist, fanning himself but perspiring noticeably.

"Hersch, come over here, meet Martin Rodriguez." I said hello and he replied, "*Mucho gusto.*" He held out a calloused, work-worn hand to shake, and he smiled warmly at me while he continued talking with my grandfather about this year's crop. He spoke Spanish and broken English while Granddaddy mumbled some Spanish words but mostly nodded his head. Their figures cut a contrasting silhouette, with my grandfather still over six feet, rather rotund in the middle, slight of hair on top, pale complexioned, with light eyes, while Mr. Rodriguez might have been five feet, eight inches at the most, lean, and dressed in field work clothes and boots, brown skin with deep dark eyes and thick black hair, unperturbed by the heat. Droplets of perspiration trickled down Granddaddy's forehead, cheeks, and neck. Mr. Rodriguez pointed to several flats, selected one, and handed it to me. Granddaddy pulled a roll of bills from his pocket, peeled off a hundred-dollar bill, and handed it to Mr. Rodriguez. He didn't take any change back, and I thought he'd made a mistake. I kept quiet, though, as I loaded the flat into the trunk. The two of them didn't seem to notice, both vigorously shaking hands and smiling as they said farewell.

Another fruit stand was on the next corner, with a sign for tomatoes this time. I didn't see any rows of tomatoes anywhere nearby, however. Granddaddy, still walking around in his stocking feet, shirt open, perspiring all over, guzzling another Coke, greeted a man. This man's name was Romero. He smiled warmly, greeted his old friend, talked for a while and offered Granddaddy a tomato from a particular flat. Taking a big bite, he splattered some of the juice on his white shirt. That taste was good enough for him and Romero handed me the flat. Granddaddy pulled out his roll, gave Romero a hundred-dollar bill, and climbed into the front seat, out of the sun.

A quarter of a mile down the road, another fruit stand featured cherries, red and yellow. Only this time I stayed close to Granddaddy, and when he went for his Coke, I asked him before the owner came, "Granddaddy, you gave those men $100 for one flat. Is that the price?"

"Nah, Hersch, a flat is a couple of bucks." He knew I'd been watching and wanted to know what was going on. "Remember when I told you about me and that Negro boy working the mule in the cotton field in Georgia?"

"Sure, it must have been hot and dusty. Like this." I gestured around.

"Right, and just as miserable. Not much 'jingle,' nothing extra. I've known some of these men for over ten years. Their work is hard—long, hot, dusty, everything I remember about that darn cotton field and mule. Overalls, no shirt, rocks in my shoes, plowing through hard red clay. Well, these guys have good produce, so I put some jingle in their pocket and maybe they have it a little easier, that's all." He was smiling again, like he knew I understood his reasoning now. He knew the man's name at this new stand, said hi to his young daughter, and finally paid $100 for a flat filled with half red cherries, half yellow cherries. Luckily, the Imperial's trunk was large, and three flats fit in easily.

We crept along the back roads of Lodi, stopping at five or six more stands. Peaches, strawberries, more tomatoes, a couple of watermelons, several cantaloupes, and more peaches (naturally). At each stop, I stayed close to him, feeling more a part of his ritual. I stood next to him with sunshine scorching the top of my head, cups of water feeding my perspiration, my eyes squinting into the old, heavily lined faces, appreciative dark eyes of old acquaintances. Most of the men I met were Mexican, and one looked Japanese. Their children helped with their parents' English while trying to broaden my grandfather's Spanish repertoire, giggling at his mispronunciations. The roll of hundred-dollar bills wasn't fazed and kept on coming; the smile on his hot, wet face continued, his conversations jovial, and his dusty, wrinkled, wet clothes a mess. The sun was repressively hot, but somehow it didn't diminish his zeal for stopping, talking, drinking six or seven more Cokes along the way, taking delight in putting a little "jingle" into hard-working hands.

The trunk of the Chrysler was large, but we couldn't squeeze in the second flat of tomatoes; they were large, juicy, and easily squished. That flat rode with us in the back seat, passed between the three of us, for the rest of the ride to Lake Tahoe. Even in the late afternoon, when we left the last fruit stand, the heat was still scorching. Granddaddy was satisfied, but his shirt and slacks by this time almost resembled work-worn overalls, moist with sweat, full of dust, wrinkled and splattered with assorted juice stains. His own hard work had provided him considerable privilege and he knew it, so he lent a hand, without mentioning to us how much giving back meant to him. He was comfortable with himself, emanating an easy confidence I strived for as a young man.

We followed Route 49 through old gold-mining towns, joined California highway 50 in Placerville, where the temperature read 103 degrees, and finally felt mild relief ascending into the Sierra

Nevada Mountains. Granddaddy dozed off and on until some-time before Meyers, when he woke, looked around, and excitedly exclaimed, "Now, be careful, Louise, be real careful, don't want a ticket. There are lots of police around here." He practically chortled when we rounded a curve, and lo and behold, a highway police car was stationed right next to the road. He faked a startled yelp and turned to us, saying, "Look out, the police!"

He'd gotten me so excited, I ducked when I saw the black and white, but quickly felt foolish when we passed it and I beheld a painted wooden cutout of a highway patrol car! The cutout was new that year, and Granddaddy delighted in joking with us. At heart he was always a jester.

At Meyers, we took a series of shortcuts, avoiding heavy traffic on Highway 50 into South Lake Tahoe, and when we regained the highway partway through town, I heard Granddaddy shout, "Quick, here, turn in here." Louise swerved into the parking lot of the Sportsman, an enormous hardware store, offering everything from light bulbs to small tools to large outboard boats and the motors to go with them. We traipsed after him, barely keeping up because he knew exactly what he wanted and where it was. He grabbed a hammer, a bag of large nails, half a dozen spools of fishing line, and then beelined to the rear, where he bought a dozen twelve-foot bamboo fishing poles and two boxes of hooks. Outside the Sportsman we ate a sandwich from a cart, somehow found room in the Chrysler to fit the poles, and continued through north along Highway 50, past Zephyr Cove, toward Cave Rock. Two hundred yards past the tunnel that goes through the rock, a small break in the highway pavement on the left marked the beginning of the road down to Granddaddy's cabin. It's easy to miss and that's good, in that snoopers miss it, traveling onward to somewhere else.

We didn't unload the Chrysler but followed his direction to gather the poles and follow him. Taking the hammer, nails, and hooks, we walked around the cabin to the steps leading down to the lake. He paused to take in the view of the sun setting behind the mountains across the lake, and almost sang, "Come on, still a couple hours of good fishing left."

Intrigued by this new development, I followed. Once on the pier, he rigged the poles with line and hooks, bent nails in an upside down "U" in eight spots on the pier, secured the poles and announced that while we fished, he was going to take a nap. "Whoever catches the first fish, we'll cook that for dinner."

He was visibly worn out. Heat and a long day on the road had done him in. I knew he was tired by how he trudged through the sand at the end of the pier and up the steps to the cabin. His pace was slow, labored, and he rested every ten steps or so. He was over seventy years old, but I'd always regarded him as invincible. A sour taste filled my mouth as I watched him climb doggedly and wearily up to the cabin. I had thought he would never weaken.

While he slept, Susan and I watched the poles farther out the pier, where the water was deep. Kit manned two poles nearer the shore, where if he fell in, we could easily pull him out. We thought he'd be happy watching minnows. I knew big fish didn't swim deep into the cove because the water was too warm. We might wait forever. The sun had set an hour ago, the light was dimming, and the temperature had cooled off only slightly. Fortunately, the large waves subsided when the sun set, the shoreline boulders were perfect for scampering on, and we could climb around while we watched our poles.

Meanwhile, Kit patiently tended his poles, hoping the ends would bob up and down, telling him he hooked a fish. Little did I suspect that would happen, but suddenly one gave a huge tug.

He yelled that he had a giant one, grabbed the pole out of the nail base, and maneuvered toward shore. He pulled out a fish at least six inches long, and he beamed with a wide-eyed smile and declared, "I have my dinner right here."

In the end, Susan and I caught nothing. Feeling skunked, we pulled our poles in the darkness and trucked them to the lake-side shed for safekeeping overnight. Louise had dinner prepared when we entered the cabin, but she acknowledged Kit's triumphant, smiling march into the kitchen exclaiming, "My catch, my dinner."

Granddaddy was awake, heard his excited cry, and made his way to the kitchen. The frying pan was loaded with lots of butter, spices, onions, and lemon, and a six-inch trout, and Granddaddy declared, "The best-looking trout I've ever seen. Good for you, Kit."

So dinner had a special flavor. Kit took his place next to Granddaddy, and although we all had small portions because everyone wanted a taste, Granddaddy declared it "the best tasting trout I've ever had." His pleasure was genuine, for Kit, with his smiling, freckle-filled face, rounded tummy, peevish humor and nature, undoubtedly tugged at memories of his middle son, our father. Family was not a topic for conversation, and that night was no exception. However, memories of my father were closer to the surface than ever before, as I would reluctantly experience toward the end of our stay.

While I slept, I kicked off my comforter more than once, squirming around through an unusually warm night for Lake Tahoe. When I awoke at dawn, it was still warm. Out on the deck I found the railings were bone dry, absent the beads of moisture that usually collected during the night. The sky was not brilliant turquoise, shrouded by a high haze that brightened the sunlight. The air was absolutely still. By breakfast time, a little before 8:00,

233

it was eighty degrees, without any breeze, and I could smell the heat rising from dry pine needles and earth. It didn't bother me because I was headed down to the lake to retrieve my rowboat, swim in the cold water, and discover who might be visiting Sky Water Lodge or the homes south of Granddaddy's pier.

After the morning had passed, I securely tied the rowboat and stood on the beach in almost tepid water, wondering if I could perspire under water. The climb up the steps to the cabin left me dripping. I crossed the deck and saw Granddaddy looking at the outside thermometer, patting his forehead with a hanky.

"It's hot, Hersch, real hot. This temp thing is either broken or it's over ninety-five degrees. Can't remember the last time this happened." His long slacks and shirts were unsuited for this heat, and I knew he wouldn't go down to the water unless he had to. Without a breeze, it didn't matter if we left all the doors and windows open. The clammy feeling made me feel that the Central Valley heat had followed us to the mountains.

"It usually doesn't last long, but this is awful. Hardly slept last night. How about you?" We exchanged our stories, and I could see how uncomfortable he was. I recalled watching him trudge up the steps from the lake. Knowing his age, plus how he had worn himself out at the fruit stands, I wanted to make sure he had his pills, especially for his heart. Louise was ever observant, and when I asked, she assured me that he did, but mentioned his labored breathing at breakfast.

I hoped the heat wave would break, but it didn't. By 3:00 the temperature read ninety-eight degrees and the air was so still, a balloon wouldn't move. The next day was the same, and the day after a degree hotter. Irritability began to infect everyone, as we milled around just to create some air movement. Granddaddy couldn't sleep at night, and trying to nap in the afternoon was

234

miserably frustrating. The high haze didn't budge, turning the lake into a steam cooker. I had the icy lake to dip into, so until afternoon I was well occupied. Inside the cabin, though, was stifling hot, and outside the sun beat down like a blast furnace. Open windows or doors made no difference day or night; the air didn't move.

On the fourth day of the heat wave, I returned to the cabin from the lake later than usual, expecting Granddaddy to be squirming in the chair next to his radio, trying to forget the heat and drift off to sleep. He was wide awake, twitching, with his eyes shut, flopping his arms when they stuck to the wooden armrests. I sat at the octagon table, opened a box of cards, and set out a game I could play by myself, waiting for time to pass. Near 5:00, his eyes opened, and he unexpectedly bounced up from his chair and began wildly waving his arms. He walked around the grand room, twisting his head as if trying to hear a distant sound. His animation caught me by total surprise, and I thought maybe something terrible had happened. Maybe he was suffering heatstroke, a heart attack, or worse. He acted like he had lost his good sense.

Suddenly he shouted, "Hersch, Susan, grab the sheets! Grab all the sheets!"

I thought he'd gone crazy. Alarmed, Susan emerged from her bedroom, saw him waving madly and shouting to "grab all the sheets off the beds." She stood rooted by the doorjamb, unsure what was going on.

He shuffled across the floor in stocking feet, nearly sliding into his bedroom, repeating urgently, "Hersch, grab the sheets, all of them. Move on. Hurry, hurry. Susan, you too."

I hesitated, still startled, watched him throw his bed cover aside, grab both sheets, and rip them off the bed. He did the same on the single bed, holding the big ball of sheets to his chest. He

235

came out in a determined rush and grinned, "Move on now, get them and follow me."

I hustled to my bedroom, not daring to fool around even if he was acting so crazy. I grabbed all the sheets I could hold. As I finished, I heard water pelting the metal sides of the shower in the bathroom. He shouted above the full blast, "Hurry up, you two, bring me your sheets!" I did, and he tossed them under the running water. "Hersch," he told me, "go get the stepladder. Quick. Hurry."

I was almost certain he'd lost it, thinking he just wanted to get wet for relief, but moved my fastest and retrieved the stepladder in a jiff. He was wringing excess water from sheets when I appeared at the bathroom door holding the stepladder. He didn't stop for an instant, barging past me, holding both arms around a huge soggy clump of white sheets. By this time his shirt and pants were soaked through. He signaled with his head to follow, and we stopped at the door leading out to the deck. He climbed the stepladder, took a wet sheet from me, draped it over the open door and pushed thumbtacks to hold it up, covering the entire doorway like he was building a kid's ghost house.

"Check on Susan, throw the rest of 'em in the shower. Soak 'em good and follow me." Susan was holding her sheets at the bathroom door, and I repeated what he said and backed up while he descended the stepladder.

We did the same thing at the other door out to the deck, located near his bedroom. He opened that door, draped a sheet over it, tacked it down, descended the stepladder, and headed for the front door. I followed, but halfway across the grand room I looked back at what I thought was a kid's playhouse and detected movement in the hung sheets. They slightly billowed into the cabin, rounding inward, catching a faint breeze!

After four miserable days of sweltering heat and stifling air, he had noticed a tender breeze from the west. We worked non-stop to mount sheets on all six doors in the cabin and some of the windows. The breeze flowed through the wet sheets, cooling the great room first. The refreshing air seeped into the bedrooms and kitchen, and it became a gentle wind as the end of daylight approached. We worked steadily, resoaking sheets and replacing drying ones with wet, dripping ones.

As we cooled down, the twinkle in his eye appeared, and he chortled. "How do you young'uns like Granddaddy's air conditioning!" He grinned, partly in relief from the heat, mostly from enjoying sharing his mountain knowledge with us.

I laughed to myself, shaking my head at my qualms, wondering why I ever doubted him. Old though he might be, his senses were as sharp as ever. Susan went so far as to nearly wrap herself in the front door's hanging wet sheet while the breeze cooled her.

The heat wave finally broke. That night all windows were open to allow cool lake air to drift throughout the cabin, lulling me to sleep. At dawn the next morning, I relished shivering on the deck, watching Lake Tahoe wake up below. A cool lake breeze was blowing from the west. I often laughed with Granddaddy later about his "air conditioning," both at Lake Tahoe and Atherton. His sharp senses added to my comfort and confidence in being with him. He was as pleased by the suspense he had created with his grandchildren and the relief of his family's laughter, as much as with the coolness his trick had created.

Granddaddy slept late, probably the first good sleep he'd gotten in four nights. I went down to the shore early in the morning and enjoyed being chilled by the cool breeze. With a lighter heart I prepared for a day of adventure, thinking I would hunt crawfish to start off the day.

Later in the afternoon, when I returned to the cabin, I found

237

myself with nothing to do. I decided to poke around. I'd explored every nook and cranny at 48 Spencer Lane and now I would do the same at Lake Tahoe. I knew a good place to start. Underneath the deck was a large storage area, enclosed by twelve-inch plank siding. The space was filled with old outboard motors; a ruined green one-person rowboat; oars, whole and broken; snowshoes; patio chairs; beach umbrellas; parts of fishing gear; tools; and lots of boxes. I quickly figured out that things had been first stored in the rear, and as time passed, each new item was stored closer to the entrance. That meant the old stuff was way in the back. I might even find boxes holding interesting memorabilia about the family. I likened the exploration to digging deeper into the geological strata of the earth, as I'd seen in a picture I had at home. The front boxes, filled with motor oil, spare parts, and extra oarlocks, gave way to rows of boxes crammed with old magazines. The covers of *Life* magazine in the 1940s looked dramatic and interesting, but they could wait. I had not yet reached the far back wall. I kept shifting boxes around, peeking inside in curiosity, until I was close. I spied a promising-looking box with what looked like a black shoelace hanging out. Three rows of boxes stood between me and the waxed box, but I forged a new path. I expected spiked baseball shoes, but sighed heavily when I opened it and found nothing but bunches of black shoelaces in a pile. I almost closed the lid, but listened to the voice in my head saying, "Nobody stores a big box of shoelaces." I pushed them aside, digging down. Yet I soon sighed again, disappointed, seeing nothing but old long baseball stockings.

The light in the far back was faint, filtering through cracks between planks, and I almost gave up. I was leery of black widow spiders as I gingerly lifted a sock out. To my surprise, it was very heavy, full of something. I spied black buckshot between the other socks. I absolutely knew I had found something, just didn't know what. The box was heavy, but I had made a path, and I lugged it out to the sunlight. Sure enough, several old, long baseball socks, some rotting, were filled with varying amounts of buckshot!

Granddaddy was inside, fiddling with the radio, probably trying to zero in on a baseball game. One corner of the box had rotted, spilling buckshot on the steps, so I wedged it against my belly as I swung the screen door open with my foot and plopped the box on the octagon table in front of him. Buckshot seeped out and rolled over the copper top, stopping at the rivets on the circumference.

"What in the world?" were his first words. "Are the stockings still inside the box?" I lifted the flaps so he could take a look. Leaning over, he roared in laughter, exclaiming, "Hersch, where in the world did you find these? Must be better'n thirty years old." He poked around until he found one stocking whole enough to lift out. It was limp and hung like a dead snake.

"Under the deck, way in the back. What are they?" I had no idea why someone would fill stockings with buckshot.

He held the stocking across both palms, lifting it up and down, as if weighing it. "Hersch, this is what I wore chasing those." He pointed to the heads of two bighorn sheep mounted above either side of the fireplace. "This is how I stayed in shape, tramping all over Wyoming and Montana chasing those critters in the winter with these on my ankles. Let me tell you, by the time I went to work in the spring, my legs were ready."

He dug deeply into the box and carefully pulled out an old sock, stiff with age, barely resembling a circle. "Hold this one, Hersch." He offered it to me and then watched my arm drop to the tabletop. It was full of buckshot and heavy. "That one I used racing the kids who wanted to make the team. I tied these around

239

my ankles and wore them the first month or so in spring. I lost a
lot of races in early training. When I finally was satisfied my legs
were ready, I took them off and flew like the wind."

He recalled particular races, telling me about the fellows he
knew would succeed and the ones who wouldn't. He had told me
on an earlier occasion that preparation, training, and determination were important, but I didn't mind him telling me again. In
my mind, I saw him racing young players, and I relished the idea
of taking off the weighted socks and flying like the wind around
the bases.

Usually, memories of his past brought a broad smile. He took
the shot-filled sock, laid it across his instep, sat up, and lifted his
foot. It didn't rise much. His brow furrowed, and he kept gazing
downward, barely moving, feeling the weight of time. When he
glanced up, he murmured, "That was a long . . . long time ago."
He was talking to himself as much as talking to me. The box of
weighted socks sat between us like a magic lantern. I fantasized
visions of seeing how fast he once was, and he had his wistful
memories of a golden time he longed for, his youth.

After the heat wave, the sunny, pleasant days passed quickly. I
filled my time rowing outside the cove, farther and farther in each
direction, looking for adventure. My liking and respect for Lake
Tahoe grew, partly because I took Granddaddy's admonitions
about the neutrality of nature to heart. Although I took risky
chances, I avoided too much injury, mainly because the lake's
beauty nurtured me. Of course, with all that rowing my muscles
grew stronger and stronger.

Late in the afternoon on the day before our departure, I was
playing a board game with Kit when Granddaddy came into the
great room and called me over. "Hersch, I need you to get something for me."

I expected to retrieve something from his car or from the storage area under the deck, but he said, pointing, "Get the ladder, it's up there." I looked up at the ceiling, which was ten or eleven feet high, and the only thing I saw was the large, round iron lamp hanging down. It held eight small lights, and the iron was worked to match the hunting scene on the fireplace screen.

He saw where my eye had settled and he corrected me. "No, no, way up, over by the chimney. I'll get the flashlight, you get the ladder." When I returned, he was standing in the small hall closet next to the front door, pointing up at a wooden ceiling panel. "Move that and you can get into the attic. Here's the light, I'll tell you where to go. Step on the crossbeams, and go slow."

I made my way into a pitch-black, musty attic, flashlight in hand. The high-pitched roof soared overhead. After I found my footing and looked around, I shouted down, "Okay, what's next?"

"Can you see the chimney? Head toward it. Don't stick your hand through the nails on the roof."

The underside of the steeply pitched roof was just above my head, and I spotted the nails holding down the roof shingles protruding inside. I trained my flashlight down at the parallel two-by-ten crossbeams as I began creeping toward the chimney. I took the opportunity to shine my flashlight all around, but the attic was empty. When I reached the granite chimney, I shouted down to him, "Okay, now what?"

He asked if I was at the chimney and I told him I was.

"Can you get around behind it?"

Most of the attic was wide open because of the high pitch of the roofline. The chimney rose along the front wall, and the space behind it was narrow and dark. I stooped, shined the light behind the granite blocks, and saw it would be a squeeze. I reported back, "Yeah, I think so, just barely."

241

I started to maneuver into the opening. Peering behind the chimney, I saw nothing but supporting two-by-fours. The space was four feet high at best, a tight fit, and the width of the granite chimney extended about six feet ahead.

He shouted, "Can you see some two-by-fours, about halfway in? One of them is newer than the rest. See it?"

He was right. The two-by-fours supporting the roof trusses next to the chimney were mostly charred with age. One was noticeably newer. I reported, "Yeah, I see it. Whadda you want me to do now?"

"There's a space at the top, two inches or so. Reach up there and yank it out."

I crawled in, reached up, and pulled. Nothing. The two-by-four didn't budge. It was wedged tight. I thought something was wrong, but heard him shout from below, "Give it a big yank, all you got."

So I did and it popped loose. I shouted, "Got it!"

"Okay, good work. Now reach inside and bring it down."

I had no idea what he was talking about, and I envisioned spiders of all kinds waiting for my hand to enter the dark. My other hand was holding fast onto the chimney stones for balance, and my flashlight rested on a crossbeam, so that was not much help. I held my breath; my fingers crawled into the dark slot. Bingo, I felt something that wasn't wood. I worked my hand around its round, smooth steel shape, and felt my throat tighten. Somehow I knew.

I pulled it out very carefully and regained my balance. I held it close and shined my flashlight up and down. Sure enough, it was a shotgun.

My breath caught in my throat. It was the same shotgun my grandfather had showed me while we were sitting in my father's Packard on our way down the side of the Snake River

Canyon to his boathouse, almost nine years ago when I was six years old. Although it was beautifully engraved, holding it jarred scary memories of that duck-hunting trip to the island. I could remember all too clearly my father forcing me to pull the trigger on the twenty-gauge, my bleeding fingers, the searing pain in my shoulder, rocks gouged into my palms, being terrified of my father's hot breath, then seeing my grandfather's hand appear, grip like a steel vise, and save me.

I gathered myself and crept back to the opening above the hall closet. Granddaddy was waiting below, and he pushed the coats aside when I shined my light on them.

"Don't worry, it's not loaded. Hand it down. I'll take the barrels, you hold the stock."

After passing him the shotgun, I climbed down the ladder and brushed myself off. As I came out of the closet, I looked around. "Where is everybody?" Susan, Kit, and Louise were nowhere to be seen.

"Went to the store, probably South Shore. Be a while." He was casually sitting in his chair, cradling the shotgun, wiping it with an oil rag.

"Come over here. Take a look. I want to show you this."

I came closer, and he continued, "Time to take this home. Been here too long."

He wiped the carved steel plate over the trigger guard, admiring what he held. "Here, let me show you something special, Hersch, look at this."

The sight of the shotgun, now standing upright next to him, grabbed my heart. Still, I ran my fingers over the carving in the steel. A hunting scene—a dog, a hunter, reeds next to water, and ducks. I managed to say, "I remember, Granddaddy."

I had startled him. "You what?"

243

"I remember. The Snake River. The duck hunt." My voice quavered.

"You remember?" He looked at me sharply.

"Yes, Granddaddy."

"Your father?"

"Uh-huh." I couldn't form a real word.

"You remember? You were so little." His disbelief faded, and he said repentantly, "Your father, he didn't mean to . . . I'm sorry . . ." He stopped as I shook my head.

"Granddaddy." It was the only thing I could think to say to make him stop.

"Hersch, your father, he . . ." He paused, trying to find his way. "Hersch, it was my fault. It was my fault. I—"

"Granddaddy, no!" I didn't want more.

"He didn't mean to . . ." His eyes searched my face. "If I'd been more . . ."

"Granddaddy!" I was certain I didn't want to hear any more from him.

The expression on my face must have said everything. Yet I was not going to melt. I reached for the strength inside of me that I'd seen in him, determined as I'd never felt before. I was not going to talk about the duck-hunting trip on the Snake River or the terrors I survived at 223 Pierce Street or my father's brutality and death. I would not stand for Granddaddy trying to carry the blame for my father. That would have forever changed everything between us. I'd lost my father; I was not going to lose my grandfather.

I quickly leaned down, put my face next to his, so he couldn't see me, so he wouldn't say anything more, and held him as tightly as I could. He wasn't sure what I was doing at first, but gradually his hand found its way around my back and I felt his grip, strong and reassuring, the one I remembered from the Snake River.

When we let go, our conversation was over. The last rays of sunlight against the knotty pine walls and ceiling gave the large room a honeyed glow. My grandfather had the sense to choke back all his explanations about what could never be forgiven.

I pulled the ottoman close to his chair. He wiped his shotgun again, put it on my lap, and leaned slightly back as I read. I ran my fingers over the inscription: "To Ty Cobb from the City of Detroit. World's Greatest Baseball Player." The date was 1926. I smiled, not at the commemorative shotgun, but at how my grandfather had listened to me. He knew that our bond grew from the trust that had developed between us, and knew I needed the same trust now. He could not take any blame. Only I could excise the scars my father left behind.

CHAPTER NINE

"So, You Met Mr. Al Stump!"

E arly one Saturday, Aunt Shirley and I were the only ones stirring except, of course, for Grandma, who always was up at 5:00, tending her garden in the coolness of early morning. I sat at the breakfast room table at my grandmother's house in Portola Valley, and Aunt Shirley stood at the Wedgewood stove, patiently watching the blue flame on the burner lick the bottom and sides of the old aluminum coffee pot. Shirley and her husband, Dixie Beckworth, and my grandmother built the home in Portola Valley together, each with their own separate wing. By now the pink-orange of dawn had already faded. As long as I could remember, Shirley used the same kind of inexpensive drip pot, even though every year Grandma bought her a new shiny automatic coffee maker of some kind. It consisted of two pots, one on top of the other, made of cheap, lightweight aluminum. The top pot held the grounds and received steaming hot water, while the bottom pot held the finished coffee. Shirley poured the steaming water over the grounds and waited.

"Want some?" she asked, engagingly, but not really expecting me to say yes.

"Sure, I'll try." I responded in as firm a voice as I could muster, since she knew I didn't drink coffee. She brought me a cup and returned to the stove to watch my reaction.

I sipped from the cup and felt my mouth revolt. "That tastes awful. What's in it?" I put the cup down and wiped the bitterness inside my mouth with my tongue and my puckered lips with the back of my hand.

"A little salt. Started drinking it this way when I was in the Red Cross in Italy during the war. Got rid of the taste of foul water. Now it keeps people away from my coffee." She flashed a sly grin, showing her wry, pointed humor. Her grin was just like her father's, filling her face to the edges.

Aunt Shirley's similarities to my grandfather ran wide and deep. Like him, she was fiercely independent, determined, intellectually active and probing, and stubborn. She had owned Shirley Cobb Books, a bookstore in Palo Alto, since she was a young woman, and was both very confident and respectful of her role in the community. She was proud of having started her own business, of knowing exactly what her customers liked. She appreciated good writing and preferred being around bright people, especially in the publishing industry. Like her father, she had a knack for knowing what people were like and what they might do. Also like her father, her temperament did not have patience with shallowness. So, in my view, which I never directly shared with her, they were so much alike, they "bumped against each other" instead of "shaking hands."

While I wiped the bitterness off my lips, she asked in an incisive tone, "How was your visit with the Old Man?"

She moved from the stove to the sink and started fussing with some dishes as she waited for me to answer. The day before I'd spent at Granddaddy's house by myself. Grandma had dropped me off early in the morning while she ran errands.

Shirley repeated her question, only this time with more force. "Well, how was it? Did the Old Man behave himself?" She viewed her father harshly, but referring to him as "The Old Man" wasn't meant to convey that he was old or feeble, but rather described someone who sat on top of a mountain, defying any and all to come up and knock him off. That's how she saw him, defiant and stubborn. She was always more than curious about Susan's or my experience with Granddaddy, for what we reported to her never fit the lens she used to view him.

"It was okay. He seemed a little tired. Maybe he didn't feel too well," I answered.

Then she said, with a point-blank inflection I'd heard before, "So, you met Mr. Al Stump!" When Shirley did not think much of somebody, she used a tone of voice that had the same effect as realizing you just stepped in dog doo with your best shoes on. It was more than disgust; it was the utter dismissal of a wretched person.

I glanced out the window, recalling the previous day with a vividness that put a grin on my face. I'd gotten up early and wandered into the kitchen. Finding nobody there, I poured myself some orange juice and sat at the kitchen table, which was painted red and had black iron legs. The clock said 7:15. The house was quiet, so I guessed that Aunt Shirley and Uncle Dixie had already left for work. Susan and Kit were asleep. I was watching some birds feeding on the ground in the flowerbed just outside the window when the back door opened. Grandma sailed in, smiling and waving to me.

She wore a smock, covered in dirt, a long-sleeve blouse, flowing skirt, rubber boots, a big hat, and rubber gloves that she took off and left on the clothes washer in the back porch. "Good morning, Hersch," she said, still smiling at me. "Hungry?" This was not really a question. She already knew I was hungry. She was just announcing her intention to fix me something good to eat. There was hardly a break in her movements from taking off her hat, removing her gloves and smock, shuffling out of her muddy boots into house slippers, moving to the stove, lighting a burner at full blast, putting a pan on it, and reaching into the refrigerator for butter, bacon, and some eggs. The pan got hot real fast, sizzled the bacon, and filled the kitchen with the familiar smell of cooking bacon. She whipped up the eggs with a little milk and poured them into a second pan on top of melted butter. Bread went into the toaster. In between moving the pans, I saw her smile, and heard the shuffle of house slippers, and a soft whistling sound.

Soon, a plate of food was set in front of me with a mound of strawberry jam on the side. The strawberries came from her garden, and the toast came from bread baked in her stove. At least three scrambled eggs, with butter oozing at the edges, six strips of bacon, a glass of milk, and biscuits left over from dinner were ready to tempt me. Grandma sat down, holding a cup about half-filled with tea. The cup was so thin, I could see light through it. She didn't drink coffee.

"I'm going to town later this morning. Want to come with me?"

I stuck a big bite into my mouth and thought for a second. "Can I go to Granddaddy's?"

"I don't know, it's kind of short notice. He might have

something planned. I don't know how he's doing." Her tone of voice was warm, but quickly firming on the side of saying no.

"He said it's okay to come anytime. Besides, I'll play outside in the jungle." I was slightly pleading, sensing I had to work my way to her saying yes.

"Jungle?" Her face showed her amusement.

"That's what we call the backyard. It's a mess of bushes and old stuff. And the pool is only half filled, has a big branch in it, so that's the swamp." My grandmother's smile widened. She smiled easily, and for her, life was like her gardens: all that was needed was good soil, water, and nurturing. So, for her grandchildren, good food, love and affection, and play were always abundant. Then she watched things grow and develop. She continued to smile as I described more of Granddaddy's backyard, playing there, and I knew I was making progress. She finally said she'd call and see if it was okay. This meant she would call Louise and make her usual inquires about Granddaddy's health, mood, and condition.

The phone was on the wall, next to the table where we were sitting; Grandma held the hand-piece two or three inches from her ear. I knew if Granddaddy answered, she would hang up. She would never talk to him. She wasn't mad, or anything I could see in that way, so I didn't understand completely. But I knew she hadn't spoken to him in years, and probably never would.

We, the grandchildren, and especially my sister, had asked Aunt Shirley to tell us why Grandma and Granddaddy never spoke to each other now. One night we were sitting in Aunt Shirley's room, talking and putting off going to bed. Susan asked what Grandma and Granddaddy were like when they were young, and what happened to cause the separation.

Shirley took a breath and started slowly, "She still loves that old . . ." Then her voice trailed off to silence in front of her small audience.

"But if she loves him, why won't she talk to him?" Susan's voice was a mixture of questioning and bewilderment.

"Your grandmother still loves him and . . ." She caught her breath, changed the subject, picked up a book, and started reading. I watched the expression on her face drift as if returning to her youth. No pages in her book turned for several minutes. She finally said, "I think it's time for you two to hit the sack. Now, scoot out of here. And brush your teeth." There was hardly any breath in her voice. We sat for a moment, but the door had closed on the past, and we had no way of pushing it open that night. I kissed Aunt Shirley and left. Susan remained, but I don't know if they talked anymore.

My reverie was broken as Grandma said firmly into the phone, "Oh, Louise. Hello, this is Mrs. Cobb. Yes, nice to hear your voice too. Just fine, everything's just fine. Louise, please ask him if Hersch can visit him today. In about an hour, maybe a little sooner. I know it's early, but just check with him. Yes, just Hersch, the others are still asleep. Yes, he's had breakfast, but will need lunch, if he can stay that long. For as long as is okay. Yes, all day is fine. Yes, yes, just ask him. Thank you."

I knew it was very awkward for Grandma to phone, but once Louise answered, the request would be made, and I hoped it was okay. I waited along with Grandma as she held the receiver a few inches from her ear, and leaned on the countertop, waiting. Finally, she became alert, listening to the voice coming from the phone.

"Oh, really. That's just what he wants to hear. No, no. I'll pack some things for him. I think I know what he'll need. Thank you, Louise. Yes, I'll drop him off in about an hour. Thank you. Good-bye."

She winked at me. "Well, Mr. Lucky, seems your grandfather doesn't have anything planned today and would love to see you. But not until after 9:00. Want to wake up Susan and Kit and ask them to go with you?"

"Not really," I answered, struggling to hide my excitement and trying to remain nonchalant.

"All right, then. Go and put on some nice long pants—and take your shorts, just in case you fall into the 'swamp.' I'll go and change, and we'll leave in a few minutes. It's early, so I hope you don't mind running some errands with me." She rubbed her hands on a dishtowel and walked out of the kitchen.

All the pans and cooking stuff would have to sit in the sink and on the stove until later. I knew that if we cleaned up, the noise would wake Susan and Kit and they would want to come with me. Grandma always understood more than she let us know.

Grandma stopped at Bing's Nursery on the way into town and bought two flats of colorful flowers. She took a little while to choose just which colors she wanted around her patio, so 9:00 had already passed when we turned into the driveway at 48 Spencer Lane. Grandma pulled slowly into the driveway, and I saw Granddaddy's black Chrysler parked in front of the garage, which was past the house on the right-hand side. There was another car, a blue sedan, parked just at the corner of the house, before the drive curved in front. I didn't recognize this car, but Grandma did.

"It looks like you have company. Louise didn't mention anybody to me." Her voice carried more worrisome concern than pleasant surprise.

She pulled around the curve to the front patio just as the large front door opened. Louise came out of the house and hurried to Grandma's side of the car. I heard, "I'm sorry, Mrs. Cobb." She was expecting a reproach, and she quickly explained. "Mr.

Stump arrived a little while ago, after you called. I didn't know he was coming today. I don't think Mr. Cobb expected him either. They're in the living room, talking. I don't think he'll stay long, so I expect everything's okay for Hersch to visit."

The engine was running, and Grandma turned and looked at me. I had never met Mr. Stump, but I'd heard his name before and knew Grandma was deciding whether to let me stay or not.

Finally she said to Louise, "You call me if anything is amiss. Understand? I don't want Hersch talking with Mr. Stump. Is that clear?" Her voice was not loud, but firmly set in this instruction.

Louise answered quickly, "Yes, Mrs. Cobb. I understand. If Mr. Stump doesn't leave soon, I'll call you."

Both Grandma's hands were on the steering wheel, and I watched her fingers massage the wheel through her white gloves as she said, "Now, Hersch, go on in and see your grandfather, but I don't want you talking to Mr. Stump. Be polite, but don't sit and talk with him. Understand?"

I didn't know quite what to say, but I nodded my head, bundled my extra clothes in my arms, reached over, and kissed Grandma on her cheek. "I'll be okay, Grandma." That was easy to say, but I sure didn't know what to expect.

I slid out, closed the car door, and watched Grandma drive away. She waved her small hand, as she passed through the gate. I felt excited and smiled. Something was going on, and I was the only one here to see it. No brother, sister, aunts, or cousins. I thought, "Granddaddy must be in a snit or something." I'd always wanted to see what Aunt Shirley was forever hinting at. "Granddaddy must be mad . . . This is going to be great." All this and more occurred in a flash as Grandma drove off. I turned toward the front door with my bundle of extra clothes, took a quick step, and bumped into Louise.

253

"Hold on, Herschel, what have you got there, extra clothes?" Her drawl was slow and low and startled me back to the present. It didn't seem to bother her that I had absently walked right into her. She was five feet nine or ten inches tall and pretty big.

I straightened up as best I could and mumbled. "Yes, ma'am, clothes, just in case I fall in the mud."

"Mud?" she asked.

"Out in the back, in the swamp. The pool, I mean. You know, if I'm playing back there." I stumbled through my sentence, getting my balance, and pulling my clothes close to my chest.

"Oh, I see. Well, let me take those, and you go on in. Mr. Cobb is expecting you. Now, go on!" She took my bundle, put her hand on my left shoulder, and guided me toward the front door. I walked off, feeling awkward and puzzled because Louise's voice didn't sound like there was a wild scene going on. In fact, she was calm as the slight breeze blowing across the yard. I picked up my stride, hit the front door step in three big leaps, and burst into the living room. When I saw Granddaddy, I stopped in my tracks.

Nothing was the matter. He was sitting in the same chair he always sat in, waving to me to come over, smiling with that silly twinkle in his eye. His voice was no different either.

"Hersch, it's good to see you. Early, though. Come over here."

By the time I reached his side, I saw what was different. There was something going on. Only, I couldn't figure out what. He was wearing his beige gabardine slacks and summer shoes, but he was still wearing his nightshirt! It had no collar, and the sleeves were three-quarter length. And he hadn't shaved. His white whiskers showed all over his face. I leaned over to kiss him, and he pulled me into a hug and my cheek rubbed against his.

254

"Ugh, your face is all scrappy, Granddaddy." I pulled away, rubbing my cheek with my left hand. "You didn't shave!"

"Oh, yeah. Been up for a while but haven't had a chance to shave. Your cheek okay?" His voice was slightly raspy too. "Had a visitor since early this morning. Got here just after you called. Sort of unexpected."

I glanced around the room. "Who's here? I don't see anybody." The door to his office was open, I noticed. The wall where Granddaddy's desk and file drawers were placed was the portion of the room I could see. Only I couldn't see his desk because a man in a blue sports coat was hunched over it, his back to me, with a drawer open in front of him. He was lifting papers out of the file drawer, putting them on the desk, and then slipping them into a dark folder lying on the desktop. I watched for a moment, and then turned to Granddaddy, just as he started talking.

"Al! Al, where are you? He was here a minute ago. Went to the bathroom, down the hall."

"There's a man in your office," I said slowly and directly.

Granddaddy shifted his whole body to look over his left shoulder toward his office. His quick movement startled me, and I stepped backward, knocking against the ottoman next to his chair. When he spoke this time, his voice sounded more like a lion than a person.

"Al. What the hell are you doing?" he bellowed. "Excuse me, Hersch," he said quietly, then yelled again, "Al, get the hell out of there. What the hell are you doing?" His face flushed fiercely red, and he was just starting to rise from his chair as the man nearly ran out of the office.

"Sorry, Ty. The door was open, and I couldn't help but admire your pictures. The signed one of you and Ruth is so great. Wish it were mine." He talked in a high, rushed tone as if to cover up being caught. I used that tone many times when I did not want an adult to know what I had been doing.

255

The stooped man was middle-aged, slightly pudgy, and noticeably puffy around his eyes. He dropped the dark folder on the sofa
at the back of the living room and stood before Granddaddy,
looking sheepish, like he wanted to dodge a verbal blast. "I'd
really like to get some more material on you and Ruth, and on
your early investments." His eyes darted toward the folder he'd
tossed onto the sofa but then shifted to me. "Oh, but who is this
handsome young man?" I looked back at him, but remained in
place. He had a full head of hair on top, an avaricious look in his
eyes that went with a forced smile, surrounded by a two-day-old
beard. The blue sports coat was soiled on one lapel, and the red
plaid shirt underneath was unbuttoned at the last button before it
tucked into his pants, exposing his white undershirt.

Granddaddy was rearranging himself in his chair. His face
was still pink with anger, the veins in his arms visibly stood out,
and his irritation was barely controlled. "Now, Al, I've told you a
dozen times, I don't want you in my office—" He didn't finish
because he was interrupted.

"Now, Ty. I'm your biggest fan and admirer. I just wish I'd seen
you play, you know, really burn those base paths. Nobody can do
that stuff today. The spikes and all." His hands were raised in surrender, moving up and down to calm Granddaddy.

"Al, I've told you about the spikes, over and over. I don't want
to talk about that. You know how it was back then. I never used
them that way—" I could tell that any patience Granddaddy had
was fading fast. His neck and face were still red, and he focused his
eyes on Mr. Stump with such intensity that he moved backward
a step. His voice crackled with a force that I could feel; it wasn't
loud, but it filled the room.

"Yes, yes, that's what I meant, Ty," the man interrupted. "I
just wish I was there. But the pictures are great. Tell me again

about Baker." His voice became even and steady, and he edged between me and Granddaddy. "And tell me about this young man. Introduce me, Ty."

Granddaddy squirmed in his seat as he regained his temper. "Al, this is my grandson, Herschel Jr. Call him Hersch. Hersch, this is Mr. Al Stump." His voice carried that resignation that grown-ups have whenever the intensity they just felt would have to wait for another time. He motioned for me to come over to him.

I moved toward Granddaddy's chair and said at the same time, "Hi, Mr. Stump." I could see his forehead was wet with little beads of sweat. I didn't offer my hand, nor did he offer his.

"Hersch, Mr. Stump is helping your grandfather write a book. It's about my life in baseball. I want the record set straight before I die." His right hand tightened around my waist. "A lot has been written about me, most of it by people who weren't there. I want the true record set down. Your granddaddy's been through a lot, and I want the truth known before I leave this world."

"Ty, you're going to be just fine," Mr. Stump jumped in. "You look great, and you've got the best doctors. You're going to be fine." He continued in an ingratiating tone, "And I've got a lot of great material. I want to get some more, though, but what we have is just great. I mean, I need some personal stuff—say, maybe I could take the bat from the office, you know, the one with the Babe's signature, and Sisler's, and yours, and take it and have it photographed. Yeah, that would be great." His voice was rushed, like a kid who was asking for ten chocolate chip cookies when he probably wasn't going to get any.

"Al, be quiet. I was just telling Hersch what I am doing. He doesn't know everything about Granddaddy. Maybe he's heard some stories. I want my record straight. Granddaddy wasn't all bad, you know." His thumb tugged on my belt loop in rhythm

257

with his voice and words, as if for emphasis. He was talking to me like he wanted to explain something important. But I didn't know specifically what in his past he was talking about, and Mr. Stump looked like a vulture about to pounce on his dying prey.

"Ty, I was just talking about the human side. You know, people want to know more nowadays. So, maybe some more personal stuff. The bat, maybe some of the nicer pictures. Signed, right. I could take them and have them copied or something. That would add a lot." He was pleading, inveigling to get the bat and photos into his hands.

"Mr. Cobb, is everything all right?" Louise had just rounded the corner from the dining room. She looked flustered, but I guessed she had wanted to wait until Granddaddy either exploded or it passed over. She stopped suddenly and exclaimed, "Oh, Mr. Cobb, you still have your nightshirt on. And with guests here."

Mr. Stump spoke right up. "Louise, maybe you should take Ty back to his room and find him a shirt, and make sure he's had his medicine." He moved out of the way and made room for Louise to approach.

"Have you had your shot, Mr. Cobb?" she asked.

"Oh, Louise, I don't know. Maybe I forgot. Al got here so early, I didn't have a chance. But it's okay, I feel just fine. We were talking about my book."

"Now, Mr. Cobb. You'll feel poorly later on if you don't have your insulin. Now, let's go take care of that. We'll be done soon enough." She sounded firm, and she was his nurse.

I knew Granddaddy took an insulin shot every day because he'd given one to himself in front of me several times. The first time had been a real surprise. I was visiting early in the morning and went back to his room before he was finished dressing. He was sitting in a chair next to his closet when I entered, and he called me over to him, told me that he was still tough as ever, and knew how to take good care of himself. At the same time, he filled a syringe by sticking the needle into a bottle, flicked a little liquid off the end, and placed his thumb on the plunger. He told me to watch. My eyes became huge when he grabbed his thigh with his other hand, bunched up some flesh, and plunged the needle into himself. He emptied the liquid into his leg, pulled the needle out, rubbed his thigh a little and looked up at me and smiled, very pleased. I felt a little sick to my stomach. I'd never seen anything like that in my life.

He patted my shoulder, gave a little laugh, and walked into his dressing room. A moment later, he came out dressed and smiling and said, "How about something to eat?" I couldn't really answer because I still felt queasy, but I followed him into the kitchen, where Louise had his breakfast waiting for him.

Louise started helping Granddaddy get out of his chair, saying, "Come, Mr. Cobb, you'll feel better with a nice clean shirt on."

He resisted a bit, but she kept talking about not wanting to call the doctor, that it would just take a few minutes and he would feel much better. She was insistent, and soon he was walking, with Louise at his elbow, down the back hallway toward his room.

After they were out of earshot, Mr. Stump turned to me and said, "Well, young Hersch, why don't we go and find some hot chocolate for you?" His voice was dripping with sweetness, and I thought of the witch in Hansel and Gretel. "Let's go see what I can find for you."

I could feel a speck of fear and excitement as I followed him to the kitchen. He opened the refrigerator, took out a glass bottle of milk, and then started going through the cupboards looking for cocoa.

He spotted the Nestlé package and put it on the drain board.

259

"You know, Hersch, your grandfather and I are good friends. He trusts me, and he doesn't have many people around him he can really trust. He wants his book to tell the whole story of his life, no matter what happened. He doesn't want anything left out, you know what I mean?"

He didn't wait for me to answer before he continued, "Perhaps you can help me. Ty might like that. I understand you spend your summers with him? Is that right?"

"W-well, yeah," I stammered a bit, and then quickly added, "but not the whole summer, just a few weeks. We usually go up to Tahoe for a while."

"Sure. That's what I meant. Just you?" I could tell he was measuring his words, like he didn't want to make a mistake.

"Oh, no," I answered, "usually me and my sister and brother. And his nurse."

"That's nice," he said. "Well, tell me, what it is like being with him? You know, the three of you and your grandfather. What's he like with you? What do you all do up there?" While he spoke, he fumbled with the cocoa, the milk, and the glass, keeping his eyes glued on me. He put a level soupspoon of cocoa into the glass and stirred. I told him I wanted more chocolate, and he put in a second huge spoonful and stirred some more, all the while forcing a wheedling smile in my direction.

"Oh, play on the beach, row around the cove, swim, ride in his Chris-Craft, fish, stuff like that," I said. "Once every few days we go out to dinner."

When I said this, he brightened up and looked eagerly right at me. "Really, is that so? Ty wants me to write some more about him getting out and about, you know that? Now, when you go out with him, does your granddaddy like a drink or two before dinner? Maybe he has some buddies he likes to have a drink

260

with?" He was stirring the glass faster and faster, acting like his question was the most natural one in the world.

"I don't know about that, Mr. Stump," I answered. He had my attention now. I saw the same narrow-eyed look as in the living room, as if I was now his prey. I sat up straighter in the chair, totally alert.

"It's okay if he drinks a little, Hersch. You can tell me about it. I'm just a little curious and need you to help me. Understand?" His voice sounded sincere as he stirred the chocolate milk absently. "Men in his day were tough. They played ball hard, and getting blocked or spiked was part of the game. They were entitled to their drinks, know what I mean?" He looked at me like a lecturer in school expecting the right answer. But it felt like a bear trap was about to spring shut.

"I've never actually seen Granddaddy drink whisky, Mr. Stump," I answered flatly. I swallowed hard because I remembered the night at the North Shore Club. Granddaddy had set his glass on the table, but it was just as full at the end as in the beginning. Mr. Stump was disappointed at me for not delivering, but what I said was the truth. I'd heard stories, and I'd read stuff, and people like Mr. Stump were always interested, but I never smelled it on him or saw it. I saw him drink a lot of Coca-Cola, but I didn't mention this to Mr. Stump.

"Maybe you didn't see him directly. No matter. I'm sure you had fun. Where do you go out?" he continued, lowering his voice.

"Well," I said, thoughtfully, wondering where this questioning was going, "Granddaddy likes the North Shore Club, and they know him there." I explained to Mr. Stump that he seldom went to South Shore, preferring the club, which was situated right on the highway going around the north end of Lake Tahoe. It was the fanciest restaurant and club at that end of the lake, and even

261

though Granddaddy's cabin was closer to South Shore, the man in charge of choosing seats for people knew Granddaddy pretty well and always greeted him by his last name. The four of us usually had a table right in front of the show.

Mr. Stump handed me the glass of chocolate milk and rocked back against the wooden drain board. He looked like he was considering how to move the conversation forward. He put the spoon in the sink and asked, "Did Ty have a lady friend up there, at the lake, I mean?"

"You mean, like a girlfriend or something like that?" I asked.

"Yeah, like that. When you went out, or to the North Shore Club."

"Nah, his nurse never even went with us," I told him. "Once in a while a friend would sit with us, and Granddaddy would talk a lot with him. A man who lives at Mr. Bliss's place. A lot of baseball stories and stuff about hunting."

"Didn't they enjoy a drink together, Hersch? You know, it would be nice to write something about Ty enjoying a good time with a friend, laughing it up and carrying on a little bit. People like to read about that stuff, you know?" He smiled broadly as he spoke.

"What 'stuff,' Mr. Stump?" I stiffened again in my chair. I didn't like talking to him anymore. I also remembered my grandmother's instruction. But I was here and felt a wave of determination to correct this man.

"I heard a story once that Ty had too much to drink at a club at Tahoe and made quite a fuss. You must have heard stories about his drinking. You have, haven't you, Hersch? The stories, I mean." He was trying to sound sincere, leaning casually against the drain board. The chocolate milk stayed in the glass in front of me, untouched. "He must enjoy a little whisky up at the lake?"

I tried to maintain an even tone, but I was angry and a little nervous. Then I suddenly recalled Granddaddy telling me about getting the other guy off balance in a situation by doing the unexpected. I decided to go in a different direction, and continued, "You know, I've been up to the lake with Granddaddy every year since I can remember. We do lots of things up there and see lots of people. Have you ever been up to the lake with him, Mr. Stump?"

"You mean, to his place at Cave Rock?"

"Yeah, to his cabin there," I replied.

"Well, not really. We've talked about it, and I expect we'll go up there together soon. I want to spend some good time with him. You know, Hersch, I'm a sportswriter. Write about lots of athletes. Tell their story. Most of them aren't as famous as your grandfather. So I've been spending most of my time lately writing and trying to get published. I really want to do this one right. Tell about his career, of course, but I want to write about what he did off the field. People really like that stuff. And, Ty—your grandfather—well, as you probably know, was a pretty colorful ball player. He still is. Has a temper, you know. There are lots of stories. Have you ever seen him really mad?" He was moving his hands back and forth in front of him, smiling, acting very friendly. He also had gotten back to probing me, hoping for family secrets.

I started thinking. From where I was sitting, I could see through the butler's pantry into the dining room, and out the window to the front yard. It was a sunny day. I turned to Mr. Stump and said, "Yeah, I did see him really mad one time." I made my voice serious, almost dramatic.

Mr. Stump's face came alive. He leaned slightly forward and said, "See, I told you. Good. Now, did he hit somebody? Tell me everything. I'd like to hear all the details. This is exactly what I'm looking for." He looked around the kitchen, as if searching for something important. "Tell me all the details, how he took this guy apart. Is there some paper in here, a note pad or something? I'd like to get this all down. Wait a minute, Hersch, I want something to write with."

He hurried over to the telephone, looked in the drawer and cupboard, didn't find what he wanted, then moved to the next set of drawers and cupboard. No luck. He didn't find a pencil or pad or anything he wanted. He was across the room when he blurted out, "Oh, shit. Just like that SOB." Then he calmed down and said, "Okay, Hersch, just tell me as clear as you can remember, how he hit the guy?"

"Well, Mr. Stump," I started very slowly, "Granddaddy didn't actually hit anybody. Probably wanted to, though, if somebody had been there." I paused, and before I could continue, Mr. Stump jumped in, questioning,

"What do you mean? He had to. I mean, what happened? Did the guy run? Tell me just the way it was, understand?"

I felt his urgency, demanding that I answer. "We arrived at the cabin just after sunset, really tired and hungry. The front door to the cabin was wide open. The window was busted and someone had broken in. Granddaddy was really mad. He rushed inside, came right back out again, and told us to stay in the car, lock the doors, and don't get out. I remember he was in his socks. He stayed inside for what seemed a long time, and I talked to Susan and Louise about what we saw. Louise said this had happened before, strangers usually looking for something to steal. They'd watch a place for lights at night, then pick one that stayed dark for a few nights, and break in during the next day. The neighbors were really too far away to do anything, and Pete, the man who watched over the place, looked in only now and then."

264   I continued telling Mr. Stump what happened. "Granddaddy came out of the house while we were talking and motioned for

me to roll down the window. He told me that nobody was inside. He said that was lucky for the guy, because he'd tear him apart if he found him.

"Nothing was taken, but Granddaddy said they were probably looking for his guns. He said they'd never find them." I knew that was true because I knew where they had been hidden.

"Guns? What kind of guns? Pistols or what?"

"I don't really know, Mr. Stump," I said, fudging a little, though I instantly remembered his shotgun from Detroit, "probably hunting guns. Like, for ducks."

"No, no, no," Mr. Stump said, "that's not what I want." He was turning away, looking out the window over the kitchen sink. I could hear him mumble, "Damn, this isn't working."

When he turned to me, his voice was a little tired. "Didn't you see him pummel somebody, sometime?"

"Pummel? What's that?" I answered.

"Beat up, knock down, attack!" He was almost pleading.

"Well, if that guy had been in the cabin . . ." I tried to imagine what Granddaddy would have done. "But, no, Mr. Stump, not really. We went places, out on the lake, had dinner with his old friends, did stuff, talked, you know, that kind of stuff."

I pretended to volunteer an interesting nugget. "One time we went to the bank in Carson City, and the owner showed us the main vault. It was huge. And inside he gave us a silver dollar. Marked 1896. Wrapped in plastic. Really cool." I casually looked up at him. "Does this help your book?"

His hands were leaning on the back of a chair, his fingers working his grip, and his mouth was clenched tight. He didn't move, except for his fingers. I didn't know what he was going to do, but I stopped worrying when I heard footsteps crossing the living room. The carpet muffled Granddaddy's steps just enough so Mr. Stump didn't hear them. When the steps hit the hard-wood floor of the dining room, Mr. Stump turned around to face the sink, turned on the water, and started washing his hands. Granddaddy's imposing figure filled the doorway to the kitchen. He wore a clean short-sleeve shirt and had shaved. He immediately walked over to Mr. Stump and pressed his body next to him, both of them facing the window. His voice was a bit muffled, but I could make out their conversation.

"Al, what the hell have you been doing? Have you been pumping Hersch?" His voice had an explosive edge to it that didn't even start to hide the fury behind it. "I told you earlier that I didn't want my grandkids quizzed. Understand?"

Mr. Stump turned a bit to look at Granddaddy and said, "Now, Ty, I wasn't doing anything like that. Fixed the boy some chocolate, that's all. We were just chatting a little."

Granddaddy didn't hesitate, took Mr. Stump by the arm, moving him along, nearly lifting him, through the kitchen. "Hersch, Mr. Stump has to go now. I'll see him to the front door. Isn't that right, Al? Don't you have something to take care of?"

Mr. Stump stammered, "S-sure, Ty, that's right. Okay, yeah, I think I'd like to go now. I'll call you later." Granddaddy kept his arm pinned and more or less pushed him out the front door. I heard some conversation and the door slam. I couldn't make out what was said, but just as quickly as Granddaddy had left the kitchen, he reappeared. He started to say something, but the doorbell rang.

Louise answered it, and I could hear Mr. Stump's rushed voice say, "Sorry, Louise, I forgot my folder. I'll just grab it off that sofa, over there. Just one second."

Granddaddy and I had walked to the dining room and just as I saw Mr. Stump start to walk into the house, I called, "I'll get it for you, Mr. Stump." I hustled in front of him to the sofa. Mr. Stump stopped in his tracks because Granddaddy was glaring at him. I took the folder off the sofa and opened it.

"Is this what you want, Mr. Stump?" Inside was an autographed photo of Ty Cobb, Babe Ruth, Tris Speaker, and Granddaddy's friend, Frank Mackey, signed by each of them, and dated.

Mr. Stump looked shocked. At the same time his hands went out from his sides like he was pleading for mercy.

Granddaddy took the folder from my hands, looked down at the picture, then at Mr. Stump, and seethed, "Get out of here, Al."

Louise was flustered, but Mr. Stump backed up through the door, turned, and left.

The next sound was the front door closing again.

Granddaddy and I went back into the kitchen. He held the folder with the autographed picture in it, as he pulled out a chair and sat down. He crossed his right leg over his left and began tapping his fingers on his knee.

He said, "Well, I guess you and Al had a little talk, huh? Did he ask a lot of questions?"

"Yeah. He wanted to know what we—no, actually, what you—did at the lake. Stuff like drinking whisky or going out. You know, stuff like that. He asked about a fight. Did you get into a fight? It was weird. He almost got mad at me, I think. What kind of a book is he writing, anyway?" I could feel my body relaxing and I was more comfortable. "Will you tell me?"

He hesitated. "Okay, sure, I guess," he replied, his voice resonant, lower. "Hersch, you know Granddaddy is not as young as he used to be. I've got doctors and they tell me I've got to take better care of myself. Before I leave this world, I want the true record of what I did in baseball put down. Now, Al has his problems and makes mistakes. He pokes around way too much and wants to

267

make things a lot bigger than they are. He asks everybody too many questions. But he's working on Granddaddy's book, and we're pretty far into it. I haven't seen the writing yet, but we've talked a lot, and he says it's coming along. I don't want to start new with someone I don't know at all. I don't have time. I just don't have time."

I knew he meant it. I remembered that when we had walked together this year, he put his hand on my shoulder, leaning more heavily on me than last year. And Louise was doing almost all of the driving. He loved his black Chrysler, but often told me how powerful it was and that it was getting to be too much car for him. I knew that he took pills for his heart, his daily shot of insulin, and strong pain medication.

"Granddaddy, that's okay," I said, wanting him to keep talking.

"You know, Hersch, I love you and Susan and little Kit. His face full of freckles reminds me a lot of your father a long time ago. I want you all to know the truth about your granddaddy, just in case." His voice trailed off when he said this, and he looked out the window above the sink for a moment.

"I played hard and I was determined. I loved baseball. I hated losing and I liked winning." His determination, his will, emerged as he remembered those days. "There were a lot of ball players who would do anything to beat me. They saw me getting better and better, and wanted to stop me. They cut my bats, ripped my uniforms, hid stuff, said things about your grandmother. Anything to get me riled up, to throw my game off. I had to be better, tougher than them. A lot has been written about Granddaddy that isn't the truth, and I want the true story set down. Understand, Hersch?" He looked directly at me. He was not so much asking me anything as making a statement.

"I think so."

As he continued, his voice reached down inside of him, became more reflective. "You and Kit are fine young men. And Susan is getting to be quite a young lady. I know you'll do well at whatever you choose to do. And you'll be determined to be the best you can be. I know that. Remember what you want, and stand up for yourself."

I could only imagine what images were going through his mind. Nobody helped him to be the best, and nobody stepped aside for him, not ever. I had read enough to know what baseball was like in the very early days, and I'd never forgotten Granddaddy's horrid red scars.

"With people like Al, you have to be careful." He was talking business now. "He's a writer and wants to do it his way. I want him to put it down the way it happened. I won't skip anything, but I want it from the way I was." He finished with a smile, but I could tell he was resigned to get the book done with the reporter he had chosen. "I just don't have time to start over with someone else."

Standing up, he got a glass and filled it with water from the old tap on the sink. "How's the chocolate milk, anyway?"

I hadn't touched it.

"Well, I'll see." He finished the glass in one gulp. "Just fine."

Silence lingered between us as he sat down. His right hand fingered the blue folder and moved it right in front of me. "Hersch, here, this photo is for you." He was pleased as I opened the folder and admired the photograph inside. Smiling, grown men. Autographed by Ty Cobb, Babe Ruth, Tris Speaker, and Frank Mackey.

"Say, let's talk about going up to the lake." Our talk about Al Stump was over for the time being. We left that old kitchen table and went into the living room and started planning our trip to Lake Tahoe.

Aunt Shirley's loud voice startled me out of my daze of reliving my introduction to Al Stump. I came back to the kitchen table in my grandmother's house. Aunt Shirley was waiting for my answer. My memories of the day before were as vivid as ever, and it took me a second to realize how I had drifted away.

She repeated herself. "I said, 'I heard you met Mr. Al Stump.' What was it like meeting an old-fashioned weasel, Hersch?"

"What did you say?" I asked. I knew she didn't think much of Mr. Stump, and her description did not really surprise me, but hearing her say it, thoroughly disgusted, caught me off balance.

"Well, Mr. Stump has been pestering the Old Man for years to let him write the story of his life, and now, I suppose, he's got his hooks in pretty far. He came around here, asking questions, but really trying to dig up any kind of dirt he could on the Old Man. Your grandfather is his ticket to being what he calls 'a real sportswriter.' He wants to use him to try to make a name for himself. That's all."

She sipped her coffee and picked up the morning newspaper, preparing to leave the room. The look on my face must have made her hesitate. "Hersch, that varmint wants to write the worst about your grandfather. He'd do anything to find any dirt. If he doesn't find any, he'll make it up, now or later. I've seen him and I know him."

"What else?" I asked, urging her to tell me more. Only once in a long while did Aunt Shirley treat any of the grandchildren like they could participate in an adult conversation.

"Hersch," she kept on, and I could see how much she was like Granddaddy, "you know that sometimes your grandfather is difficult, and over the years we've had our bouts. He's had his ups and downs, and I've seen most of them. Al Stump tried to be polite when he showed up a couple of years ago, but he got tired of asking baseball questions. He wanted dirt on the Old Man's personal life. He cornered Charlie one morning before you got here this summer. Blocked the driveway with his car; when she tried to drive out, she had to stop, and he rapped on her window, yelling, trying to badger her into talking to him. Scared the wits out of your grandmother. Luckily, I was home and saw what he was doing. I rushed out and shooed him away. Last year he tried to bribe Hank, our gardener. You know Hank works for Charlie three days a week and for the Old Man two. Well, Stump wanted Hank to go through the Old Man's garbage looking for liquor bottles. Hank likes the Old Man and refused. Stump was furious and tried to get the Old Man to fire him. Ha, I heard about that!"

I saw how angry she was getting. "It's none of his business, but he got pretty pushy and I stopped it all. Told him he wasn't welcome around here, and if he didn't stop, I'd talk to the Old Man and that would be the end of his chance to get famous. He got my message."

She went on, "I told the Old Man that Stump would use him to write a book and say anything to make himself famous. I think he understands, but the Old Man wants his story told before it's too late. That's all. I'll bet Al shook all over when your grandfather found him talking to you." She was beaming with a knowing smile.

"Yeah, he did. And he stopped and left the house pretty quick," I answered, knowing what she said was as personal as she was going to get about Granddaddy. She realized that his relationship with his grandchildren was vastly different than she had experienced as a child of his, over forty years ago. It must have puzzled and irked her to hear about his bond with his grandchildren, but she never tried to derail the warmth that existed on both sides. Oddly, I felt she was pleased for the Old Man, whether she liked it or not, but knowing that her father and his grandchildren shared what she had missed—an acceptance, caring, and wide affection.

"I think that's enough," she said, turning to leave the kitchen with the newspaper. "Put this stuff in the sink, please." She paused at the door, turned slightly toward me, genuinely offering, "You really get along with the Old Man, don't you? Trust him, huh?"

"Yeah, I do," I quietly answered, and on her face developed the gentlest, warmest smile that I'd ever seen.

That was the sort of family secret that a reporter would never want to learn. My grandfather's biographer was interested only in what was negative about Ty Cobb's family. Perhaps the past had been bitter. I could count myself as one of the people most directly affected by the family's tragedies. But in this life we all have a chance to overcome what hasn't worked out. Granddaddy had taken Susan, Kit, and me under his wing, and because of what we had built with him, we were going to turn out all right.

CHAPTER TEN

July 17, 1961,
and Beyond

Late in the afternoon on July 17, 1961, my mother gathered my sister, brother, and me in the breakfast room and told us that Granddaddy had passed away. An announcer came on the radio and said many complimentary things about Granddaddy and his career, and then played "Take Me Out to the Ball Game" twice. My eyes filled with tears, and I felt my chest swell up. I was overcome by affection and love, but I feared my guide and protector was forever lost to me. When the announcement was over, my mother abruptly stood up and left the room, not saying anything to us.

Ty Cobb died at Emory Hospital in Atlanta, Georgia. For the two weeks prior, he had tumbled in and out of consciousness. When he finally passed, my aunts Shirley and Beverly decided that the funeral would be held immediately, with only family members present. Nevertheless, nearly three hundred Little League and Middle League ball players showed up and lined the

273

streets leading to his mausoleum in Royston, Georgia. Nobody from Major League Baseball was invited. However, three close comrades—Ray Schalk, Mickey Cochrane, and Nap Rucker—made the journey for their old friend and were waiting at his mausoleum when his body arrived.

Sadly, I did not attend the funeral, nor did my sister or brother. My mother refused to pay for us to travel to Atlanta.

I was a senior in high school. Earlier in the year, using my own money, I applied to three colleges and was accepted at two. However, throughout the entire process my mother steadfastly told me that she was not going to pay for any of them. The local junior college was good enough for me. I was certain my hopes of attending college were dashed. I rode my bicycle over to visit Allan Hancock Junior College and tried to feel positive about it. Yet the next day, around noon, my sister called loudly that I was wanted on the phone.

A man introduced himself as Mr. Edward Brannan, senior trust officer at the Trust Company of Georgia. He told me that my grandfather had left me money in his will, and I could use this money for my "education, health, and maintenance." I only heard the word "education." My heart leapt in appreciation that my grandfather had known exactly what I needed and provided it again, just as he had so many times in the past. What's more, when I finished college, I still had enough money left to pay for graduate school. Granddaddy had made sure I could fulfill whatever life dreams I had for myself.

For many years after finishing school and entering the work world, I struggled to feel comfortable in groups, small or large. The emotions I had repressed lay in wait in a deep cave. The protective barriers I developed in order to shield myself from my father and mother now stood in the way of my relationships.

Much of what I learned and took with me from my summers with my grandfather served me well. However, I shared with him a deep reluctance to trust others.

In the middle of my life I was living alone in Berkeley, California, paying attention to work, when Susan M., a business colleague, asked me if I wanted to play tennis with her and her husband. I absentmindedly said yes, and arrived at their club thinking the three of us would hit around together and then have a beer. Susan arrived with a girlfriend, both giggling, and said, "Herschel, meet Lyn Jason. She's your partner today. Let's find Tom and get going." We started playing and I became more and more nervous, not because of the tennis, but because I realized I really liked Lyn.

That was the beginning. Two years later, when I was forty-six years old, we married. While dating, Lyn always told me, "Hersch, kids are part of the deal." She was younger than me, but had passed up having children thus far, so I thought her idea would fade. It didn't. Two years later, Madelyn, our daughter, was born, and two years after that, Ty, our son, was born. Madelyn was born with a smile, ready for fun and adventure. Ty was born with a warm, mild manner. From the beginning, he was curious and smart, with a huge smile and joyous sense of humor. I realized very quickly that I was blessed and that children and my wife are the true gifts in my life.

Madelyn loves adventures, has lots of energy, and trusts life. Not blindly, but with her eyes open. I learned from her how this works. She is direct with people, positive in her attitude and comments, and balanced if things don't work out. This approach works very well, and I've tried to adopt it too. Her confidence has grown over the years, with Lyn continually supporting her next steps and me following Lyn's lead. When she was accepted by the

275

college she desired, she reserved her dorm room that night and started packing up her things the next day even though classes didn't begin for months. She was ready for her next adventure.

Ty has always shined with a wide smile, laughing often, and loves his many friends. His sports teammates are his natural buddies. When Ty was ready to play T-ball, I went to the local schoolyard with a good friend and his son with our registration papers. I handed the sheet to Ty to give to the dad organizing the sign-in.

The dad read Ty's sheet and said, rather loudly, "Ty Cobb, you sure that's your name?"

Ty quickly answered, "Yes sir, Ty! That's my dad," and pointed to me.

The dad turned to me, "Ty Cobb? The Ty Cobb?"

"Yep. The Ty Cobb. Only he's the great-grandson." I knew I was giving a short answer, but I didn't know whether I'd burst out with tears or laughter, I was so overcome with emotion. I felt so very lucky having a son who was confident, happy, and just bursting to join in with his friends, play ball, and love life. I've often called upon my memories and experiences with my grand-father for guidance and have always found some. When Ty was born, I had no role model except Granddaddy, so I build upon that and it's worked pretty well. My son's good nature and ease with friends has helped.

"Well, Ty," the dad continued, "are you a lefty or righty?"

Ty looked over at me with a big question on his face. "Your great-grandfather batted lefty, Ty."

"I'm a lefty," he stated firmly.

And that's the way he bats, throws, and shoots a basketball today. Ty continues to flourish, as does Madelyn. He loves team sports (football, basketball, and baseball), especially basketball. He is quietly confident, competitive on the court, loves to laugh, plays for the love of the game, and relishes team victories. He's been a captain on all his teams, and in high school he was selected to First Team All-League in football, basketball, and baseball. At college he plays basketball in Division III.

Madelyn loves horses and plays polo. She was captain of her college women's polo team for three years and led them to compete in Intercollegiate Polo Championships four years. She continues to share this interest with Lyn, and both play competitively.

As for me, I notice the patterns, how the pendulum has been righted, as if I've struck a sacred bell and the reverberations have emanated forward and back, finding a balance.

The summer I retrieved Granddaddy's engraved shotgun from the attic at the cabin, we were set to return to Atherton the next day. He slept late, did not hurry packing, and, after lunch, around 2:00, told me he decided he was not returning to Tahoe that summer and he wanted to take the Chris-Craft to Sierra Boat Works, put her in dry dock for the winter. He asked me if I would come with him.

I looked at the lake. Large waves and whitecaps as far as I could see. "Sure. Now?"

"Yes." He wore a summer shirt, slacks, and street shoes. We went down to the boathouse, dodging water splashing up between the planks on the pier as waves roared to the beach. He slowly maneuvered the craft backwards, out of the Quonset hut that had served so well.

He kept the engine low and our speed slow, our bow slicing sharply through five-foot waves as we picked up speed. I hoped for smooth water farther out.

"This is rough," I said.

"It'll calm down. We should be there in about an hour; it's only eight miles," he answered, not addressing my concern.

277

I watched the whitecaps, recalling how many times he had told me about Lake Tahoe being part of nature. We trudged through the choppy waves, careful to keep the bow pointed into them, slicing and rocking, bow, then stern. I didn't like it at all.

Twenty minutes went by. The waves easily crashed over the bow into the cockpit and second seat, making it nearly impossible to see. Cave Rock rested far behind us and Sierra Boat Works was beyond sight. The waves were relentless, just as he had told me, spraying crisscross over us and the engine compartment. Everything was drenched, including us, when the engine chortled and sputtered to a stop.

Granddaddy shouted over the wind and waves, "Too much water in something, or we've bounced so much there's air in the line."

I hoped he knew. He grabbed a yellow canvas life vest and secured it around my chest. "Where's yours?"

He grabbed two others, tried them on, and they were pitifully small. "Hersch, it's okay. I'll have a look." He climbed into the second row of seats, opened the covers to the engine compartment, and stuck his head high and low.

I thought, "Air in the lines, or water in something." I knew nothing about marine engines. He handed me an oar and told me to paddle off the side and keep the bow pointed into the waves. I pulled hard as the boat rocked helplessly. He leapt back and forth, hitting the start button, then shifting valves, adjusting lines, wiping parts around the engine. He went back and forth a dozen times with no result, sweating profusely in the cold wind and crashing waves.

When he stopped to take a break he was heaving and gasping. I worried. He looked up at me, sucking in air, with the damndest look on his face and said, "Don't worry, Hersch, we'll be fine." It didn't seem so. I realized the situation—me in a life vest a mile from shore, him in street clothes with five-foot whitecaps crashing over our craft, bouncing us around in icy water like a cork.

He caught his breath, grabbed a splashing wave, wiped the cold water over his face, and leapt back from the engine compartment to the front seat to try again. Nothing. He shouted, "We're going to put her sideways, with the waves, keep the tail in the water. Got it?" He rushed back to the engine, wedged himself between the seatback and engine compartment, thrust his arms deep along the sides of the engine, and moved around furiously. He wiped down everything he saw, adjusted a valve, and hollered, "Get behind the wheel. Push the starter when I tell you."

I secured the oar, jumped behind the steering wheel, foam and spray blowing in my face off the tops of whitecaps, and twisted around to watch him. Pretty soon, he looked up, shouting, "Now!" I pushed the button hard and held it. She sputtered, coughed, then caught, rumbling to a soft roar. "Oh, what a pretty sound," I thought. He was over me instantly, adjusting the throttle on the steering wheel while I slid aside. She picked up some revs and he gained control, pointing into the waves, slowly turning back, toward Cave Rock.

I moved next to him, pushing my body close, grinning. The waves at our back pushed us along, he being careful not to fight them. He put his arm around me, saying, "Hersch, it's Lake Tahoe, it's nature, just like I told you. We'll call the guys at Sierra; they can pick up the boat tomorrow. I didn't choose a good time. You know, I'm not invincible."

I was with my grandfather, Ty Cobb. In my mind, invincible.

At ECW Press, we want you to enjoy this book in whatever format you like, whenever you like. Leave your print book at home and take the eBook to go! Purchase the print edition and receive the eBook free. Just send an email to ebook@ecwpress.com and include:

GET *the*
*e*BOOK
FREE*

* the book title
* the name of the store where you purchased it
* your receipt number
* your preference of file type: PDF or ePub?

*PROOF OF PURCHASE REQUIRED

A real person will respond to your email with your eBook attached. And thanks for supporting an independently owned publisher with your purchase!